Simple Tally 8.1

By

Asok K Nadhani
Kisor K Nadhani

BPB PUBLICATIONS
B-14, CONNAUGHT PLACE, NEW DELHI-110001

FIRST EDITION 2007

ISBN 81-8333-189-0

Distributors:

MICRO MEDIA
Shop No. 5, Mahendra Chambers,
150 D.N. Road, Next to Capital Cinema
V.T. (C.S.T.) Station,
MUMBAI-400001 Ph.: 22078296, 22078297

COMPUTER BOOK CENTRE
12, Shrungar Shopping Centre, M.G. Road,
BANGALORE-560001 Ph: 25587923, 25584641

MICRO BOOKS
Shanti Niketan Building, 8, Camac Street,
KOLKATTA-700017 Ph.: 22826518, 22826519

BUSINESS PROMOTION BUREAU
8/1, Ritchie Street, Mount Road,
CHENNAI-600002 Phone: 28410796, 28550491

DECCAN AGENCIES
4-3-329, Bank Street,
HYDERABAD-500195
Phone: 24756400, 24756967

MICRO BOOK CENTRE
2, City Centre, CG Road,
Near Swastic Char Rasta,
AHMEDABAD-380009 Phone: 26421611

BPB PUBLICATIONS
B-14, Connaught Place, **NEW DELHI-110001**
Phone: 23325760, 23723393, 23737742

INFO TECH
G-2, Sidhartha Building, 96 Nehru Place,
NEW DELHI-110019
Phone: 26438245, 26415092, 26234208

INFO TECH
Shop No. 2, F-38, South Extension Part-1
NEW DELHI-110049
Phone: 24691288, 24641941

BPB BOOK CENTRE
376, Old Lajpat Rai Market,
DELHI-110006 PHONE: 23861747

Published by Manish Jain for BPB Publications, B-14, Connaught Place, New Delhi - 110 001 and Printed by him at Akash Press, Delhi.

Trademark

Cross References

A related topic is cross referenced as Ref 99.9.9 (e.g Ref 4.3.1). The First figure after Ref refers to the Chapter Number, followed by section (and sub section) number of the topic.

Similarly, Figures (illustrations) are referred as Fig 9-99 (e.g Fig 4-12). The first part shows the Chapter Number and the second part shows the serial number of the figure in the chapter.

Preface

Now Tally speaks in multiple Languages simultaneously. You can work in English or in any of 9 Indian Languages.

This book is written in simple & lucid way, for starters who do not have any prior knowledge of any accounting software. Yet it covers the entire gamut of Financial & Materials Accounting, right from Accounts & Inventory Masters creation, Invoice & Voucher entry, Accounting & Inventory Reports, Final Accounts and move to next year's accounts.

All the steps are lucidly explained with numerous illustrations, aided by commented labels for quick learning at first glance. A number of exercises have been placed at the end of each chapter with solved answers at the end, which would be helpful for students learning Tally and appearing for certification examinations.

We are sure, this book will also be patronised by our valued readers like our previous books on Tally.

We welcome your valuable suggestion to make the book more useful

Asok K Nadhani
akn@nadhani.com

Kisor K Nadhani
kisor@nadhani.com

2nd October 2006

Contents at a Glance

Table Of Contents

Part - I

Basic Accounts

Installation

1

After you buy Tally, you get a CD containing the Tally 8.1 software. The first task is to install the software in your computer. The process of installation is described in this chapter.

1.1 System Requirements

To install Tally 8.1, your computer system should meet the following minimum requirements

1.1.1 Hardware Requirements

Tally recommends minimum hardware as follows:

Processor	Intel Pentium III and Higher
Memory	64 MB RAM or more
Free Hard disk space	30 MB Minimum
Monitor Resolution	Recommended 1024 X 768 or higher

As Tally performs better with more memory, a free Hard Disk of at least 40 MB will make multilingual feature perform better.

1.1.2 Operating System Requirements

Different version of Windows OS will support Indic languages as follows:

Operating System	*Support for Indian Scripts in Windows Versions*
Windows 98, Windows 95, windows ME	Supports Tally 8.1 but does not support Unicode. You can use in English only but not with any Indic language.
Windows NT	Supports Unicode but does not support Indic Languages
Windows 2000	Support Unicode and Hindi, Marathi, Tamil (Indic Languages)
Windows XP	Supports Unicode and Hindi, Marathi, Tamil, Telugu, Kannada,Punjabi, Gujarati (Indic Languages)

Windows 2003	Supports Unicode and Hindi, Marathi, Tamil, Telugu, Kannada,Punjabi, Gujarati (Indic Languages)
Windows XP Service Pack2	Supports Unicode and Hindi, Marathi, Tamil, Telugu, Kannada,Punjabi, Gujarati, Bengali, Malayalam (Indic Languages)

So, to get full support of Indic Language, you need Windows XP with Service Pack 2.

Before installation, you should :

- Have administrator rights on your computer to install Tally.
- Have all rights (create, write, update, modify and delete) for the Application, Data, Configuration and Language directory.

1.2 Tally 8.1Installation

Insert the Tally Software CD in Drive and click install.exe

You will get the Installation Welcome screen (Fig 1-1)

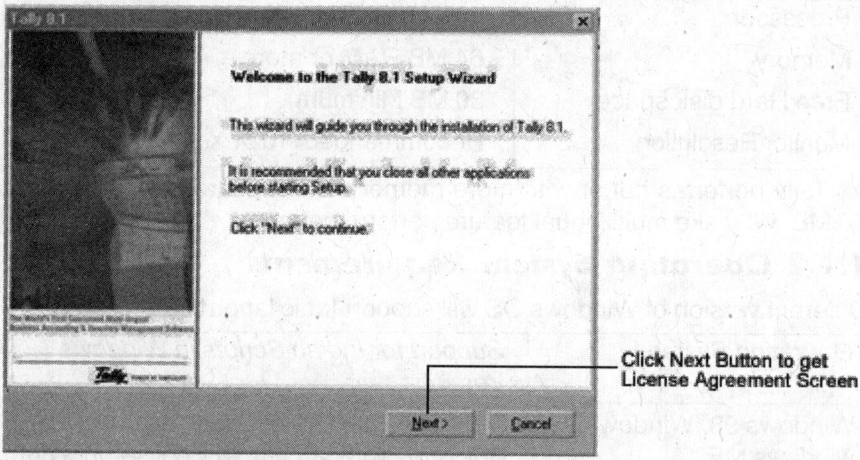

Fig 1-1: Tally 8.1 Installation Wizard – Welcome Screen.

At *Welcome* screen (Fig1-1), click *Next* Button to get *License Agreement* screen (Fig 1-2)

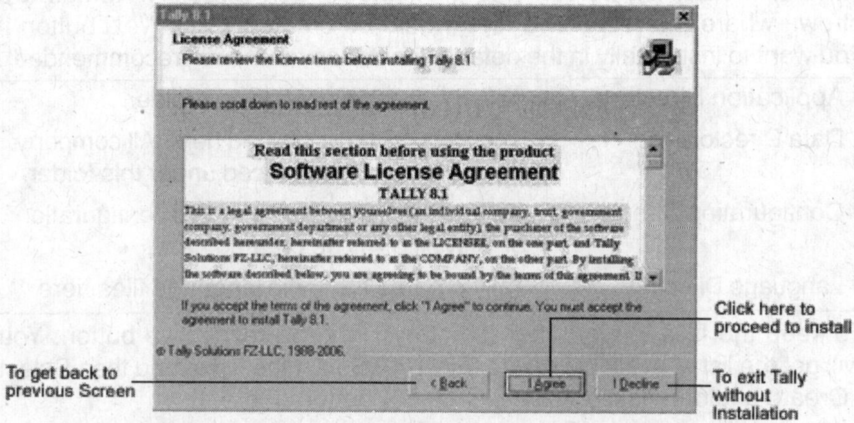

Fig 1-2: Tally 8.1 License Agreement screen.

At *License Agreement* screen (Fig 1-2), you get the following buttons

Button	*Action*
I Agree	Click here to proceed to install.
Back	To get back to previous screen (Fig 1-1)
I Decline	To quit from Tally 8.1 set up without installation

Click *I Agree* button (Fig 1-2) to accept the License agreement and get the *New Installation* screen. (Fig 1-3)

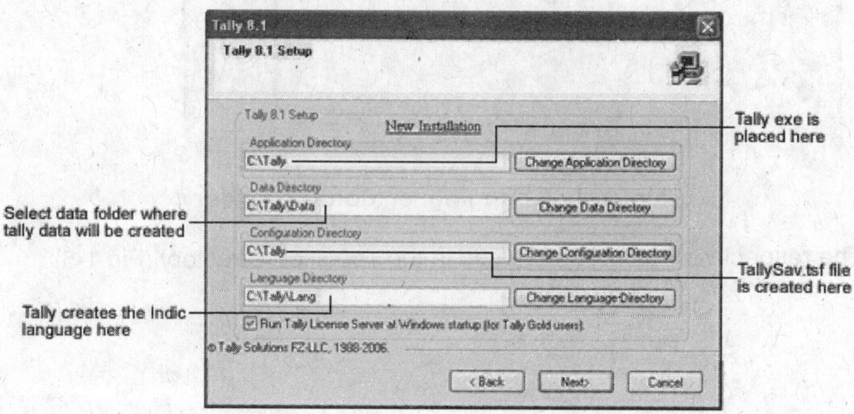

Fig 1-3: Tally 8.1 New Installation set up screen (with default Directory Names)

At New Installation screen (Fig 1-3), the default Directory Names are shown where the respective files would be created. Click *Next* button if you want to install Tally in the default directories as shown (recommended).

Application Directory	*Tally81.exe* is placed in this folder.
Data Directory	The Data folder is created here. All company data folders will be placed under this folder.
Configuration Directory	*TallySav.tsf* (Containing saved configuration of Tally) file will be created here.
Language Directory	Tally creates the Indic language files here

To keep the files in any other directory, click the respective button. You will get the list of available drives (Fig 1-4). Select the Drive and then Select / Create a folder, as necessary. Click OK button (Fig 1-4).

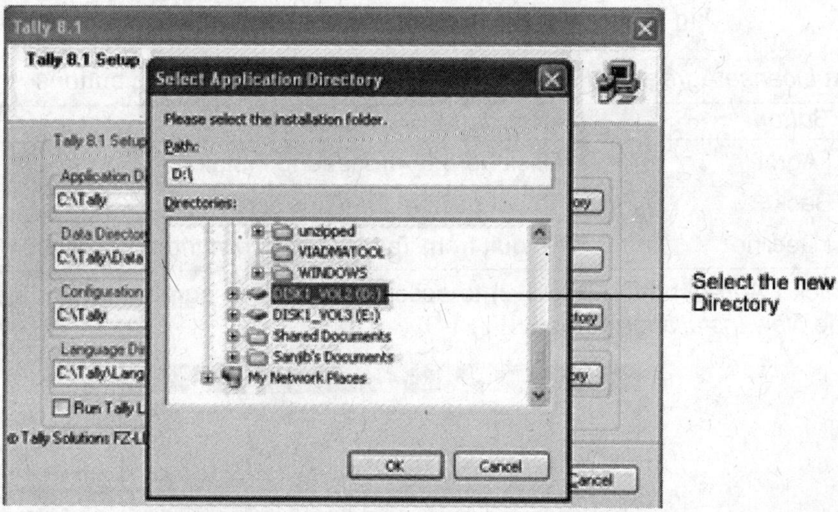

Fig 1-4: Changing of default Folder

The respective files will be created in the specified Directory (Fig 1-5)

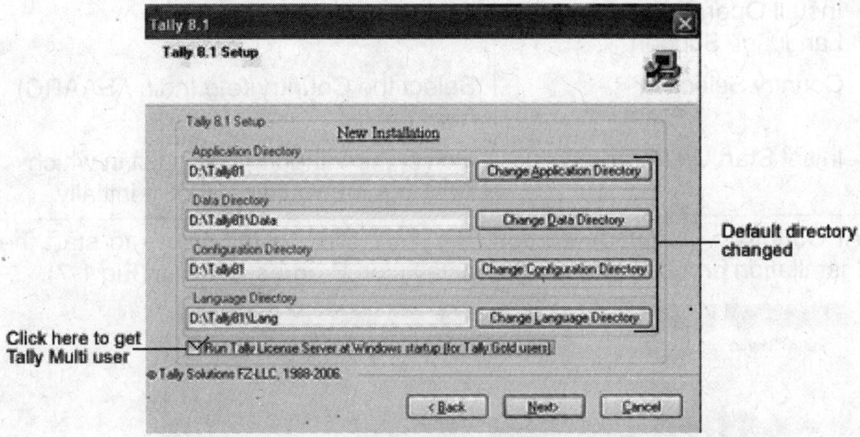

Fig 1-5: Tally 8.1 New Installation set up screen (with changed Directory Name)

New Installation screen. (Fig 1-3), click *Next* button to get the Country / Language selection screen (Fig 1-6). For installation of Tally Gold (in multi user environment) check the box *Run Tally License Server at Windows Startup for Tally Gold Users* (Fig 1-5).

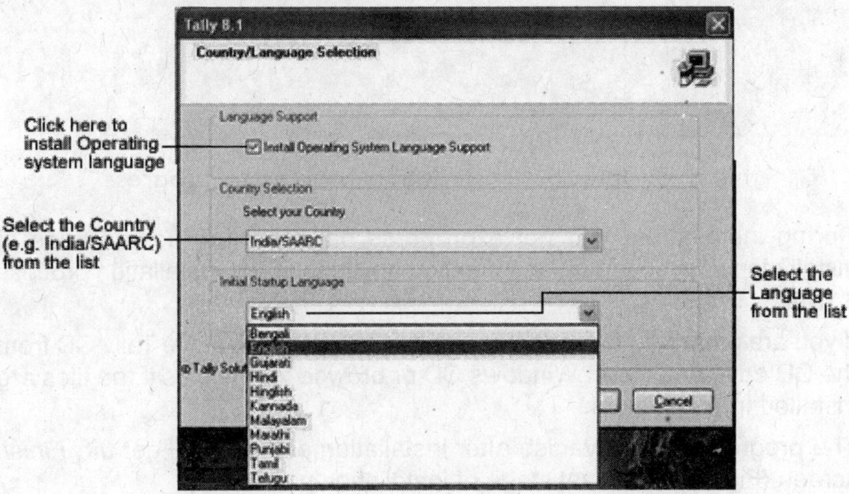

Fig 1-6: Country & Language Selection screen.

At Country / Language screen (Fig 1-6), at the respective field, select as follows :

Install Operating System Language Support	Check this checkbox
Country Selection	Select the Country (e.g India / SAARC) from the list
Initial Start Up Language	Select the Language from list in which Tally screen would be shown initially.

At Country / Language screen (Fig 1-6), click *Install* button to start the Installation process and get the Installation Progress screen (Fig 1-7).

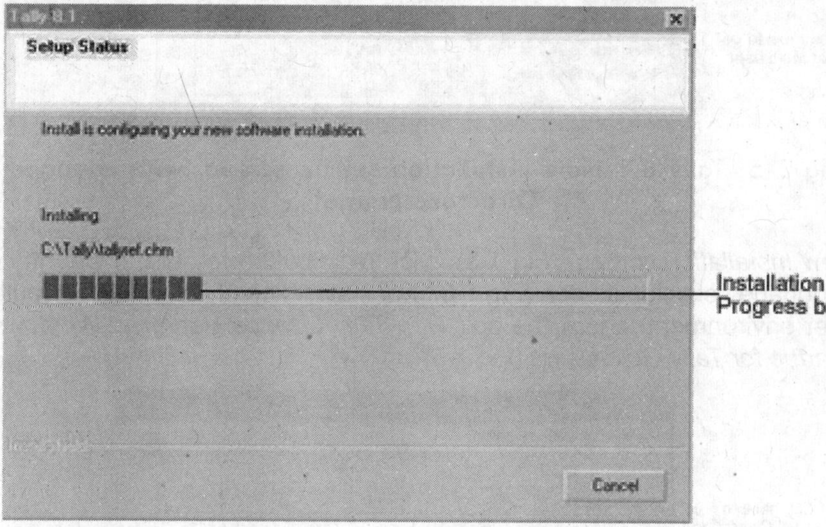

Fig 1-7: Tally 8.1 installation process in progress

During installation, you get a progress bar showing the progress of installation (Fig 1-7). Wait and don't do anything till the installation process is over.

If you are prompted to insert Windows OS CD, then remove Tally CD from the CD drive and insert Windows CD or browse for the files if the files are installed in the system.

The progress bar will vanish after installation and you will get the *Finish* screen (Fig 1-8), the last stage of installation process.

At Finish screen, click *Finish* button (Fig 1-8). You get back to the desktop and the Tally icon will appear in the Desktop and Taskbar (Fig 1-9).

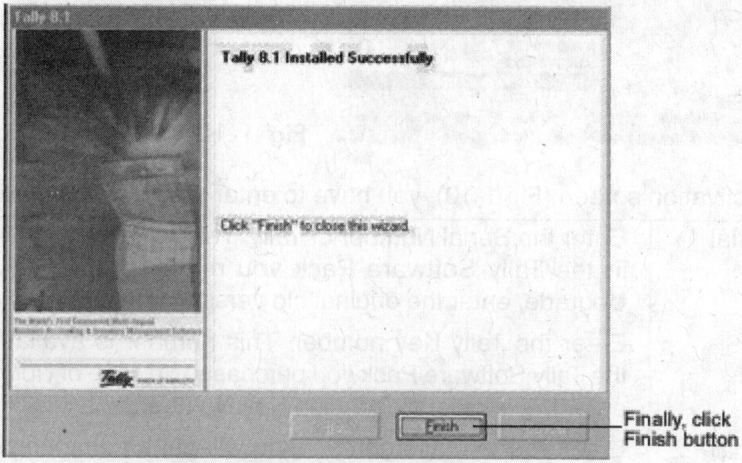

Fig 1-8: Tally 8.1 Installation Final step.

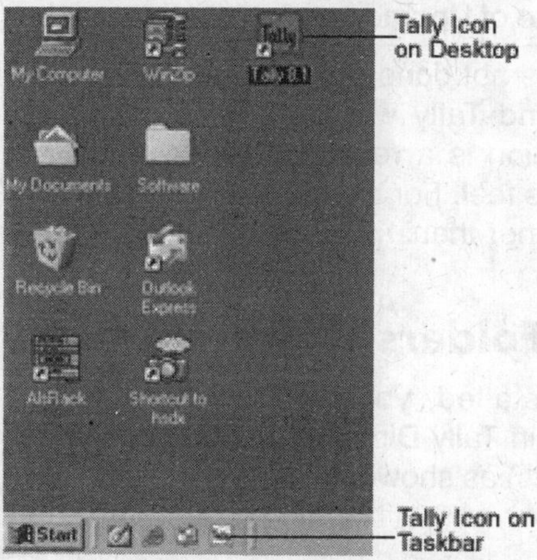

Fig 1-9: Tally Icon at Desktop & Task Bar.

1.3 Loading Tally

You can load Tally either by clicking on the *Tally icon* on Desktop or on the Taskbar (Fig 1-9). Using Tally icon at Taskbar you can conveniently switch between concurrent running applications without existing Tally.

1.4 Activation

After Installation (as explained above) or Upgradation (Ref 2.2), when you load Tally first time, you get the Activation screen (Fig 1-10).

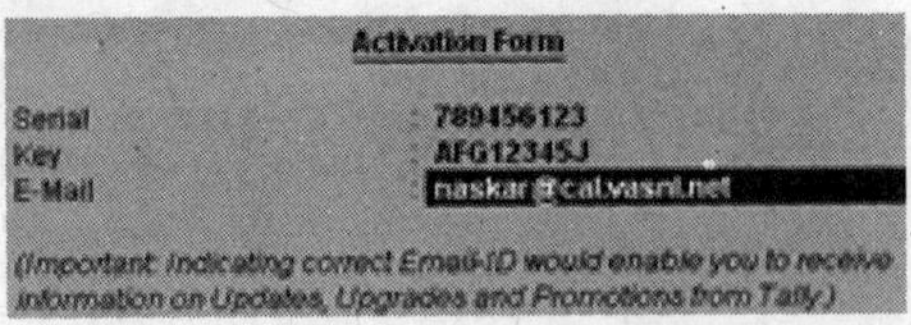

Fig 1-10 : Activation Screen

At Activation screen (Fig 1-10), you have to enter the following details :

Serial	Enter the Serial Number of Tally. This number is available in the Tally Software Pack you purchased. In case of Upgrade, enter the original old version serial number
Key	Enter the Tally Key number. This number is available in the Tally Software Pack you purchased. In case of Upgrade, enter the original old version Key Number.
e-mail	Enter your e-mail address. You will get a communication from Tally through this e-mail address. In case of Upgrade, enter the same e-mail address that you specified at the time of Upgrade at Registration screen (Fig 2-15).

If the Activation is not done properly, you will get EDUCATIONAL at the serial number and Tally will work as Educational version (Ref 8.2). Educational version is a restricted version, just for evaluation of Tally software to get its feel. For example, in EDUCATIONAL version, you can not enter Date other than 1, 2 & 31 and you do not get the Multi Printing Menu (Ref 21.1).

1.5 Tally Folders & System files

After Tally is installed, you get the following folders and files in Tally Directory (if you accept default Directories) as shown in Fig 1-11.

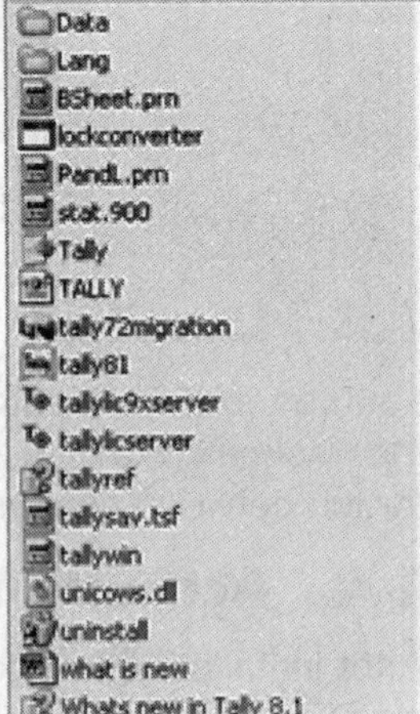

Fig 1-11: Tally System Folders & Files

Self Test Questions

STQ 01.1: What is the minimum hardware requirement to run Tally 8.1

STQ 01.2: Can you work in Gujrati in Tally under Windows 2000

STQ 01.3: How to place the Tally System files in following directory locations (mention the respective fieldname in New Installation set up screen) :

Data at d:\Tally\81data, Tally at c:\tally81, Tallysav file at c:\tally81, Tally language file at *c:\tally81\language*

STQ 01.4: What information are needed to be entered to Activate Tally 8.1. What happens if you do not enter then properly in Activation screen.

Upgrading Tally 2

In Chapter 1, we have shown how to install Tally 8.1 when you buy a new Tally 8.1 software. If you are an existing Tally user of older version (like Tally 7.2), then you need not buy a new Tally license rather you can upgrade the older version of Tally to 8.1 by paying upgradation fee.

2.1 Tally Currency coupons

To upgrade, you have to buy Tally Currency coupon (from Tally Authorised Dealers) of the requisite value. The coupons come in several denominations (like a 1800, 900 etc). For example, if the upgradation charge for Tally Gold for 7.2 to 8.1 is Rs 4500, then you may buy two coupons of 1800 each and one coupon of Rs 900 to make up 4500 (1800+1800+900).

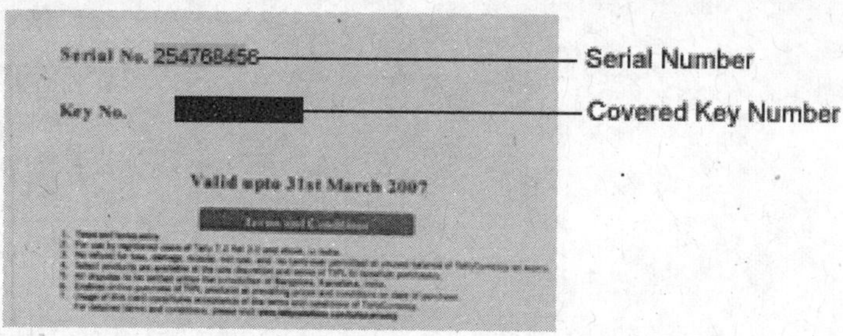

Fig 2-1: Tally currency coupon (unscratched)

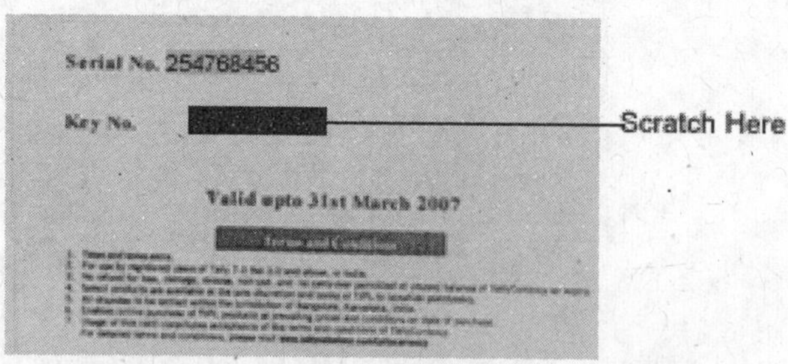

Fig 2-2: Scratching Tally currency coupon

Each coupon envelop contains a scratch card with a serial number and covered key number (Fig 2-1). You have to scratch to uncover the Key

Number (like the kind of scratch card you get for pre paid Phone coupons), as shown in Fig 2-2 to get the Key Number uncovered (Fig 2-3). You will have to type the Key Number (Fig 2-10) at the time of on-line upgradation described later.

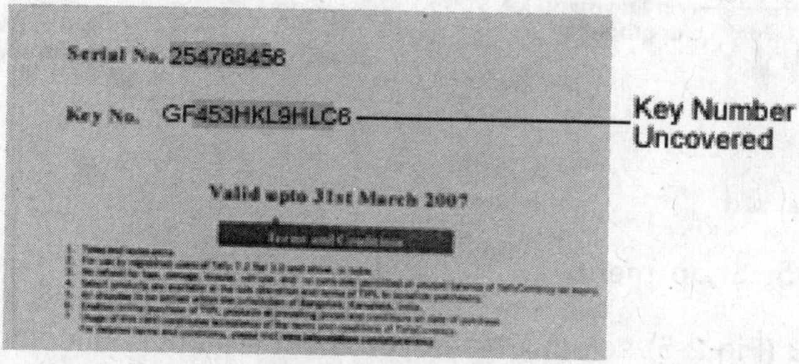

Fig 2-3: Tally currency coupon (unscratched)

2.2 Upgradation Process

The steps to upgrade existing Tally 7.2 ver to Tally 8.1 ver are explained here. First get connected to internet and start the process explained next, step by step, very carefully.

Load Tally 7.2. At Gateway of Tally screen, click F12: Configuration to get Configuration Menu (Fig 2-4)

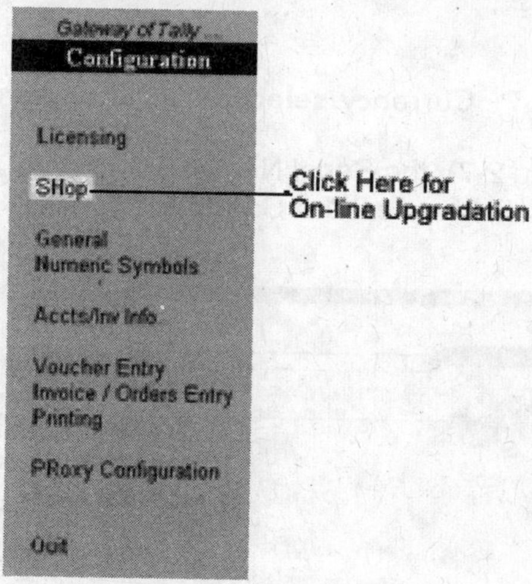

Fig 2-4: Tally Configuration Menu

At Configuration menu (Fig 2-4) select *Shop* to get *Shop* Menu (Fig 2-5).

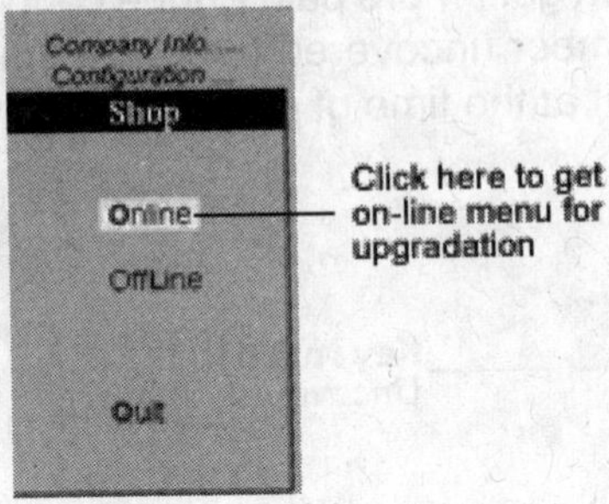

Fig 2-5: Shop menu

Fig 2-6: Online menu

At Shop Menu (Fig 2-5) select *Online* (you must remain connected with Internet), to get *Online* Menu (Fig 2-6)

At Online Menu (Fig 2-6) select *Buy* to get *Shop* screen (Fig 2-7).

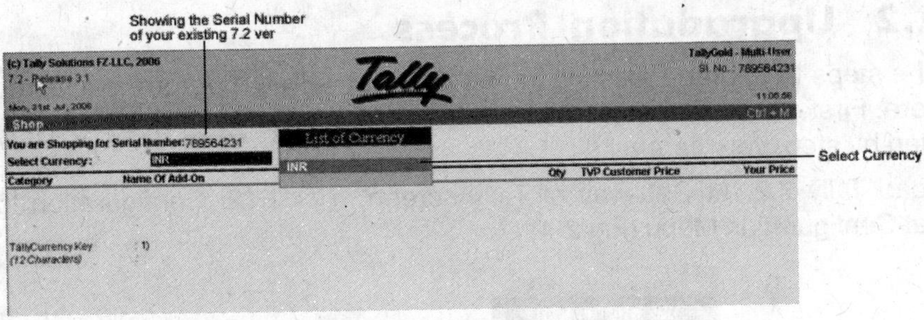

Fig 2-7: Currency selection at Shop screen

At *Shop* screen (Fig 2-7), the Serial Number of existing 7.2 ver is shown. At *Select Currency* field, select the Currency (e.g INR), as shown in Fig 2-7

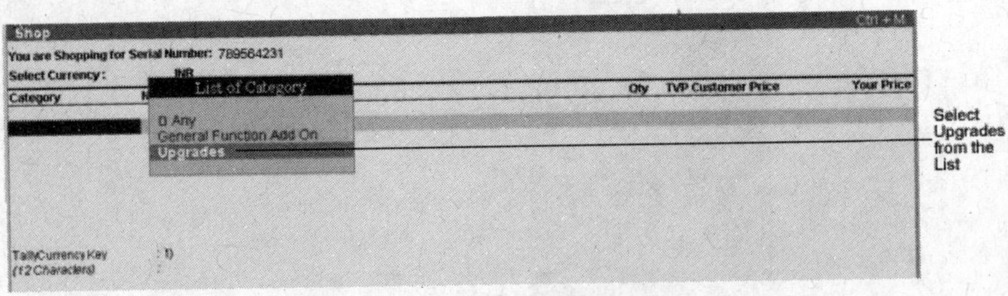

Fig 2-8: Upgrade option selection at Shop screen

Next, in the Shop Screen, at Ca*tegory* field, select *Upgrades* from the list (Fig 2-8)

Fig 2-9: Upgrade Item selection at Shop screen

Now select the respective upgrade option from the *List of Add Ons* (depending upon the existing User level (Silver/ Gold etc) as shown in Fig 2-9.

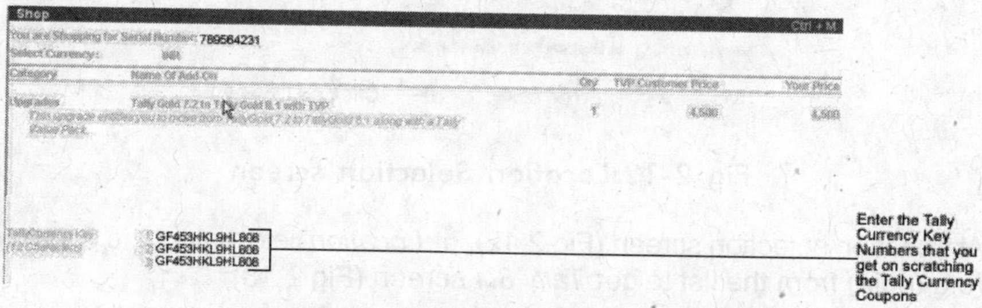

Fig 2-10: Tally Currency Key Number entry

Now you get a prompt to enter the Tally Currency Key Numbers (Fig 2-10) that you got on scratching the Tally Currency Coupons (Fig 2-3). You should enter the Key Numbers one by one, in each line (Fig 2-10).

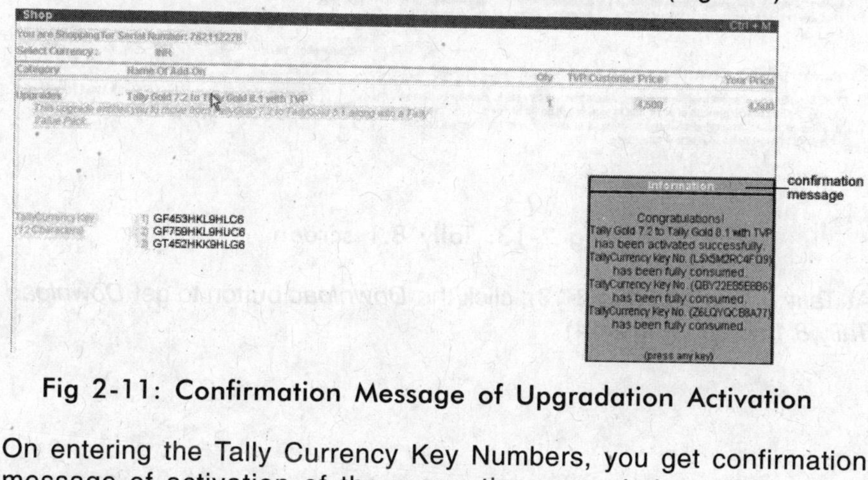

Fig 2-11: Confirmation Message of Upgradation Activation

On entering the Tally Currency Key Numbers, you get confirmation message of activation of the respective upgradation scheme and consumption of Tally Currency Numbers (Fig 2-11)

Having completed entry of all Key Numbers, press any key to get connected to Tally Website and get the *Location* selection screen (Fig 2-12)

Fig 2-12:Location Selection screen

At Location selection screen (Fig 2-12), at *Location* field, select the Country (e.g India) from the list to get *Tally 8.1* screen (Fig 2-13)

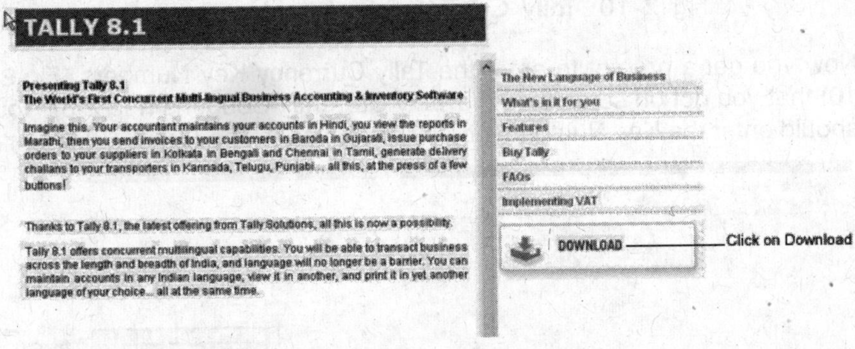

Fig 2-13: Tally 8.1 screen

At *Tally 8.1* screen (Fig 2-13), click the *Download* button to get *Download Tally 8.1* screen (Fig 2-14)

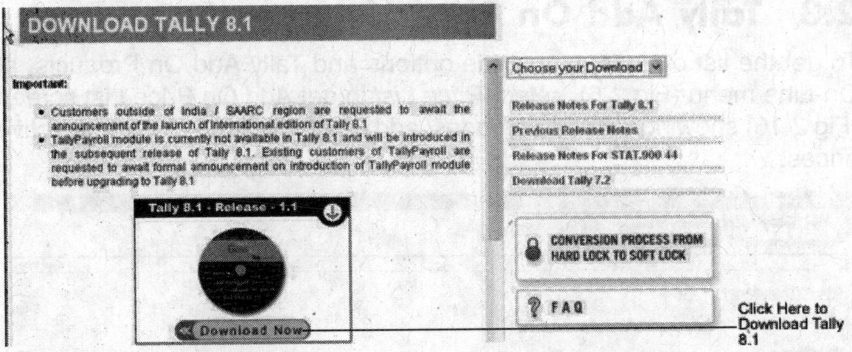

Fig 2-14: Download Tally 8.1 screen

At *Download Tally 8.1* screen (Fig 2-14), click the *Download Now* button at Tally 8.1 box to get the Tally 8.1 Registration screen (Fig 2-15).

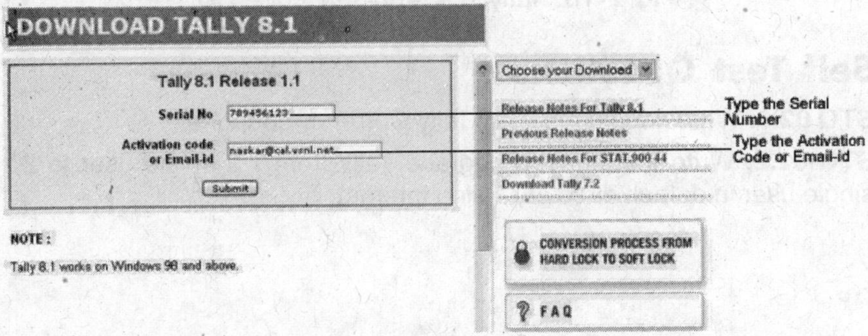

Fig 2-15: Tally 8.1 Download submission screen

At Download submission screen (Fig 2-15), enter the following to Download the Tally 8.1 Upgrade

- At Serial Number field, enter the Tally Serial Number (your old version serial number) very carefully.
- At Activate Code e-mail id field, enter your e-mail id carefully. This e-mail id will have to be entered at the time of Activation of Tally (Ref 1.4)

Now click at *Submit* button List (Fig 2-15)

Cheers! You have finally downloaded the Tally Upgrade. Now Install Tally 8.1 as described in Chapter 1 (Ref 1.2).

Enjoy working with new Tally 8.1 and experience the excitement of Multi Lingual Tally.

2.3 Tally Add On Price List

To get the list of various upgrade options and Tally Add On Products, at On-Line menu (Fig 2-6), select *Price List* to get Add On Price List screen (Fig 2-16) showing various upgrades/ add on products and their respective prices.

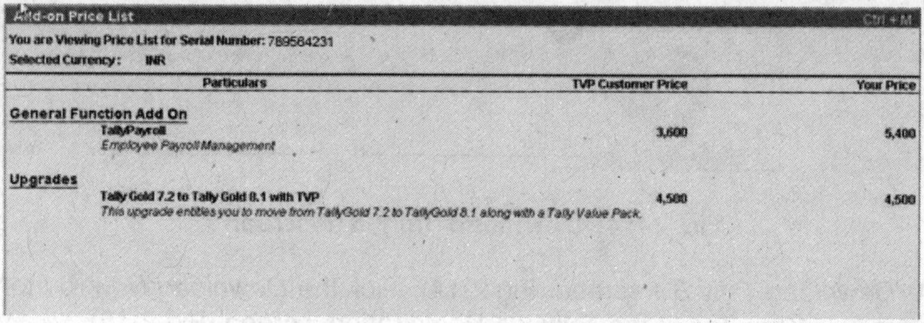

Fig 2-16: Tally 8.1 Add On Price List

Self Test Questions

STQ 02.1: What do you mean by Tally Currency coupons.

STQ 02.2: Write the steps to upgrade Tally from 7.2 single user to 8.1 single user in default directory, using Internet.

Data Migration

3

Data of Tally 7.2 ver cannot be used in 8.1 ver directly. You have to convert the 7.2 ver data into 8.1 format through Data Migration tool

Before Migration, you must get Tally 8.1 activated (Ref 1.2). You cannot migrate data in EDUCATIONAL version.

3.1 Data Migration Utility

At Tally System file folder (Ref 1.3), click the tally72migration file (Fig 3-1) to get the Data Migration screen (Fig 3-2).

Alternately, you may load the migration tool from Start>Programs>Tally 8.1>Tally Migrate Data

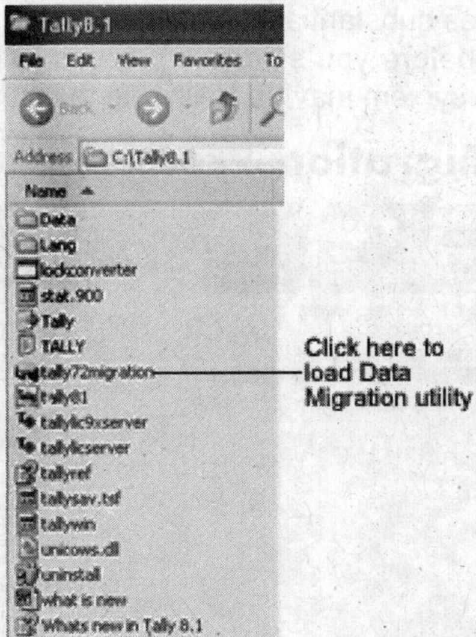

Fig 3-1:Tally Folder showing the Tally System files

The Data Migration screen contains 2 parts (Fig 3-2). In the left part, you get Migrate Company Menu. In the right part, Migration information get displayed as the Migration process goes on.

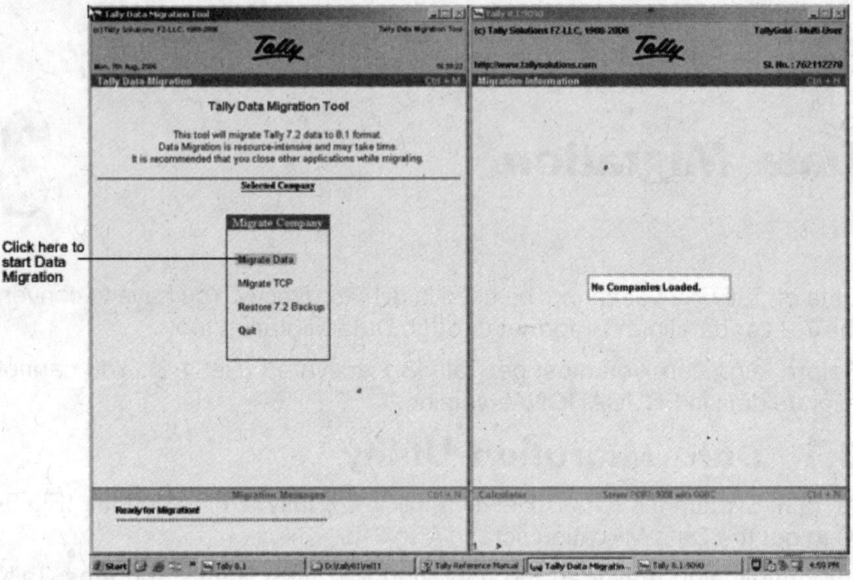

Fig 3-2: Tally Data Migration screen

As the process takes substantial computer memory, you should close all other applications before you start this process (otherwise the process may be slow or the system may hang up due to insufficient memory).

3.2 Data Migration Process

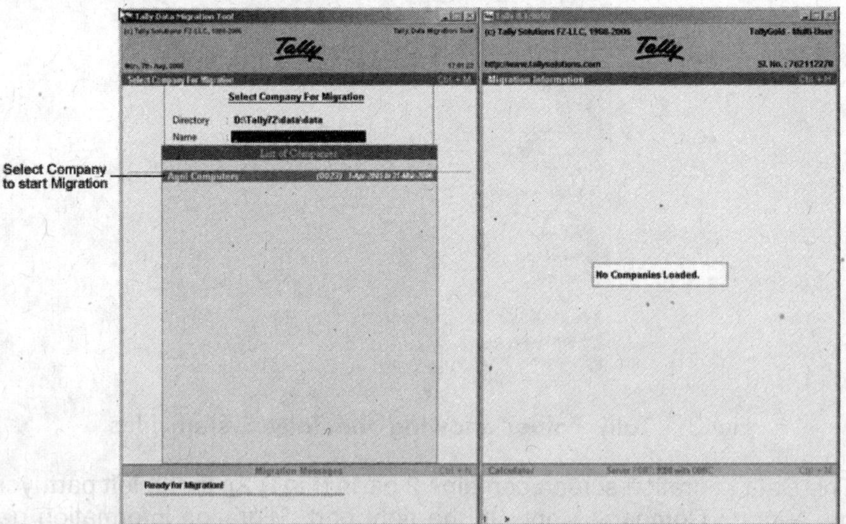

Fig 3-3: Selection of Company for Data Migration

At Migrate Company Menu (Fig 3-2), click *Migrate Data* to get *Select Company for Migration* screen (Fig 3-3).

At *Select Company for Migration* screen (Fig 3-3), select the Company for which data to be migrated from 7.2 to 8.1 ver

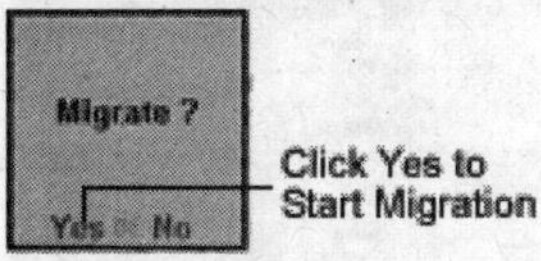

Fig 3-4: Data Migration confirmation

After the data is loaded, you get a confirmation screen (Fig 3-4). Click *Yes* to confirm.

At the right side, statistical figures about the migration data are shown (Fig 3-5).

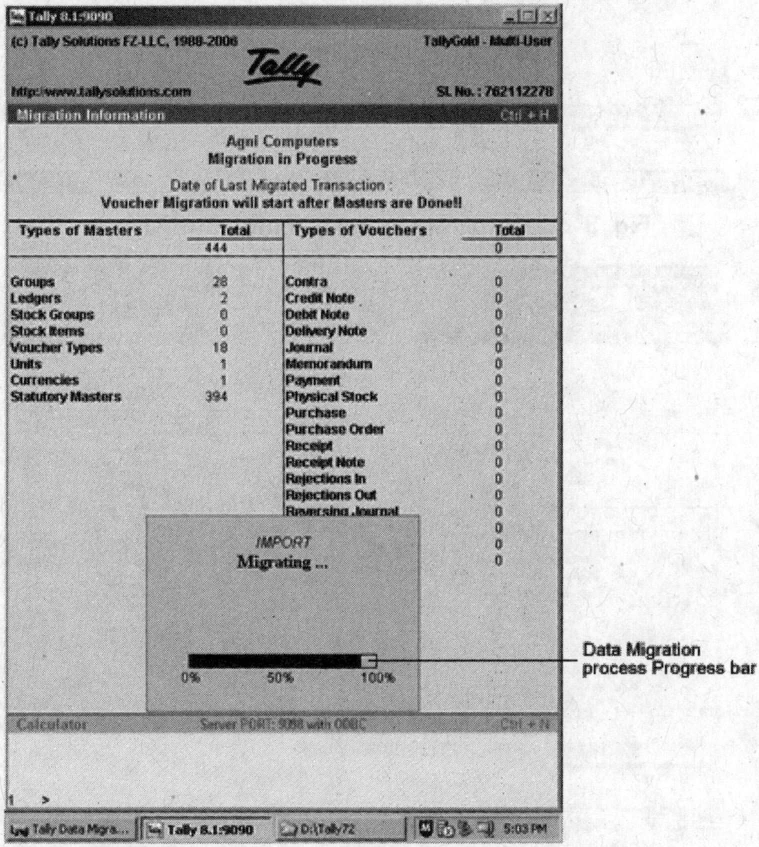

Fig 3-5: Data Migration Process Messages

During the Migration process, the progress bar shows progress stages (Fig 3-5). Also messages about the stages of migration appear.

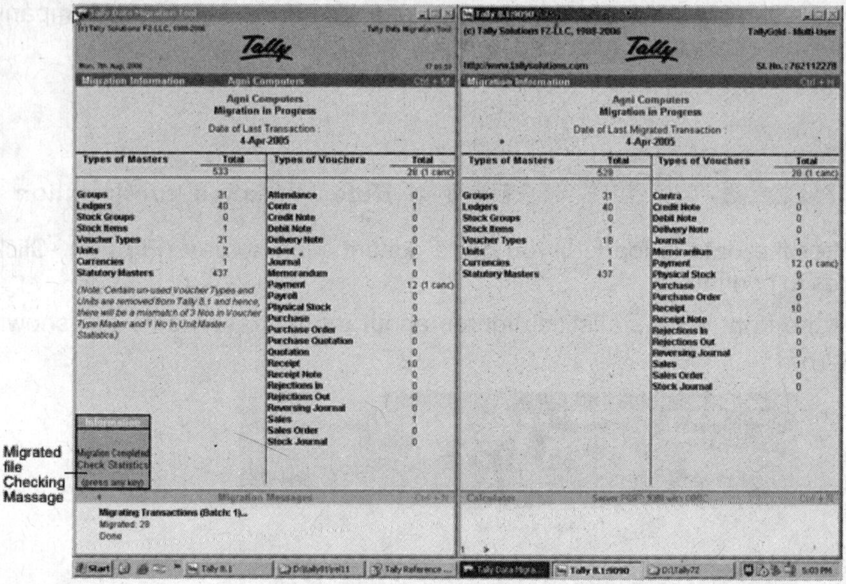

Fig 3-6: Data Migration - Final Statistics

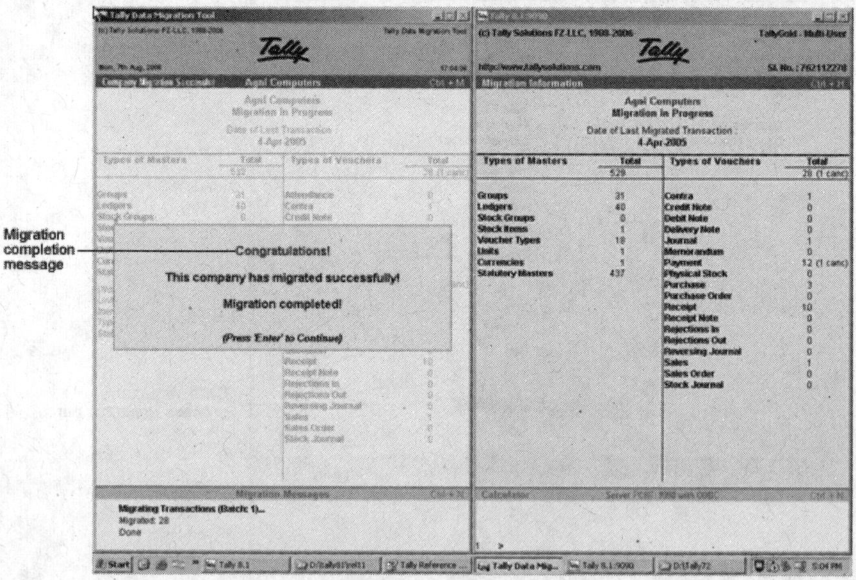

Fig 3-7: Migration completion message

At the end of Migration process, the two panes show the comparative statistics of Data of 7.2 ver & 8.1 ver (Fig 3-6). You see an information in the box to compare and ensure that all data have been migrated properly.

Having compared the statistics at both pane (Fig 3-6), press <enter>. If the data has been migrated properly, you get a Congratulation message (Fig 3-7). Pat your back for having such a great job done so easily and nicely!

Press <Enter> to get back to the Migrate Company Menu (like Fig 3-2).

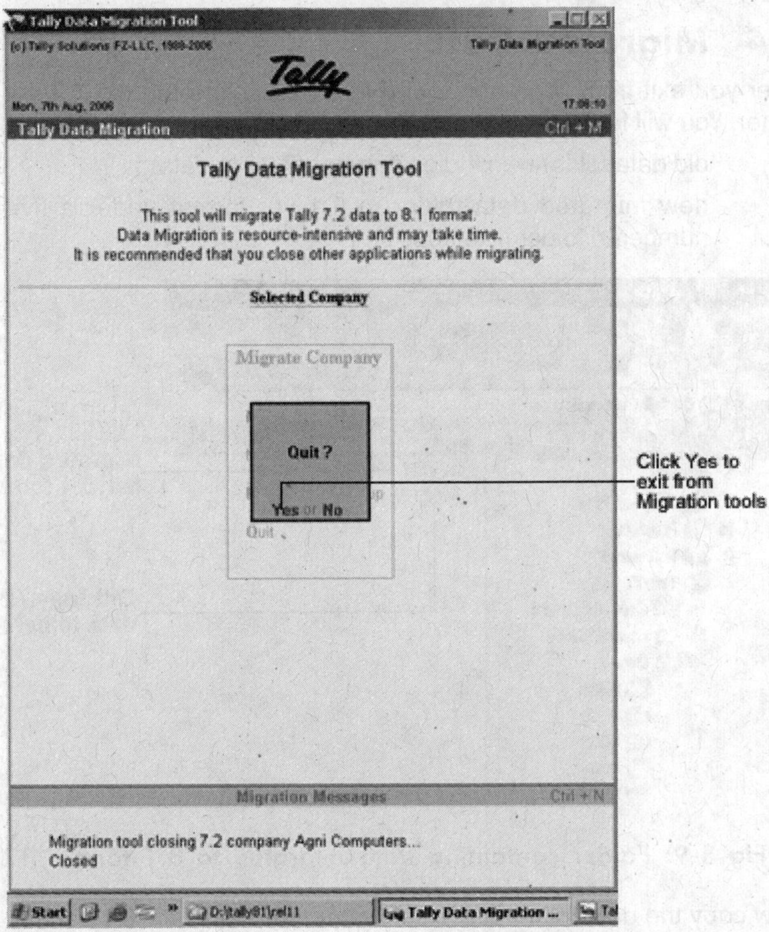

Fig 3-8: Exiting from Migration tool

Press <Esc> to get Quit box (Fig 3-8) to get a confirmation screen (Quit box) to exit from Migration application (Fig 3-8). Type Y to quit from the Migration utility and you get back to the Operating System screen.

3.3 Data Migration Error Messages

If any error is encountered during the process, the info is displayed in the Error Messages pane at the Calculator Area. The partially migrated data will be deleted and you will have to re-start the process once again from beginning.

3.4 Migrated Data

After you exit from Migration tool (Fig 3-8), explore the old 7.2 ver data folder. You will find 2 data folders there (Fig 3-9).

- old data folder with 4 digit number (7.2 ver data)
- new migrated data folder in 8.1 ver format under a five digit numbered folder (like 00001)

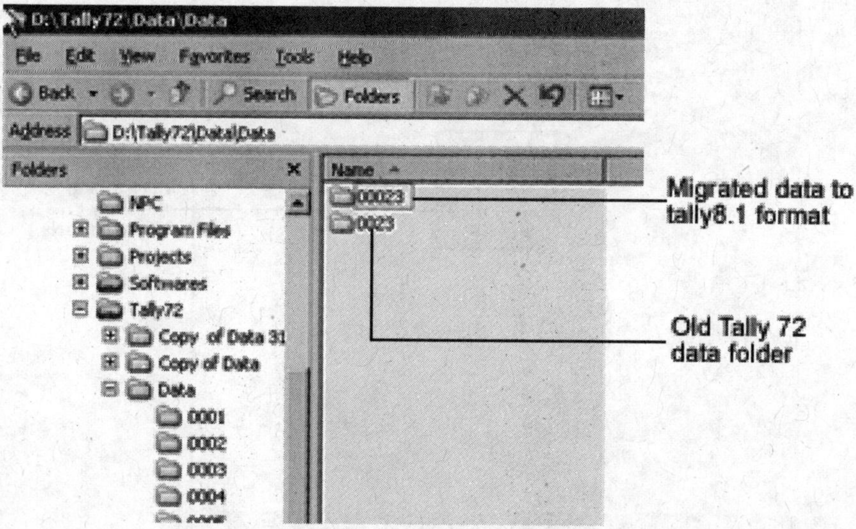

Fig 3-9: Folder containing data migrated to 8.1 format_12

Now copy the data folder in 8.1 data directory. Run Tally 8.1 version. You will now be able to open the Company in 8.1 ver as usual.

Self Test Questions

STQ 03.1: When you can use Tally 7.2 data into Tally 8.1.

STQ 03.2: What is the name of migration utility file. How you can load it.

STQ 03.3 : You have all 7.2 ver data placed in a folder d:\tallydata72 and you have placed all 8.1 ver data in a folder d:\tallydata81. Explain the steps to convert the data of a company from 7.2 ver and place the converted data in 8.1 data folder.

4

Language Setup

Tally 8.1 is a multilingual software. Depending upon the operating system, Tally works in English (available in all flavours of Windows), Hinglish (English vocabulary in Hindi scrip) and 9 other Indic languages (Ref 1.1.2)

4.1 The Start up Language

When you load Tally (Ref 1.3) first time, you see the Gateway of Tally displayed in the language selected at the time of installation (Fig 1-6)

4.1.1 Language Configuration

To change the language, click <u>L</u>:Language button at the vertical button bar (Fig 8-3) or press Alt+L to get the language selection list (Fig 4-1), displayed in the same language.

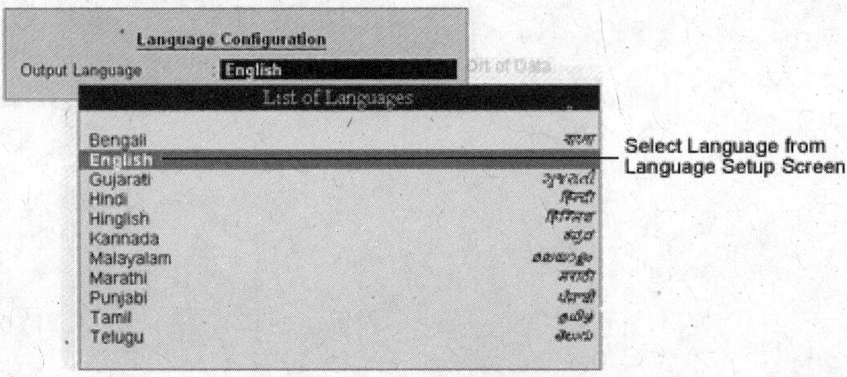

Fig 4-1: Language Selection

Now select the language that you like to work with henceforth. Consequently, all Tally Menu, Forms etc will be displayed in the selected language (this is known as current language). At any point of time, you may again change the current language in the same way (click L:Language and select the language). You will continue to work with the selected language (even when you load Tally next time) till you change the language again

4.1.2 Tally Main menu in different languages

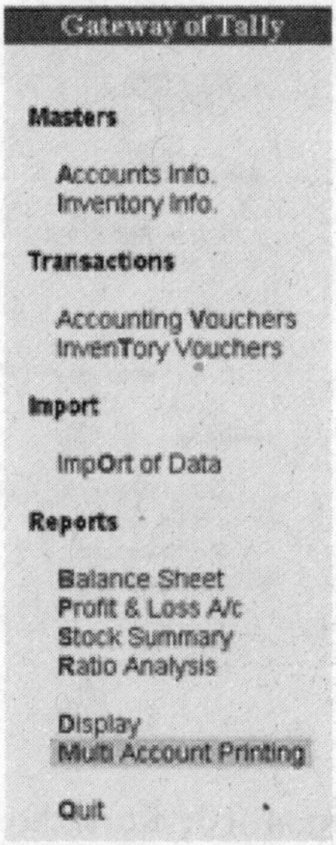

Fig 4-2: English Menu

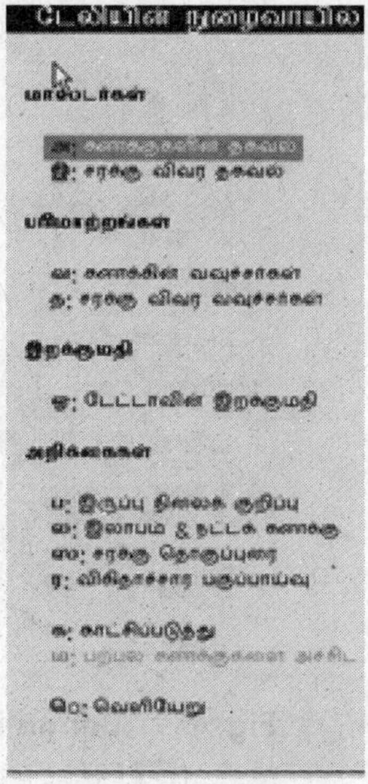

Fig 4-3: Tamil Menu

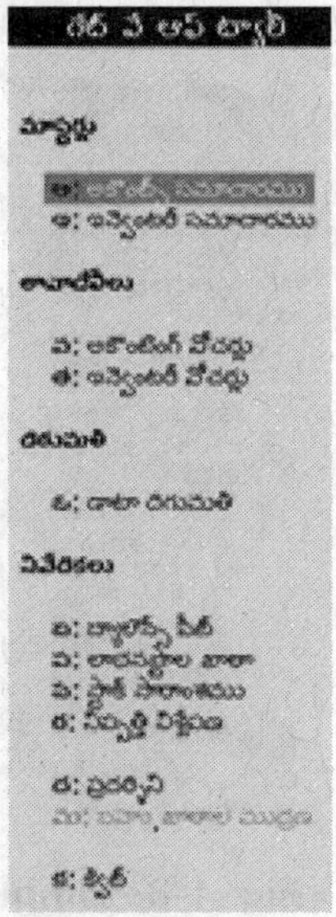

Fig 4-4: Telegu Menu

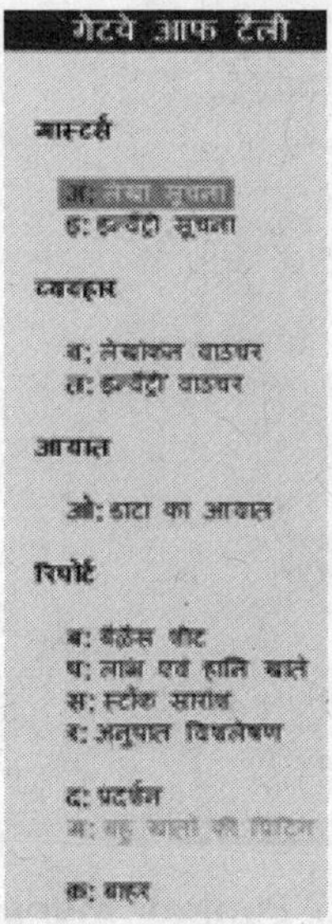

Fig 4-5: Hindi Menu

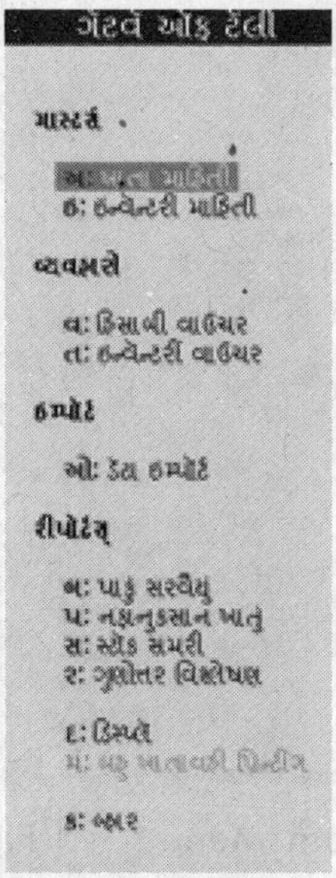

Fig 4-6: Gujrati Menu

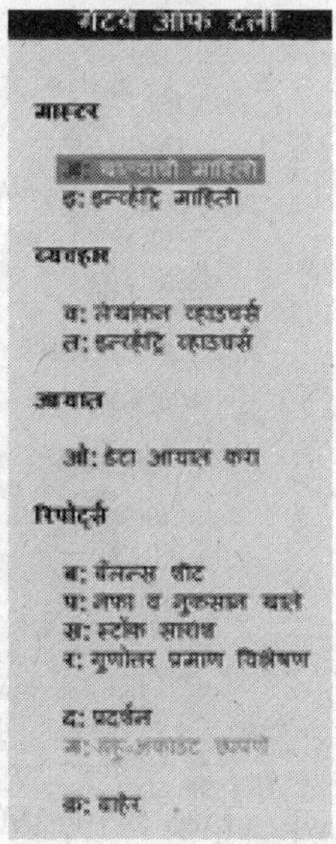

Fig 4-7: Marathi Menu

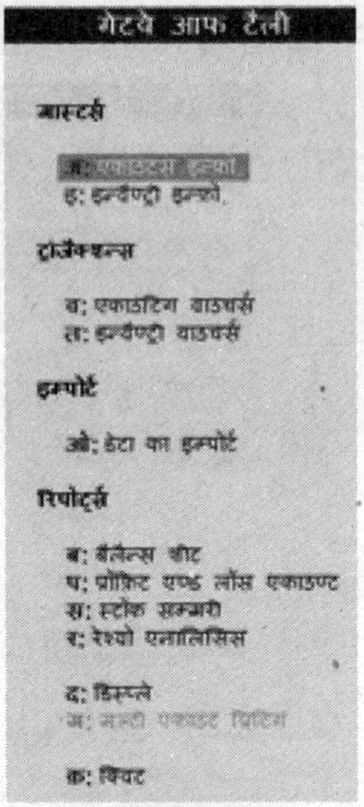

Fig 4-8: Hinglish Menu

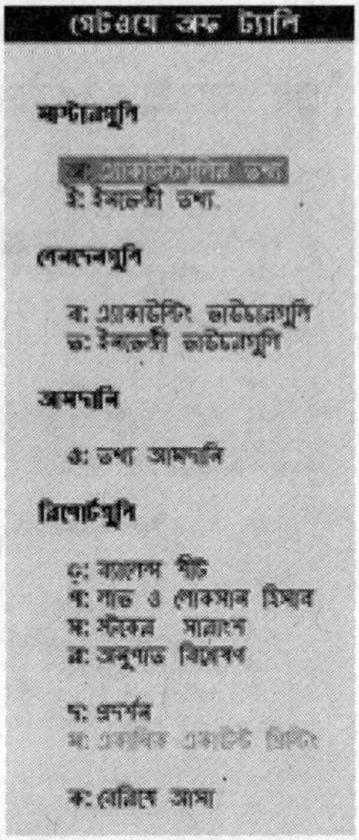

Fig 4-9: Bengali Menu

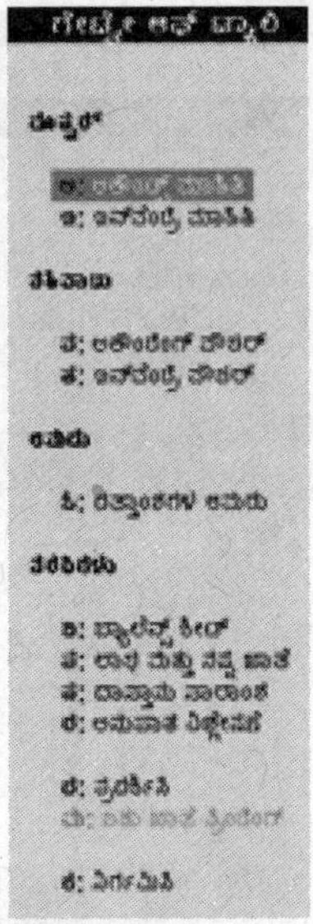

Fig 4-10: Kanadian Menu

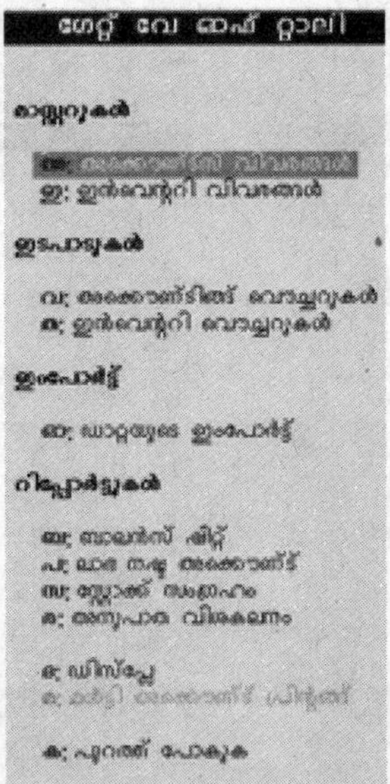

Fig 4-11: Malayam Menu

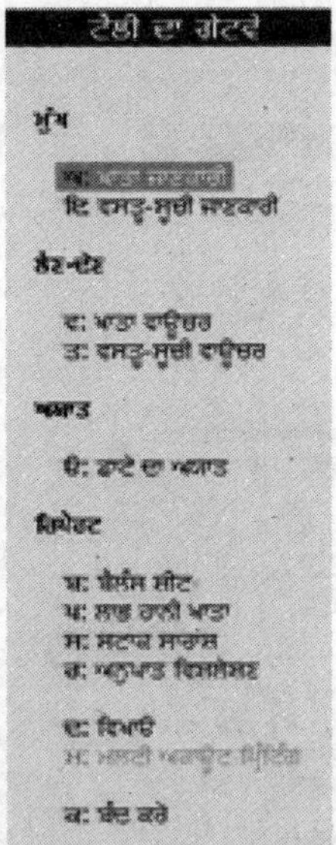

Fig 4-12: Punjabi Menu

After you select the language, you will get the Gateway of Tally in the selected language. Fig 4-2 to 4-12 shows the Tally Main menu in different languages. When you start Tally next time, you will again get the Gateway of Tally in the same language in which you were working when you closed Tally last time.

Self Test Questions

STQ 04.1: At the time of installation, you have selected Hindi language. Now, you want to work in Bengali. How do you change.

Multilingual Operation 5

In chapter 4, you have seen how you can set the language and work in the language of your choice. Everything gets changed to into the selected language. So, you can do all your work in any one of the available language in Tally. All available languages other than English are collectively called *Indic* language.

5.1 Current Language

When you create a Company, Tally internally creates all the initial masters (Reserved Groups, Ledgers etc) in all the available languages, but displays in the current language set.

So, there are 3 types of Languages active at any point of time :

- **Output Language :** The Language set up by L:Language button is the current *Output Language* (Ref 4.1). All data are displayed in this language
- **Keyboard Language :** The Language set up by K:Keyboard button is the current *Keyboard Language*. All data entered is displayed and stored in the current Keyboard Language (Ref 5.2)
- **Print Language :** The language selected through the vertical button bar (Fig 5-17) in Printing Dialogue while displaying / printing a report.

Tally can concurrently work in different languages and you can dynamically switch any or all of these languages whenever you like. Thus at any point of time, you may specify 3 different languages for Output, Keyboard & Printing. Thus while working in English, you may enter data in Hindi and print a Report in Tamil, all at same time. Tally translates the displays and transliterates the data in the specified language on the fly, dynamically (Fig 5-19)

5.2 Keyboard Language Set up

When you select a language, all internal Tally info like Menu, Reports, Forms are displayed in the selected language (called the *current language*). However, the data is entered by user in the Keyboard Language. By default, the current language also becomes the keyboard language.

So, when you enter text data (like Name etc), it is shown in the current language (numeric data are always in English, even in text fields).

To enter data in a different language, click *K:Keyboard* button at the horizontal button bar (Ref 8.3) to get Keyboard language selection list (Fig 5-1). Now select the language from the list, all text data entered will be in selected language script.

You can change the *Output* Language at Menu Level only but can change the *Keyboard* language at entry and printing screen also.

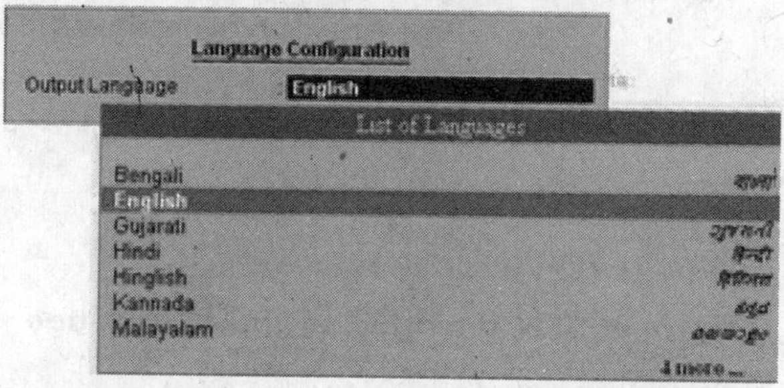

Fig 5-1:Keyboard Language selection

5.3 Reserved Accounts

When you create a Company, all the default Masters (like Reserved Groups etc) are internally created in all the available languages (depending on the operating system). So, the Reserved Accounts may appear in any of the current language, the user created master appear only in the languages created.

5.4 Data Input in Indic Language

When you set the keyboard in any Indic Language, you may enter data in the selected language with your English keyboard in phonetic mode. It is simple & intuitive. A little experiment and practice will do.

The following table shows a typical example of script in Hindi (setting Keyboard Language – Hindi). The corresponding letters to be typed in the English keyboard are shown in the next column.

भारत	bharat	प्रफुल्ल	prafull	तनमय	tanamay	ऋसि	R^isi
बसन्त	basant	निसिथ	nisith	गौतम	gautam	ऋशि	R^ishi
बसन्ट	basanT	तन्मय	tanmay	गौटम	gauTam	ऋषि	R^iShi

The text data that you enter will be entered in the keyboard language selected (numeric will always be shown in English, irrespective of Language or Keyboard selected). For example, if you select Tamil as Keyboard language in the ledger entry screen, Ledger names typed will be displayed in Tamil (irrespective of the current Language)

5.5 Hot keys in Indic language

In Indic language, you have to press the respective key. For example, in Hindi Y/N dialogue box (Fig 5-2), you should press H for *Yes* (not Y). In the same way, other hot keys may be different as per the corresponding key in the selected Indic language.

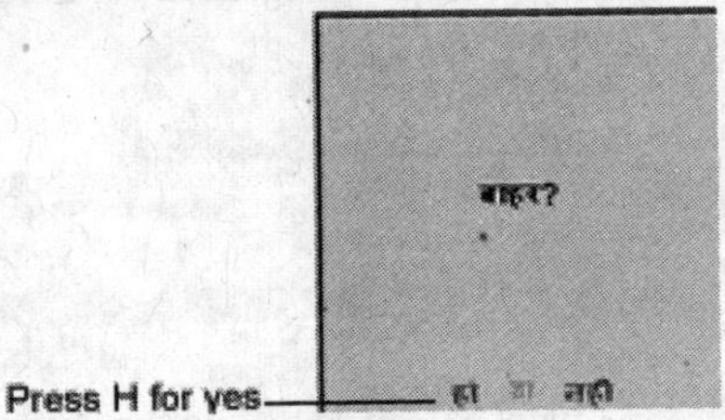

Fig 5-2: Y/N dialogue in Indic language

5.6 Selection of Item from keyboard

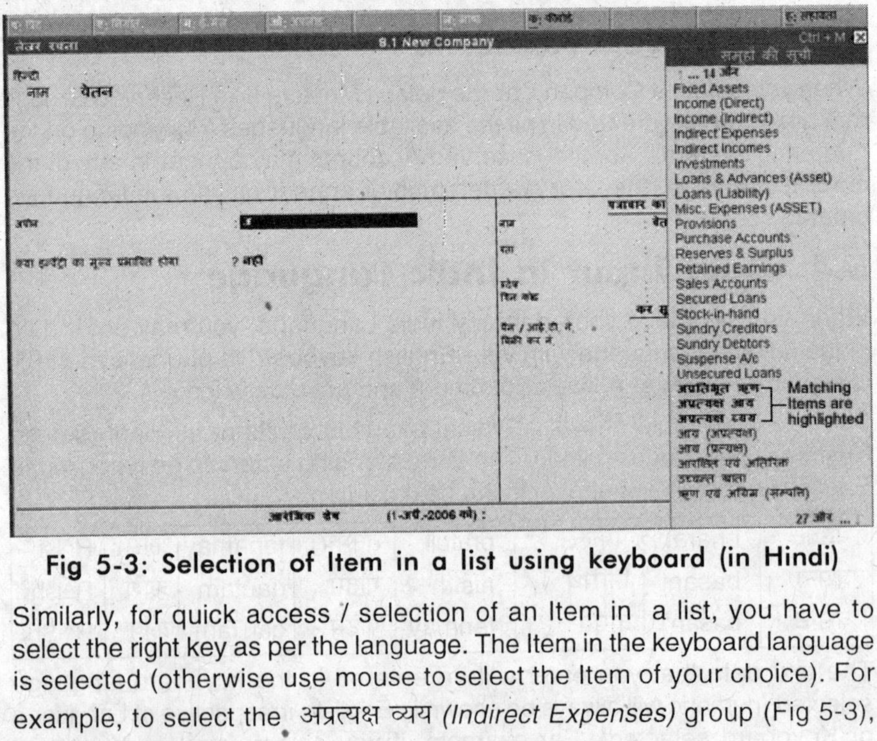

Fig 5-3: Selection of Item in a list using keyboard (in Hindi)

Similarly, for quick access / selection of an Item in a list, you have to select the right key as per the language. The Item in the keyboard language is selected (otherwise use mouse to select the Item of your choice). For example, to select the अप्रत्यक्ष व्यय *(Indirect Expenses)* group (Fig 5-3), you have to type A (the Hindi equivalent letter A for अ (A=अ). All the Items starting with ¥ will get highlighted. You should not type I for *Indirect Expenses* when the keyboard language is Hindi.

5.7 Masters Creation

As has been explained, all reserved masters are internally created by Tally in all the languages. So, you may get the reserved masters displayed in any language.

To get the newly entered masters created by the user also available in any language (like Reserved Masters), you should enter the Name in the respective language also in Master Creation screen, as explained.

5.7.1 Multi Language Masters creation configuration

At Gateway, click F12:Confgure>Accts Inv Info to get the Masters Configuration screen. Set *Yes* at *Allow Language ALIASES alongwith Names* (Fig 5-4)

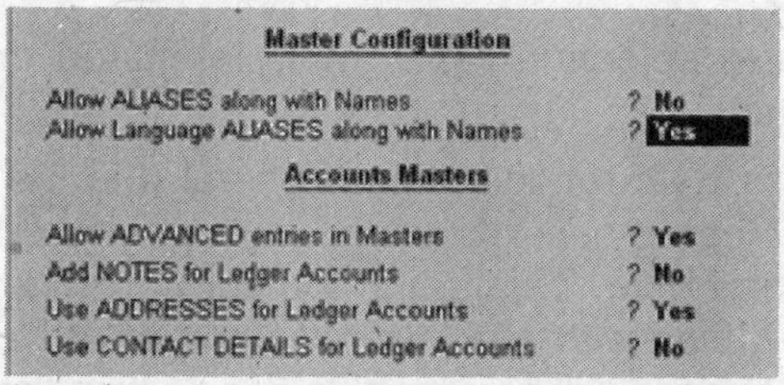

Fig 5-4: Multi Language Masters configuration

5.7.2 Multi language Masters Creation

Now, when you create a new master, you get the current language name (Fig 5-5). Enter the Name in the current language. Having entered the Name in the Current language, you will get the list of language to select from (Fig 5-6). Select the language and enter the Master name in that language for the same Master (Fig 5-7) This way, you may continue to enter Name in multiple languages for the same master (Fig 5-8). Finally select *End of List.*

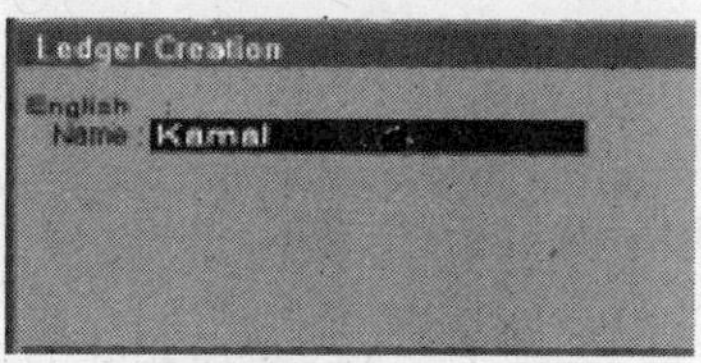

Fig 5-5: Entry of Name in current language (English)

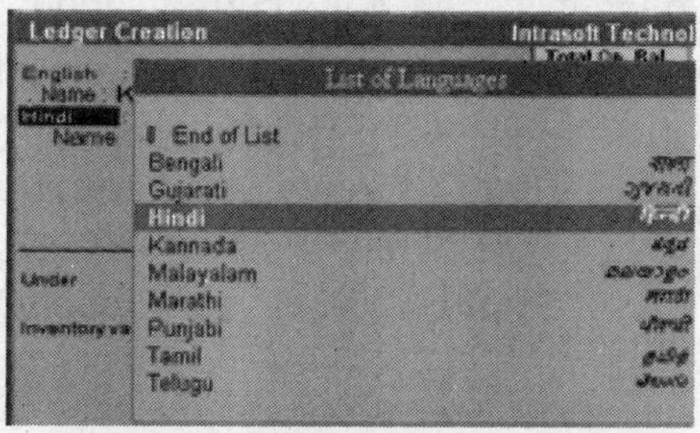

Fig 5-6: Selection of Hindi language

Having entered the master name in multiple languages (Fig 5-8), you will get the names in those languages also in drop down selection list of masters (Fig 5-3) in vouchers and other screens.

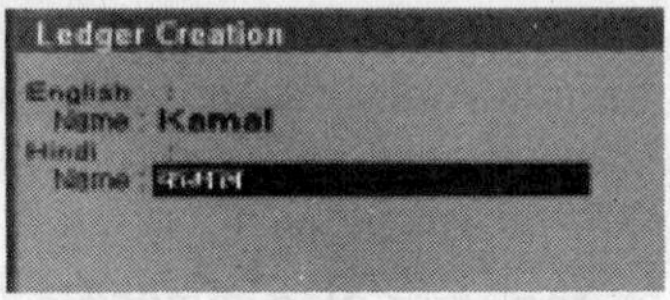

Fig 5-7: Entry in Name in languages

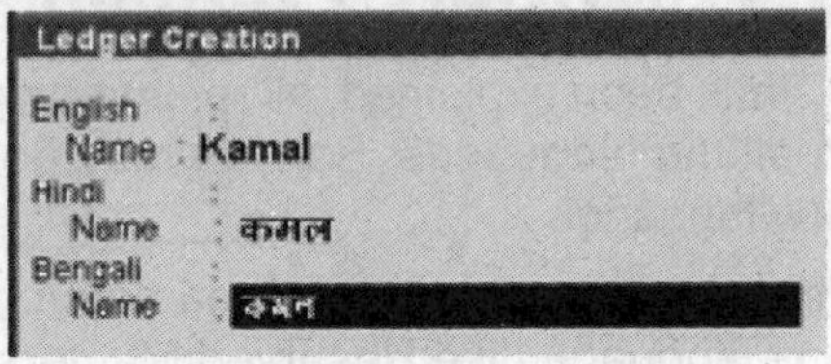

Fig 5-8: Master in multiple another language

5.8 Multi Language Masters List configuration

You may configure selection list of multi language masters through configuration set up

At Gateway, press F12:Configuration>General (Fig 5-9) and set Yes at *show tables with Masters only in current Language* you will get the Masters (Default Master and User created) in the current language only. If you set *No* at *Show tables with Masters only in current Language,* then all masters in all languages will be available in selection list.

Let us assume, few masters are created in Hindi and few masters in Tamil.

Now, when you set *No* at the configuration option (Fig 5-9), you will get the list of all masters in all languages (i.e all reserved masters in all languages and all user created masters in Tamil & Hindi), as shown in Fig 5-10.

When you set *Yes* at the option, you will get the list of masters in the current language only (i.e all reserved masters in the current language and all user created masters in the current language only.

So, in this case, if the current language is :

- **English :** You will get only the reserved masters in English (because no other master has been created in English)
- **Hindi :** You will get all reserved masters in Hindi and all the user created masters in Hindi
- **Tamil :** You will get all reserved masters in Tamil and all the user created masters in Tamil

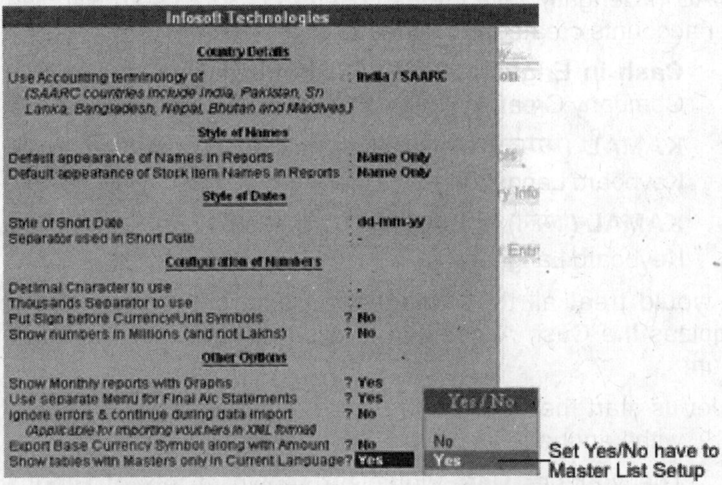

Fig 5-9: General Configuration

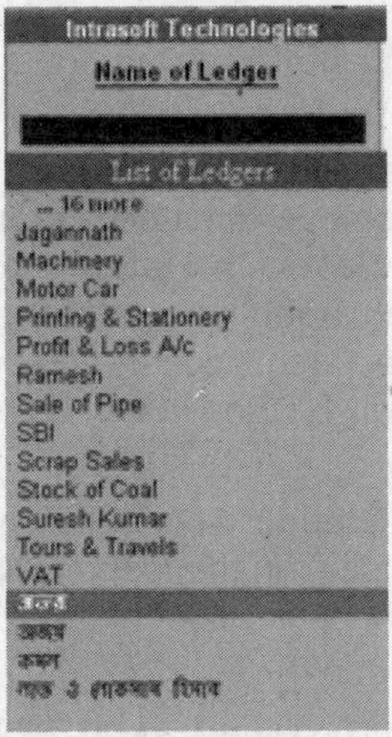

Fig 5-10: Master list in all Languages

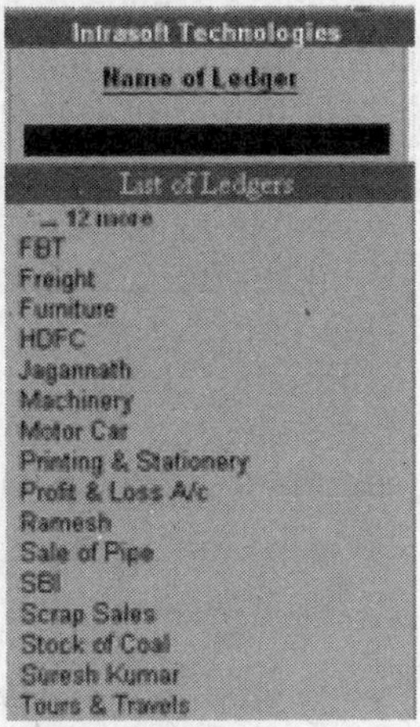

Fig 5-11: Master list in English only

5.9 Multi Language Voucher Entry

Now let us see a Payment Voucher entry in single entry mode. Let us assume that the current language is Hindi & current keyboard language is Bengali . We also assume that all default accounts were created in English (the default language at the time of creation of the Company). Later on, 2 separate Ledger Accounts: कमल (KAMAL in Hindi) and কমল

(KAMAL in Bengali) were created (Ref 5.7). So, to start with, we have 3 ledger accounts created :

- **Cash in English :** This is auto created by Tally at the time of Company Creation
- **KAMAL (कमल) in Hindi :** Created by user setting *Hindi* as Keyboard Language
- **KAMAL (কমল) in Bengali :** Created by user setting *Bengali* as Keyboard Language

Tally would treat all the 3 ledgers as different ledger accounts and recognizes the Cash Account in English as its Reserved Cash Ledger Account

Now let us start the Payment Voucher entry in Single Entry mode (Ref 12.2.2), with Language as Hindi & Keyboard as Bengali.

- The voucher Date would be shown in mix of Hindi (current language) & English (Fig 5-13). The Date & Year (numeric data) would be shown in English, but the month part (e.g May) would be shown in Hindi (the current language). The Day would be shown in Hindi (current language).
- In the Header Account, only Cash Account in English would be available in list (Fig 5-12), because no Cash Ledger (only Cash / Bank Ledger accounts are displayed in Header Account of Payment Voucher) account has been created in any other language. So, you can select the Cash Account in English and the selected Ledger account will be shown in English (the language in which it is created).
- Now in Line Account, you will get 2 ledger Accounts (one KAMAL in Hindi & Another KAMAL in Bengali), in the ledger selection list (in Line Account, only Non cash / bank accounts are available, so Cash Account will not be displayed).
  - ➢ In first line account, select The Hindi KAMAL (कमल) ledger and enter 2300 at amount column. The KAMAL ledger in Hindi would be displayed and a balance of 2300 Dr would be shown in Hindi (figures in English), the current language.
  - ➢ In second line account, select The Bengali KAMAL (কমল) ledger and enter 2500 at amount column. The KAMAL ledger in Bengali would be displayed and a balance of 2500 Dr would be shown in Hindi (figures in English), the current language.

This indicates that the 2 KAMAL ledger accounts created separately in different language, are, in fact, treated as different ledgers by Tally, though in reports in an indic language, they may appear similar (Fig 5-13)

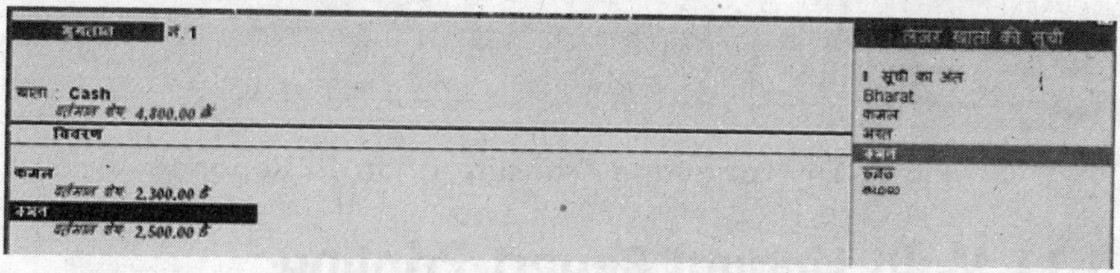

Fig 5-12: Ledger selection from list

Now enter the Voucher Narration. The text letters will be entered in Bengali (current Keyboard language) and numeric figures will be entered in English, within the Narration field (Fig 5-13).

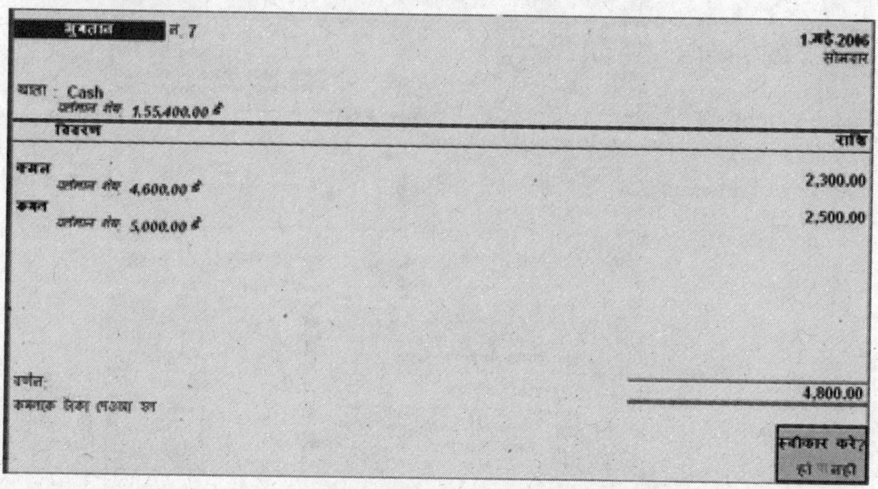

Fig 5-13: Voucher entry in Hindi Language (Bengali Keyboard Language)

5.10 Transliteration

When you view a report in any Indic Language, the data entered in Indic language are transliterated in the current Indic language. So, in the report taken in Hindi, both ledgers (कमल in Hindi and কমল in Bengali) will be shown in Hindi, with their respective figures (Fig 5-14). So, in the report, though the 2 Ledgers appear similar, in fact they are different ledger accounts (that is why they are shown separately with their respective Balance).

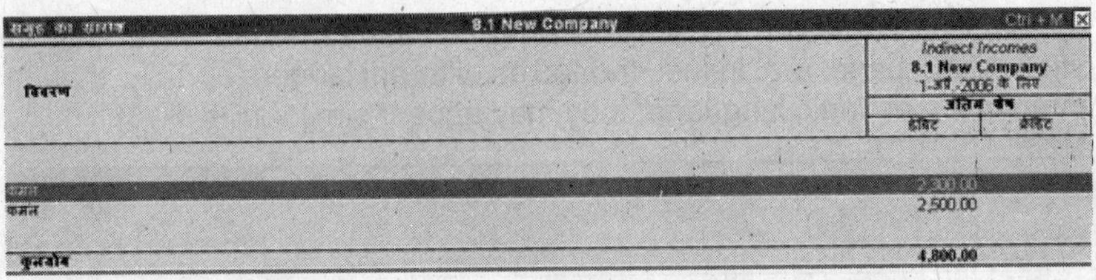

Fig 5-14: Language Transliteration in Reports

5.11 Multi Lingual Report Printing

To print a report in any language, at Print dialogue screen, click *Print Language* button at the vertical button bar (Fig 5-17) and select the Print Language (like Fig 5-1)

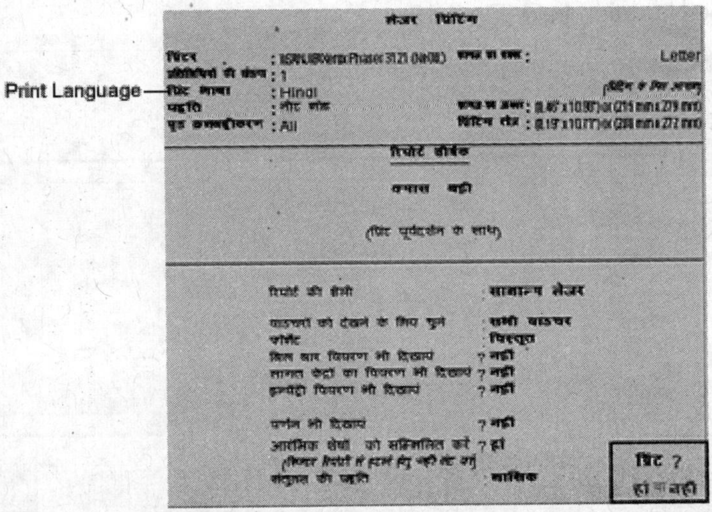

Fig 5-15: Report Printing dialogue in Hindi

The print dialogue Box will be displayed in the current language (Fig 5-15) but the Report will be printed in the selected Print Language.

The data entered in an Indic language will be transliterated in the selected Print Language but data entered in English will not get translated and will be shown in English only (Fig 5-16).

Fig 5-15 shows the Print Dialogue Box in Hindi and Fig 516 shows Report in Hindi.

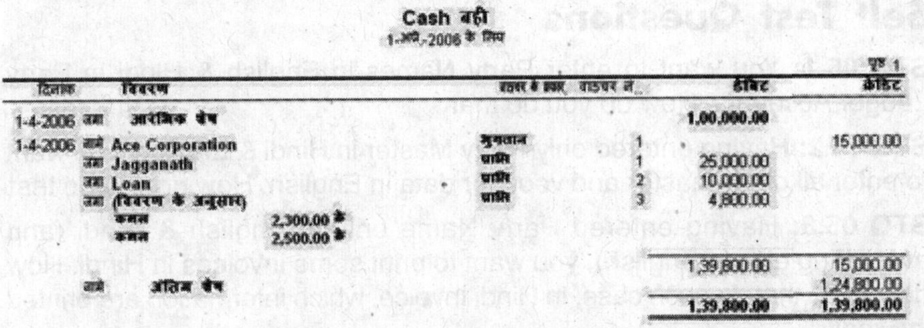

Fig 5-16: Report in Hindi

The default Title will appear in current language. To change Report Title & Subtitle in any other language, click K:Keyboard from the horizontal button bar and select the language (Fig 5-1). Now click *Titling* Button at Vertical Button Bar (Fig 5-17 – the button names are displayed in the current language) and enter the Report Title & Sub Title in the Keyboard Language (Fig 5-18)

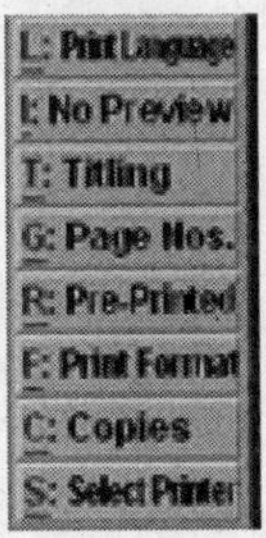

Fig 5-17: Title Button at Vertical button Bar

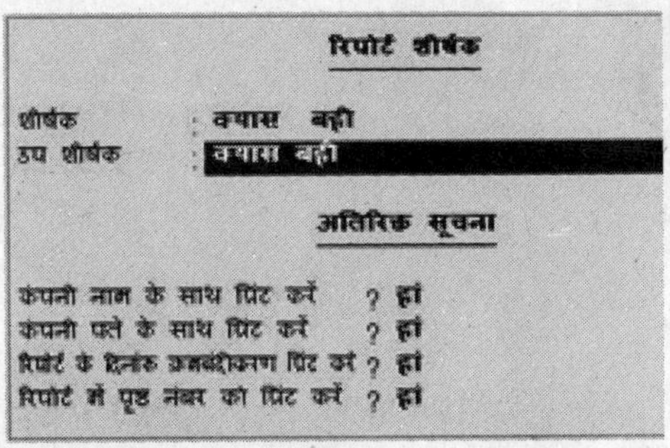

Fig 5-18: Report Sub Title entry in Hindi

Fig 5-19 shows the Report in Bengali (in Print Language) and Sub Title in Hindi. The data in Indic language are transliterated in the Print Language.

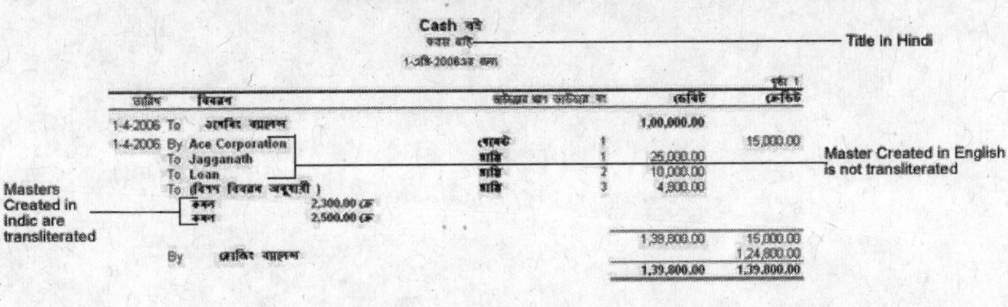

Fig 5-19: Report Preview

Self Test Questions

STQ 05.1: You want to enter Party Names in English & Hindi in Party Ledger Accounts. How do you do that

STQ 05.2: Having entered only Party Master in Hindi & English, you want to enter all other master and voucher data in English. How do you do that

STQ 05.3: Having entered Party Name only in English & Hindi (and everything else in English), you want to print some invoices in Hindi. How do you do that. In such case, in Hindi Invoice, which information are printed in Hindi.

Basic Concepts of Acccounting 6

Accounting is about managing resources (like Money, Materials). It involves identifying, recording, analyzing and presenting information about Money & Materials to form an opinion about the performance or status of an enterprise for better decisions.

The task of accounting may be classified in 2 stages. Recording & Analyzing.

Recording : The first task of accounting starts from recording an activity which can be discreetly expressed in terms of money. The activity may actually involve Money (for example Payment of Salary), Materials (like Issuing Materials from Stores to Works for Production) or both (Cash Sales of Goods) and is expressed in terms of money affecting the financial position.

Record of each individual activity is called *Voucher*

Analyzing : It involves compiling & summarizing the basic records to present information in desired manner

The presented information derived from the records (Vouchers) is called *Report*

We have already stated that Accounting is about managing Money & Materials. In the first part of the book, we exclusively discuss about Financial Accounting (only about Managing Money). In second part of this book, we will discuss about managing Materials also.

6.1 Basic Foundation of Accounting

The basic task of accounting involves :

- Finding the net gain / loss of financial activity during a stated period. This information is presented in a report called *Profit & Loss Statement*
- Ascertaining the status of what is owned, owed and the assets held. This information is presented in a report called *Balance Sheet*

6.2 Basic elements of Accounts

Having identified the concept of Accounting, it is easy to find the following basic elements of accounting, represented in a financial report (the results of Transactions recorded in Vouchers)

- *Income & Expense* which contribute to Net Gain / Loss in terms of Money
- *Liabilities & Assets* representing what is *owed* & what is *owned*, in terms of Money

So, any financial transaction will result in :

- Increase / decrease in Income or Expense
- Increase / decrease in Liabilities or Assets

Or any sort of combination of some or all of the above

For any entity, the Liabilities represent 2 elements. Money contributed by the owner, called *Capital* and money supplied by others (other than owner). So, the enterprise, which is considered to be distinct from the Owner for the purpose of accounting, owes money to Owner (represented by *Capital*) and to others (represented by *Liabilities*).

The Net Increase or decrease in Income / Expense (normally called *Profit* or *Loss*) is finally absorbed into Capital.

As there are rules of arithmetic, there are rules of Accounting. The Liabilities and Assets will always be equal. In simplest terms, the net profit (excess of Income over expenses) is added to the Capital Account and the Net Loss (excess of Expenses over Income) is reduced from the Capital Account

To explain the concepts stated above, we will take up 3 simple examples about Accounting – recording a *voucher* (the financial transaction) and reflecting it in a *report*.

- Madhu, a student, who maintains his accounts of money received from his parents and maintains his accounts of expenses and other financial transactions.
- Somnath, an employee, who maintains his accounts of Salary, Other Income and household expenses & his investments
- P K Das, an accounting professional, maintains the accounts of his profession and his personal expenses, investments etc.

Madhu : A student

Madhu, a first year B Com student, starts his accounts from Rs 1000 received from his father on 1st April 06, considered as Income, by which he creates his own Capital. So, he has a cash of Rs 1000 to start with.

So, his starting Balance Sheet would be

Liabilities	*Rs.*	*Assets*	*Rs.*
Capital	1000	Cash	1000

He now opens a savings Bank Account with State Bank of India, with an initial deposit of Rs 500. The effect of this transaction is :

Account affected	*Effect of the transaction*	*Rs*	*Rs*
State Bank of India	Increase in Asset	500	
Cash	Decrease in Asset		500

Through this transaction, the asset *Cash Account* is decreased and another asset Bank Account is increased by Rs 500.

The Balance Sheet after this transaction would look like :

Liabilities	*Rs.*	*Assets*	*Rs.*
Capital	1000	Cash	500
		State Bank of India	500
Total	**1000**		**1000**

During April 06, he spends Rs 200 for books, Rs 100 for Conveyance, Rs. 150 in Restaurants in cash

The effect of this transaction is :

Account affected	*Effect of the transaction*	*Rs*	*Rs*
Books Purchase	Increase in Expense	200	
Conveyance	Increase in Expense	100	
Fooding Expenses	Increase in Expense	150	
Cash	Decrease in Asset		450

The Profit & Loss Statement for the period 1-4-06 to 30-4-06 will look like:

Expenses	*Rs.*	*Income*	*Rs.*
Books Purchase	200	Contribution Received from Father	1000
Conveyance	100		
Fooding Expenses	150		
Net Income transferred to capital Account	550		
Total	**1000**		**1000**

And the Balance Sheet as on 30-4-06 would look like:

Liabilities	*Rs.*	*Assets*	*Rs.*
Capital (1000-450)	550	Cash	50
		State Bank of India	500
Total	**550**		**550**

In May 06, he gives coaching to a Std II student and earns 600 rupees, in cash.

The effect of this transaction is :

Account affected	*Effect of the transaction*	*Rs*	*Rs*
Coaching Fees Received	Increase in Income		600
Cash	Increase in Asset	600	

The Profit & Loss Statement for 1-4-06 to 31-5-06 will now look like :

Expenses	*Rs.*	*Income*	*Rs.*
Books Purchase	200	Contribution Received from Father	1000
Conveyance	100	Coaching Fees Received	600
Fooding Expenses	150		
Net Income transferred to capital Account	1150		
Total	**1600**		**1600**

The Profit & Loss Statement now tells the details of his income and the expenses and the net Income.

And the Balance Sheet as on 31-5-06 would look like :

Liabilities	*Rs.*	*Assets*	*Rs.*
Capital (1000-450+600)	1150	Cash	650
		State Bank of India	500
Total	**1150**		**1150**

The Balance Sheet shows the net position of all his assets and owned capital.

Now since he has started earning, he feels that he will not take any money from his parents as contribution. If he needs money, he will take as loan and refund from his earnings. On 1-6-06, he takes a loan of Rs 2000 from his Brother in Cash, deposits the money (Rs 2000) in Bank account and. During June 06, he pays Examination fees of Rs 1000 to his college, by cheque

The effects of the transactions in June 06 are:

Account affected	*Effect of the transaction*	*Rs*	*Rs*
Loans taken from Brother	Increase in Liabilities		2000
Cash	Increase in Asset	2000	
State Bank of India	Increase in Asset	2000	
Cash	Decrease in Asset		2000
Examination Fees	Increase in Expenses	1000	
State Bank of India	Decrease in Asset		1000

The Profit & Loss Statement for 1-4-06 to 30-6-06 will now look like :

Expenses	*Rs.*	*Income*	*Rs.*
Books Purchase	200	Contribution Received from Father	1000
Conveyance	100	Coaching Fees Received	600
Fooding Expenses	150		
Examination Fees	1000		
Net Income transferred to capital Account	150		
Total	**1600**		**1600**

You find that the P & L Statement shows the details of Income & Expenses only while the Balance Sheet tells about the Assets & Liabilities

And the Balance Sheet as on 30-6-06 would look like :

Liabilities	*Rs.*	*Assets*	*Rs.*
Capital	150	Cash	650
Loan from Brother	2000	State Bank of India	1500
Total	**2150**		**2150**

Somnath: An Employee

Somnath, a salesman in a manufacturing firm, starts maintaining his accounts from 1st of April 2006. His earning comprises Salary received from his employer and from Bank deposits and other investments

To begin with, he first compiled all his assets and liabilities at the start of 1st April 2006.

Liabilities	*Rs.*	*Assets*	*Rs.*
Loan from Employer	6000	Investment in Shares	10000
		Fixed Deposits in Bank of India with accrued Interest	14157
		National Savings Certificate with accrued Interest	10343
		Balance lying in SBI Savings A/c	12300
		Cash in Hand	3400
Total	**6000**		**50200**

So, the net of Assets and Liabilities would comprise his Capital. The Balance Sheet as on 1-4-2006 looks like :

Liabilities	*Rs.*	*Assets*	*Rs.*
Capital	44200	Investment in Shares	10000
Loan from Employer	6000	Fixed Deposits in Bank of India with accrued Interest	14157
		National Savings Certificate with accrued Interest	10343
		Balance lying in SBI Savings A/c	12300
		Cash in Hand	3400
Total	**50200**		**50200**

On 30th April 2006, he gets a cheque of Rs 11250 towards his salary (Salary - Rs 12000, PF deduction – Rs 120, I Tax Deduction – Rs 100, P Tax deduction – Rs 30, Loan Recovery – Rs 500).

The effect of the transactions are explained below :

Account affected	*Effect of the transaction*	*Rs*	*Rs*
Salary earned	Increase in Income		12000
P F Cont – Own	Increase in Assets	120	
I Tax - TDS	Increase in Assets	100	
P Tax	Increase in Expense	30	
Loan Repayment	Decrease in Liability	500	
SBI Savings Account	Increase in Asset	11250	

You find that PF and I Tax deductions have been treated as Asset. This will help him to keep records of PF deductions on a continuous basis. At the end of the year, when he gets a statement of PF, he may account for Employers Contribution and the Interest accrued on them. I Tax paid is also will be accounted for at the end of year treating his total I Tax Liability as Expense after adjusting the I Tax already deducted. The P Tax deducted is naturally treated as Expense.

The P L statement for the period 1.4.2006 to 30.4.2006 will look like :

Expenses	*Rs.*	*Income*	*Rs.*
P Tax	30	Salary	12000
Net Profit transferred to Capital A/c	11970		
Total	**12000**	**Total**	**12000**

And the Balance Sheet as on 30.4.2006 will look like :

Liabilities	*Rs.*	*Assets*	*Rs.*
Capital (44200+11970)	56170	Investment in Shares	10000
Loan from Employer (6000-500)	5500	Fixed Deposits in Bank of India with accrued Interest	14157
		National Savings Certificate with accrued Interest	10343
		P F Cont - Own	120
		I Tax - TDS	100
		Balance lying in SBI Savings A/c(12300+11250)	23550
		Cash in Hand	3400
Total	**61670**		**61670**

On 12th May 2006, he withdrew Rs 5000 from his Bank Account through ATM and paid in Cash as follows: House Rent – Rs 3600, Rs 2800 for household expenses, Bought a scooter costing Rs 35000 through HDFC Bank Loan and paid Rs 3000 as first instalment. On 31.5.2006, the Bank charged Rs 630 towards Interest on Loan on Scooter for the month and debited in Loan A/c

The effects of the transactions are explained below:

Account affected	*Effect of the transaction*	*Rs*	*Rs*
SBI Savings Bank A/c	Decrease in Assets		5000
Cash	Increase in Assets	5000	
Household expenses	Increase in Expenses	2800	
House Rent	Increase in Expenses	3600	

Cash	Decrease in Assets		6400
Purchase of Scooter HDFC Bank Scooter Loan	Increase in Assets Increase in Liabilities	35000	 35000
HDFC Bank Scooter Loan SBI Savings Bank	Decrease in Liability Decrease in Asset	3000	 3000
HDFC Bank Scooter Loan Interest Paid on Scooter Loan	Increase in Liabilities Increase in Expenses	 630	630

On 31.5.2006 he got the same salary for May 2006, as he received on 30.4.2006. Now prepare the P L Statement and Balance Sheet as on 31.5.2005 after considering the receipt of salary.

The P L statement for the period 1.4.2006 to 31.5.2006 will look like :

Expenses	*Rs.*	*Income*	*Rs.*
P Tax	60	Salary	24000
Household Expenses	2800		
House Rent	3600		
Interest on Scooter Loan	630		
Net Profit transferred to Capital A/c	16910		
Total	**24000**	**Total**	**24000**

And the Balance Sheet as on 31.5.2006 will look like :

Liabilities	*Rs.*	*Assets*	*Rs.*
Capital (44200+16910)	61110	Scooter	35000
Loan from Employer	5000	Investment in Shares	10000
Loan on scooter (35000-3000+630)	32630	Fixed Deposits in Bank of India with accrued Interest	14157
		National Savings Certificate with accrued Interest	10343
		P F Cont – Own(120+120)	240
		I Tax – TDS(100+100)	200
		Balance lying in SBI Savings A/c (23550 +11250– 5000 - 3000)	26800
		Cash in Hand (3400+5000-6400)	2000
Total	**98740**		**98740**

P K Das : Accountant

P K Das, an Accountant provides accounting services and consultancy to its clients. He started accounts from 1.4.2006. He had his Balance Sheet ready as on 31.3.2006, to start with.

Liabilities	*Rs.*	*Assets*	*Rs.*
Capital	3,68,800	Furniture (At Cost 145000, less Accumulated Depn – 14500)	1,30,500
Term Loan from SBI	60,000	Public Provident Fund including accrued Interest	1,72,500
Rent Payable	3,000	National Savings Certificate including accrued Interest	33,500
		Deposit with Electricity Co	6,300
		Deposit for Office Space	30,000
		Sundry Debtors	18,000
		HDFC Current A/c	36,350
		Cash	4,650
Total	**4,31,800**		**4,31,800**

He summarized the accounts for the period for 1.4.2006 to 31.3.2007 as follows:

- He raised professional bills for Rs 1,35,000 during the year
- He received Rs 1,43,000 from his clients against his service bills and Rs 400 as interest from one of his client for paying the bill late. He takes all such payments by Cheque only and banks his cheques in HDFC current account.
- He paid Rent Rs 18000 including the outstanding rent of Rs 3,000 due on 31.3.06. SBI charged him Rs 5300 towards interest on Term Loan and debited to the Term Loan account. He also repaid Rs 6000 towards Term Loan.
- He incurred Cash business expenses on account of Conveyance – Rs 3200, Postage – 620, Telephone / Mobile – Rs 4300. During the period, he withdrew Rs 6000 to meet cash expenses from HDFC current a/c.

The effect of the transactions are shown below:

Account affected	*Effect of the transaction*	*Rs*	*Rs*
Sundry Debtors	Increase in Assets	1,35,000	
Professional Fees earned	Increase in Income		1,35,000
Sundry Debtors	Decrease in Assets		1,43,000
Interest received	Increase in Income		400
HDFC Current A/c	Increase in Assets	1,43,400	
Rent paid	Increase in Expense	15,000	
Outstanding Rent	Decrease in Liabilities	3,000	
HDFC Current A/c	Decrease in Asset		18,000
Interest Paid on Loan	Increase in Expenses	5,300	
Term Loan from SBI	Increase in Liabilities		5,300
Term Loan from SBI	Decrease in Liability	6,000	
HDFC Current A/c	Decrease in Asset		6,000
Conveyance	Increase in Expense	3,200	
Postage	Increase in Expense	620	
Telephone / Mobile Exp	Increase in Expense	4,300	
Cash	Decrease in Asset		8,120
Cash	Increase in Asset	6,000	
HDFC Current A/c	Decrease in Asset		6,000

The P L Statement for the period 1.4.2006 to 31.3.2007 would look like

Expenses	*Rs.*	*Income*	*Rs.*
Rent paid	15000	Professional fees earned	1,35,000
Interest Paid on Loan	5300	Interest received	400
Conveyance	3200		
Postage	620		
Telephone/Mobile Exp	4300		
Net Profit transferred to Capital A/c	106980		
Total	**135400**	**Total**	**1,35,400**

And the Balance Sheet as on 31.3.2007 will look like

Liabilities	*Rs.*	*Assets*	*Rs.*
Capital (368800+ 106980)	475780	Furniture (At Cost 145000, less Accumulated Depn – 14500)	1,30,500
Term Loan from SBI (60000+5300-6000)	59300	Public Provident Fund including accrued Interest	1,72,500
		National Savings Certificate including accrued Interest	33,500
		Deposit with Electricity Co	6,300
		Deposit for Office Space	30,000
		Sundry Debtors (18000+ 135000-143000)	10,000
		HDFC Current A/c (36350+ 143400-18000-6000-6000)	1,49,750
		Cash(4650-8120+6000)	2,530
Total	**5,35,080**		**5,35,080**

At the end of year, he provided Depreciation on Furniture @ 10% on net depreciated value. He also wrote off Rs 2000 as Bad Debt as one of his clients left the city and is not likely to pay off.

The effect of the transactions are shown below

Account affected	*Effect of the transaction*	*Rs*	*Rs*
Depreciation	Increase in Expenses	13,050	
Furniture	Decrease in Assets		13,050
Sundry Debtors	Decrease in Assets		2,000
Bad debt	Increase in Expenses	2,000	

The revised P L Statement for 1-4-2006 to 31-3-2007 looks like

Expenses	*Rs.*	*Income*	*Rs.*
Rent paid	15000	Professional fees earned	135000
Interest	5300	Interest	400
Conveyance	3200		
Postage	620		
Telephone/Mobile Exp	4300		
Depreciation	13050		
Bad Debt	2000		
Net Profit transferred to Capital A/c	91930		
Total	**135400**	**Total**	**135400**

And the revised Balance Sheet as on 31.3.2007 will look like

Liabilities	*Rs.*	*Assets*	*Rs.*
Capital (368800+ 91930)	4,60,730	Furniture (At Cost 145000, less Depn – 27550)	1,17,450
Term Loan from SBI	59,300	Public Provident Fund including accrued Interest	1,72,500
		National Savings Certificate including accrued Interest	33,500
		Deposit with Electricity Co	6,300
		Deposit for Office Space	30,000
		Sundry Debtors (10000-2000)	8,000
		HDFC Current A/c	1,49,750
		Cash	2,530
Total	**5,20,030**		**5,20,030**

So, you have understood the basic concepts of accounting about how to organize financial information into Profit & Loss Account (to know the Profit / Loss for a specified period) and to get balance Sheet (to know the Assets & Liabilities on a given date). In this short brief, you have seen that transactions are posted into entities (called ledgers / account groups) that are represented in the Balance Sheet & P L Statement.

In later chapter in this book, we will see how to create the entities (Account Ledger & Account Groups), how to record the transaction in Vouchers and how to get the P L Statement and Balance Sheet compiled from the Transactions (Vouchers) into the respective entities (Accounts Groups & Ledger Accounts).

Self Test Questions

STQ 06.1 State the nature of following accounts (Liability, Asset, Income, Expense)

(a) Stock of Goods for sale

(b) Motor Car held in stock by a car dealer

(c) Motor Car used by a Doctor

(d) Depreciation

(e) Sales

(f) Purchase

(g) Professional Fees earned by a lawyer

(h) TDS deducted by the company from payment to a contractor (in Company's Book)

(i) TDS deducted from the contractors bill (in Contractors Books)

(j) Professional Tax deducted from salary (in employees books)

(k) Loan Taken

(l) Loan Given

(m) Drawings by Proprietor from the Business (in the books of Business)

(n) Customer account (whom goods have been sold on credit)

(o) Supplier account (from whom goods have been purchased on credit)

(p) Term Loan taken from bank

(q) Overdraft from bank

(r) Current Account with bank

(s) Debenture issued by the company

(t) Share Capital of the company

(u) Share of the other companies purchased (for investement)

STQ 06.2 For each of the following transactions, state the effect of accounts

Example: Conveyance expenses Rs 500 paid in Cash

Conveyance A/c	Increase in Expenses	500	
Cash A/c	Decrease in Assets		500

i. Depreciation on Motor Car Rs. 2000

ii. Cash Sales of Rs 1000

iii. Goods for Rs 4000 Purchased from A K Enterprise on Credit

iv. Professional Fees of Rs 200 earned in Cash

v. A K Tewari billed for Professional Fees for Rs 1000

vi. Rs 3960 paid in Cash to an employee towards Salary (Rs 4000) after deducting Rs 40 towards Professional Tax

vii. Rs 2200 received in cash towards Cash Sale of goods (Rs 2000 sale value, Rs 200 Sales Tax charged). The Sales Tax collected is to be deposited to the Government

viii. Rs 20000 received by cheque from A K Saha towards Loan, deposited with bank of India current account.

Company Creation

7

Having installed Tally, you will now create the first Company in Tally

7.1 Tally Company

In Tally, the term *Company* represents any entity for which an independent set of Accounts is maintained. It may be a Company, Partnership Firm, H.U.F, Individual, NGO, or even a Branch Office for which a set of Account is maintained. If a Company maintains separate sets of accounts for its Branches, then each Branch will be treated as a separate *Tally Company*.

So, in Tally, the Term *Company* is any entity for which you keep a separate Set of Accounts.

7.2 Tally Company Creation

To create a Company, click *Create Company* at Company Info Menu (Fig 7-1 & 7-2)

- **Creating the First Company** : After installation of Tally, you get the *Company Info* menu (Fig 7-1). Click *Create Company* at *Company* to get Company Creation screen (Fig 7-3).
- **Creating more Companies** : Later on, to create a Company, at Gateway (Fig 8-1), click *F3: Cmp Info* button at vertical button bar (Fig 8-9) to get *Company Info* Menu (Fig 7-2). Select **Create Company** to get Company Creation screen (Fig 7-3).

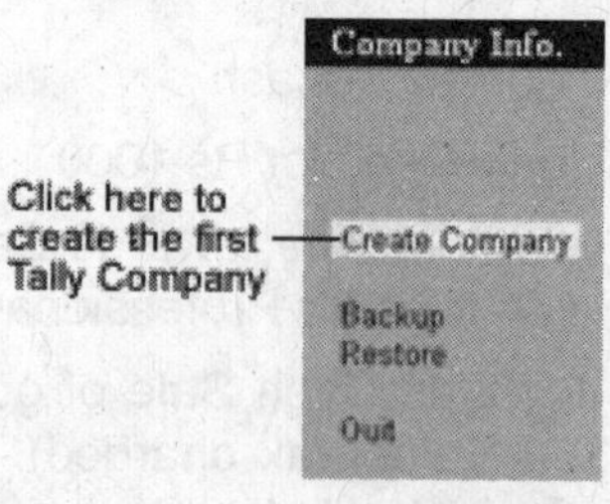

Fig 7-1: Company Info Menu (when no Company is created)

Fig 7-2: Company Info Menu

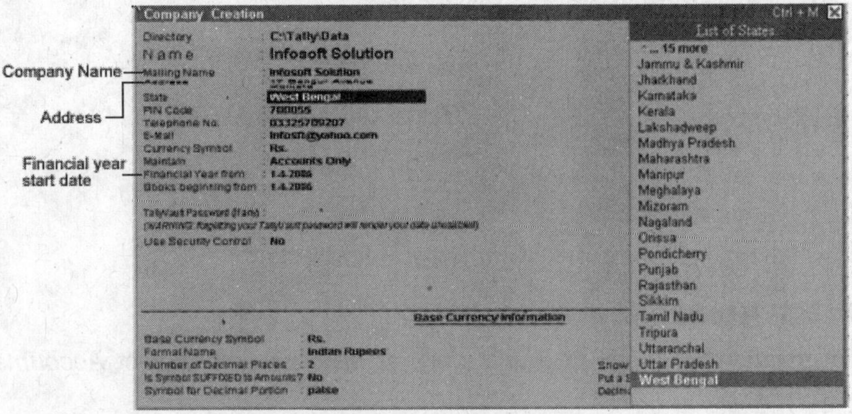

Fig 7-3: Company Creation

We now explain the steps of entry.

7.3 Company Particulars

At the top part, enter the following information regarding the new Company you are creating (Fig 7-3).

1. Company Name
2. Address
3. Maintain (modules)
4. Financial Year From

Fig 7-3 shows the completed entry of company creation screen. You may enter only the above 4 fields and leave default value at other optional fields (explained later). You must enter Company Name, Module Name (Maintain) & Financial Year from. Entry of Company Address is optional. You may enter them later on through Company Alteration (Ref 7.7.2).

7.3.1 Company Name

Enter the Name of the Company at *Name* field (Fig 7-4). This Name is displayed at all Company selection lists and internal Reports.

7.3.2 Company Address

Enter the complete mailing address line by line (Fig 7-4), as you like to print in Invoice etc (you may enter address in many lines). Press ↵ and type the address in the next line. Press ↵ in a blank line to terminate Address entry and move to the next field.

- **State** : Select the State from the list (for India only)

PIN Code : Enter the PIN Code

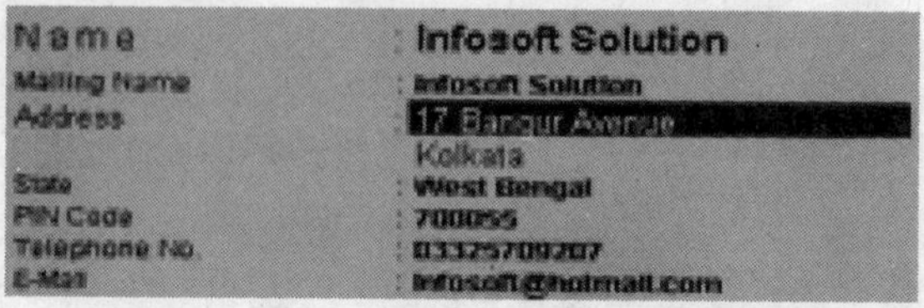

Fig 7-4: Company Address entry

7.3.3 Accounting Modules

To maintain Financial Accounts only, at *Maintain* field, select *Accounts only* (Fig 7-5).

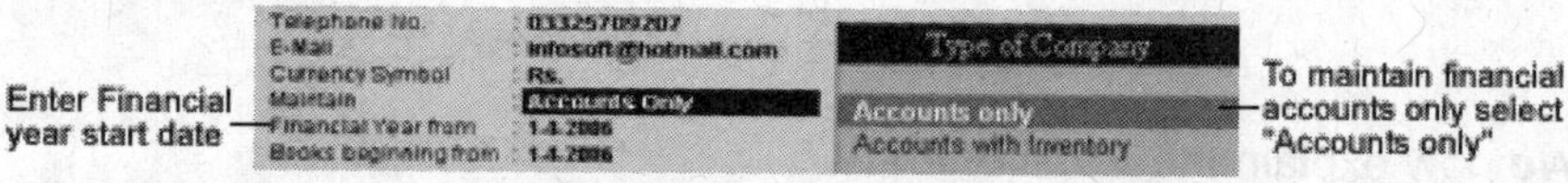

Fig 7-5: Selection of Accounting Module

7.3.4 Financial Year Starting Date

At the *Financial Year From* field (Fig 7-5), enter the Beginning Date of *Financial Year*. If you follow April-March Financial year, enter 1st April of the beginning year (e.g. 1-4-2006). In fact, you may enter any date as *Financial Year From (like 24-10-2005)* and Tally would close the books exactly 12 months from the date you enter here (e.g. 23-10-2006).

7.4 Saving the Company Profile

Finally Tally asks for your confirmation to save the Company Profile as entered. Click *Yes* (or press *Y*) to save the information (Fig 7-6), create the Company, folder & data files for it, else press *N* (or Click *No* to modify any data). You may also press Ctrl+A to save quickly.

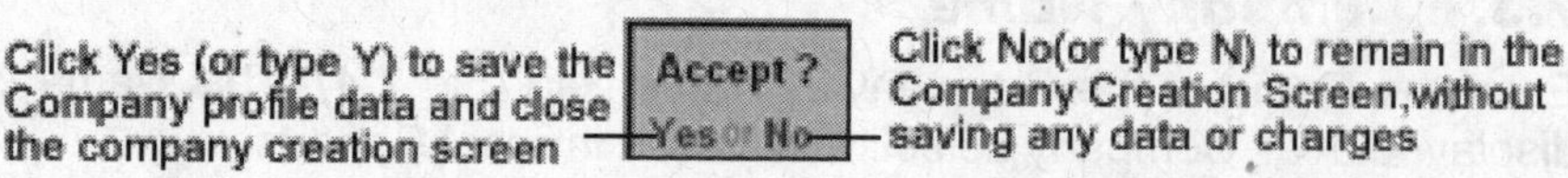

Fig 7-6: Confirmation for Saving Company Profile

The new company created is auto selected and *Gateway of Tally* appears (Fig 8-1). Name of the Company is now displayed under *List of Selected Companies.*

7.5 Company Additional Particulars

Apart from the above, you may also enter the following additional particulars (Fig 7-3) at the time of creation or later on through Company Alteration (Ref 7.7.1)

7.5.1 Telephone Number

Enter the Telephone Number preferably with City Codé prefix (Fig 7-4)

7.5.2 E-mail Address

Enter the e-mail address of the Company, if any (Fig 7-4). This address will be picked up at sender's e-mail address when you e-mail any report.

7.5.3 Company Mailing Name

The Company Name is carried at Mailing Name also (if you blank it out, Tally will fill it up with the Company Name).

Here enter the Company Legal name (if different from *Company Name*). This would be printed in all external documents (like Invoice, Money Receipt) etc.

While a Company Name must be unique, two or more companies may have same Company Mailing Name (Fig 7-7/ 7-8).

The Company Name & Company Mailing Name may be different when you create several Tally Companies for the same Legal Company. For example, you maintain separate Tally Companies for HO, Branch of same legal company, in one computer, e.g Infosoft (Calcutta) & Infosoft (Mumbai) for the legal company InfoSoft. So, in such case, enter the Company Legal Name (e.g.Infosoft) at mailing name for both the Tally Companies. Company Name cannot be duplicate but Mailing Name may be duplicate.

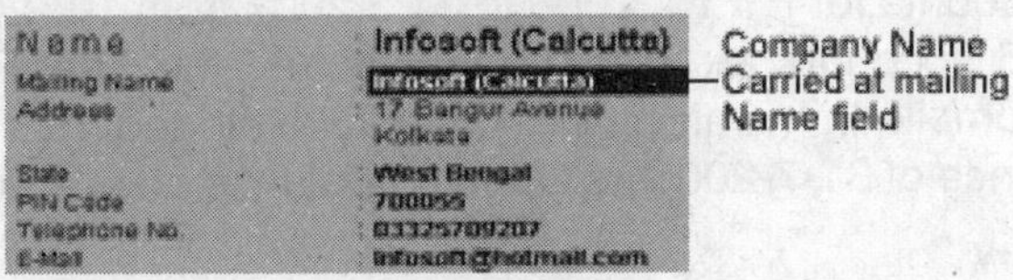

Fig 7-7: Company Name carried at Mailing Name field

Fig 7-8: Changed Mailing Name

Fig 7-7 shows the Name carried at Mailing Name and Fig 7-8 shows the changed Mailing Name.

7.5.4 Books Beginning Date

At *Books Beginning From* field, the *Financial Year From* Date is carried (Fig 7-9). If you start Accounts in Tally for the first time, from middle of the Financial Year (say you start Accounts entry in Tally from 1.8.2006 for FY 1.4.2006 to 31.3.2007) then change and enter the books starting date (i.e 1.8.2006 at *Books Beginning From* field), as shown in Fig 7-10. This field cannot be left blank.

The *Books Beginning Form* Date must be within 12 months from the date entered at *Financial Year From*. For example, if you enter 1-4-2006 at *Financial Year From*, you can enter any date between 1-4-2006 to 31-3-2007 at *Books Beginning From* (Fig 7-9 & 7-10).

Fig 7-9: Books starting from

Fig 7-10: Books starting from Mid Financial Year

You cannot enter any voucher prior to books beginning date (Fig 7-10). The ledger Opening balance should refer to the Books Beginning from Date.

Even if you start from the middle of the Financial Year, you may keep the Books Beginning Date same as Financial Year from Date. Enter the Opening Balance as per the date from which you start the Accounts in Tally.

Example:

You start accounts for FY 1.4.2006 to 31.3.2007 from 1-8-2006 (1-4-2006 to 31-7-2006 accounts are done manually and the Trial Balance as on 31-7-2006 compiled). In Tally, the accounts are started from 1-8-2006 with Closing balance of 31-7-2006 as Opening Balance of 1-8-2006.

Now, you may :

- Enter 1-4-2006 at Books Beginning From Date, or
- Enter 1-8-2006 at Books Beginning From Date.

In both cases, you must enter the Ledger Opening Balance as on 1.8.2006. In first case (Books Beginning From Date is 1-4-2006), accidentally someone may enter a voucher of date prior to 1-8-2006 (Tally would not be able to detect it). But in second case (*Books Beginning From* Date is 1-8-2006).Tally would prevent entry of any voucher dated prior to 1-8-2006.

7.6 Company Data

When a Tally Company is created, Tally creates a data folder at the specified data directory and allots a company serial number in 5 digit (like 10000).

7.6.1 Company Data Directory

Tally shows the current data directory name to store the data and skips this field. To keep Company data in any other place, press <backspace > (or <Shift> + <Tab> buttons) to move cursor to *Directory* field and enter the Path (Fig 7-11) where you wish to keep data files for the Company (Tally would create the Directory, if not existing).

Fig 7-11: Directory Name in Company creation

7.6.2 Company Number

For each data path specified at Directory field (Fig 7-11), Tally allots a 5 digit consecutive serial number starting from 10000, for the new company created, called *Company Number*. The Company Number is shown against the Company Name in parenthesis in the list of Companies during Company Selection (Fig 7-16).

7.6.3 Data Folder

Tally creates a Data Folder as per the allotted Company Number (like 10000) at the Directory specified at Directory field (Fig 7-12)..

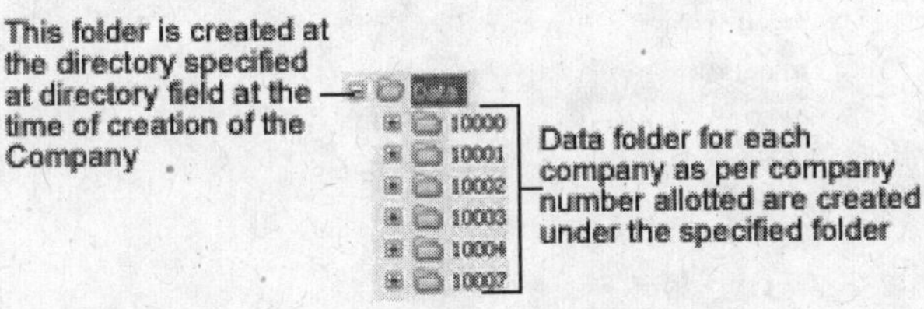

Fig 7-12: Tally Data Folder

7.7 Alteration / Deletion of Company

After creation of Company, or even after entering Master or Voucher data, you may change some information that you entered at the time of Company Creation, or fill up which were left blank.

Click *F3:Cmp Info* button at Gateway to get Company Info menu, select **Alter** from Company Info menu (Fig 7-13) and select the Company from list of selected Companies (if more than one Company is selected) to get the Company Alteration Screen (Fig 7-14).

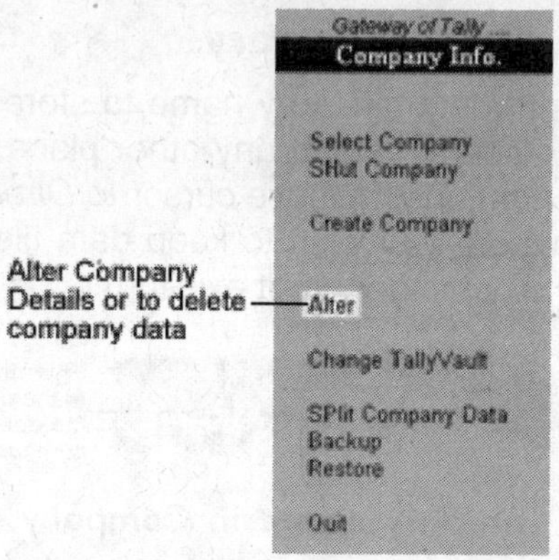

Fig 7-13: Company Info menu

7.7.1 Alteration of Company

At Company Alteration screen (Fig 7-14), you may carry out necessary alteration (or fill up any blank field left earlier). The Directory is not shown in Company Alteration screen. So, you cannot modify the Data Directory Name after creation of Company.

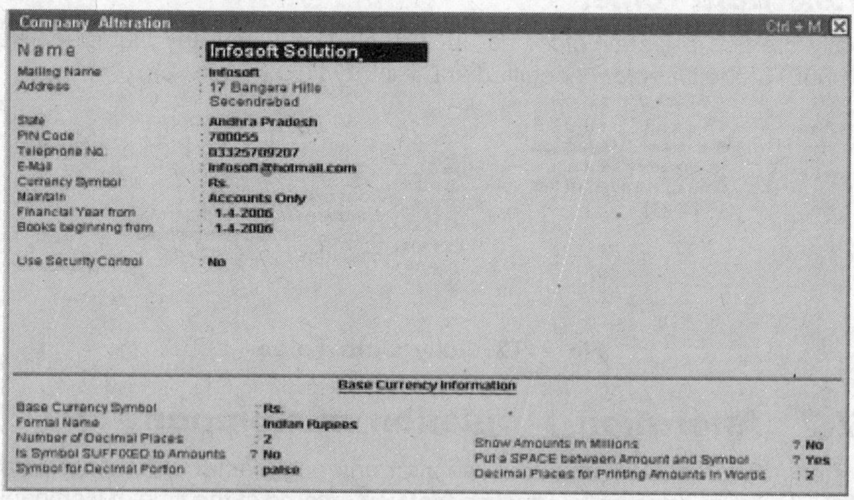

Fig 7-14: Company Alteration Screen

You cannot change Currency symbol data (cursor will skip the fields). After Opening Balance entry / voucher entry, Do NOT change the *Financial Year From* Date as it may render your previous *Data* unusable.

Press Ctrl+A to save the modified information immediately.

7.7.2 Deletion of Company Data

To *Delete* the currently active Company, press Alt+D, at Company Alteration screen (Fig 7-14). A confirmation '*Delete ? Yes or No'* appears. Type *Y* (*Yes*) to confirm Deletion. Next, you again confirm *Yes* at *Are you sure?* (Fig 7-15*)*. The Data files of the Company are deleted.

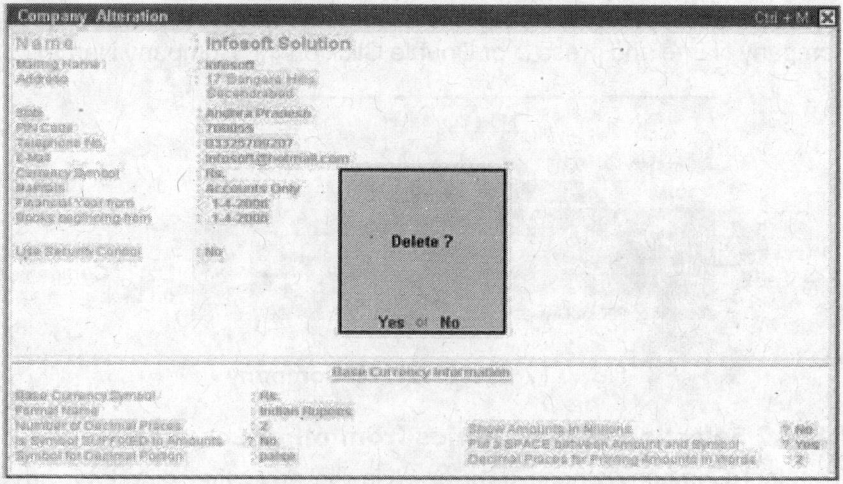

Fig 7-15: Company Deletion in Alteration mode

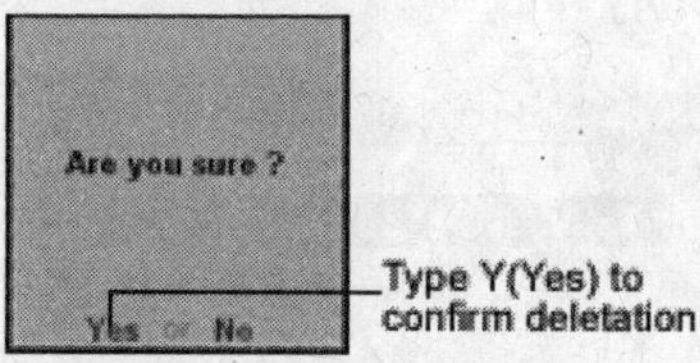

Fig 7-16 Deletion Confirmation

You CAN NOT get back a Deleted company. The data folder of the Company also gets Deleted. Therefore you should take *Backup* (Ref 22.1) before *Deletion* of a Company.

7.8 Selection of Company

To work with any Company, you have to first get the Company *Selected.* You may get a Company selected in 2 ways :

- Selection of Company
- Re-selection of a selected Company

7.8.1 Selection of Companies

Depending on the location of Data, there are 2 ways of Selection of Company. At Gateway, Click *F1: Select Cmp* button (or press F1 key) to get the Select Company screen (Fig 7-17)

7.8.1.1 Selection of Companies from Current Location

The list of *Companies on disk* at the current directory (as specified in the Directory statement in Tally.ini file) appears in alphabetical order (Fig 7-16). Now select the Company from the list (move the cursor on the Company Name and press ↵ or Double Click on the Company Name)

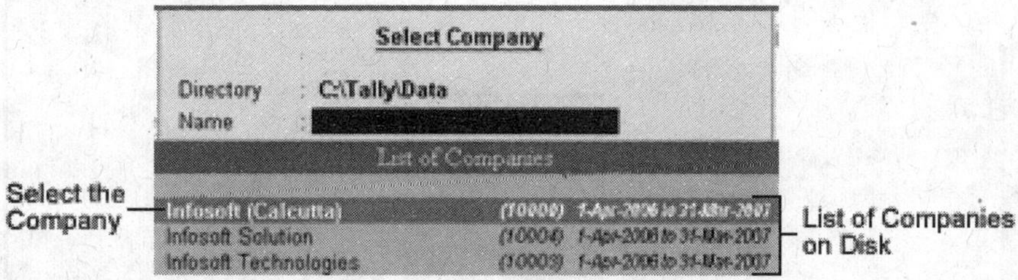

Fig 7-17: Selection of Company

7.8.1.2 Selection of Companies from other Location

To select Company whose data are lying in any other directory, press <backspace> key to get the cursor at the Directory field (Fig 7-18) and type the desired directory name.

Fig 7-18: Data directory name for selection of Company

Name of all the companies whose data are lying in the specified directory (referred as *Company on Disk*) will be listed. Now select the desired Company (Fig 7-19) from the list (move the cursor on the Company Name and press ↵ or Double Click on the Company Name).

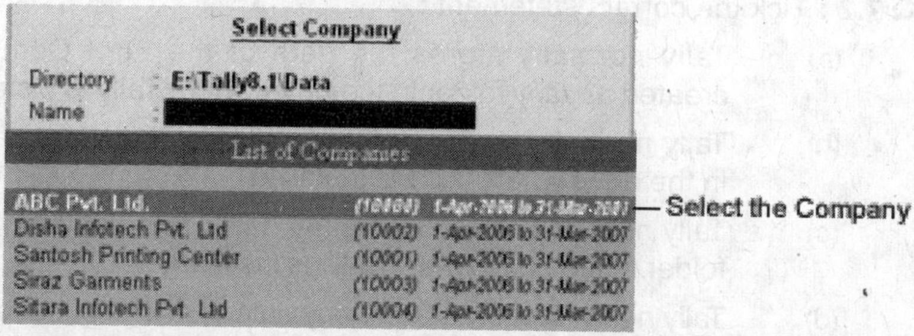

Fig 7-19: Selection of Company from specified directory

This way, you may select several Companies, one by one. The last selected company becomes the *Active Company* (Ref 8.4.4) and shown in bold at list of selected Companies (Fig 8-7).

7.8.2 Re-Selection of Company

If the company was previously selected but not currently active, you may click on the company in the list of selected companies (Fig 7-20) to quickly select it again.

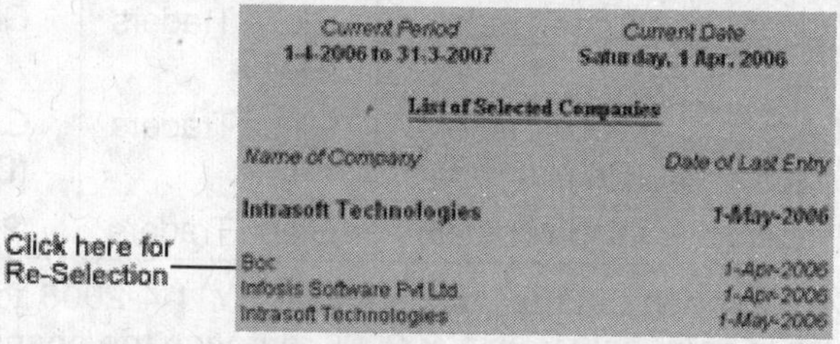

Fig 7-20: Re-selection of Company

Self Test Questions

STQ 7.1: After installation of Tally, to create the first Company: (select the correct option)

(a) Select *Create Company* option (the Company Creation menu appears automatically with *Create Company* selected as default)

(b) You get Gateway of Tally Menu by default. Click F3:Cmp Info to get Company Info Menu and select *Create Company*

(c) You directly get the Company Creation screen

(d) Click F1 and select *New Company* option

STQ 7.2 : Tick the correct statement :

(a) Tally normally stores the data of the First Company created at *Tally* folder in the drive where Tally is installed

(b) Tally normally stores Company data at *Tally\ data* folder in the drive where Tally is installed

(c) Tally normally stores Company data at *Tally\ data*\10000 folder in the drive where Tally is installed

(d) Tally normally stores Company data at 10000 subdirectory under the folder where Tally.ini file is lying.

STQ 7.3: Globe Traders likes to maintain separate Accounts for their Calcutta HO and Delhi Branch at Calcutta HO office. Tick the correct options to enter the Name & Mailing Name for the 2 Tally Companies for HO & Branch Office

	For Calcutta HO		**For Delhi Branch**	
	Name	*Mailing Name*	*Name*	*Mailing Name*
A	Globe Traders (Cal)	Globe Traders (Cal)	Globe Traders (Delhi)	Globe Traders (Delhi)
B	Globe Traders (Cal)	Globe Traders	Globe Traders (Delhi)	Globe Traders
C	Globe Traders	Globe Traders (Cal)	Globe Traders	Globe Traders (Delhi)
D	Globe Traders	Globe Traders	Globe Traders	Globe Traders

STQ 7.4 : A Company starts Accounts for FY 1-4-2006 to 31-3-2007, starting voucher entry only from 1-8-2006, entering the opening balances of all ledgers as on 1-8-2006. Tick the best option to enter the respective data at Company Creation screen :

	Financial Year From	*Books Beginning from*
A	1-Apr-2006	31- Mar –2007
B	1-Apr-2006	1-Aug-2006
C	1-Apr-2006	1-Apr-2006
D	1-Aug-2006	1-Aug-2006

STQ 7.5: To Delete the currently active Company, At Gateway of Tally (tick the correct option):

A. Click F3:Cmp, select *Alter*, select the Company and press Alt+D

B. Select F3:Cmp, select the Company, select *Delete*

C. At Gateway of Tally Menu, select the Company, press Alt+X

D. At Gateway of Tally Menu, select the Company, press Alt+D

STQ 7.6: When the Company Name and Mailing Name are different? Explain with example

STQ 7.7: What is Books Beginning from Date? When it differs from *Financial Year From* Date.

STQ 7.8: How you can place data of each company in different directories?

STQ 7.9: How you may Delete the data of a Company?

Gateway of Tally

8

Having created a Company, on loading Tally every time, you get the Gateway of Tally. This is the entry point to get to the desired part of the Tally you want to work with.

So, it is important to get familiarized with the various elements of Tally Gateway

8.1 Components of Gateway of Tally

The *Gateway of Tally* screen (Fig 8-1) contains 7 major areas:

- Product Info
- Horizontal Button Bar
- Current Status
- Tally Menu
- Vertical Button Bar
- Tally Calculator / Command line
- Footer Line

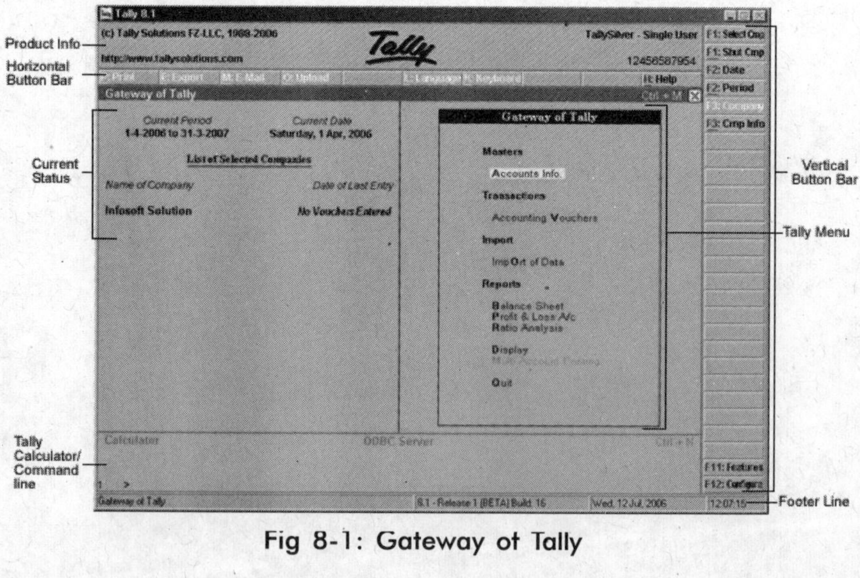

Fig 8-1: Gateway of Tally

Brief details of each Area of the Gateway of Tally screen (Fig 8-1) are explained below:

8.2 Product Info

At the top part of Gateway of Tally screen (Fig 8.1), you get the following general particulars (Fig 8.3), regarding the loaded Tally software:

- **Software Name** : Name of Software (Like Tally 8.1)
- **Copyright Notice**: Copyright Notice (like © Tally Solutions FZ-LLC,1988-2006).
- **User Level** : User Level (like Tally Silver – Single User).
- **User Serial Number**: Registration Serial Number (or EDUCATIONAL when unregistered).
- **Link to Tally Website** : Tally Website Name. Clicking on it will directly load the Tally Website (when connected to Internet)
- **Logo :** Tally Logo

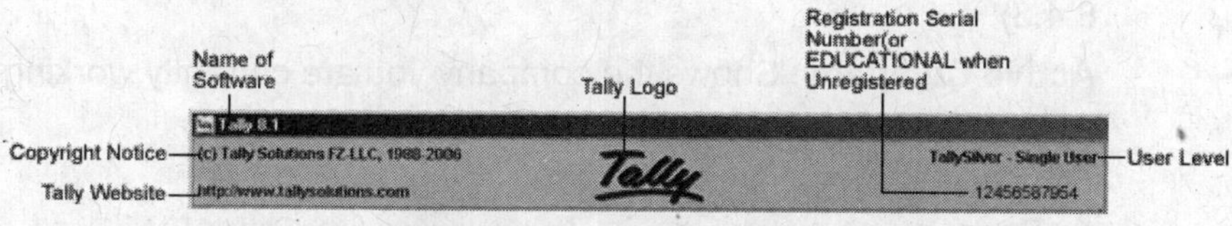

Fig 8-2: Product Info

8.3 Horizontal Button Bar

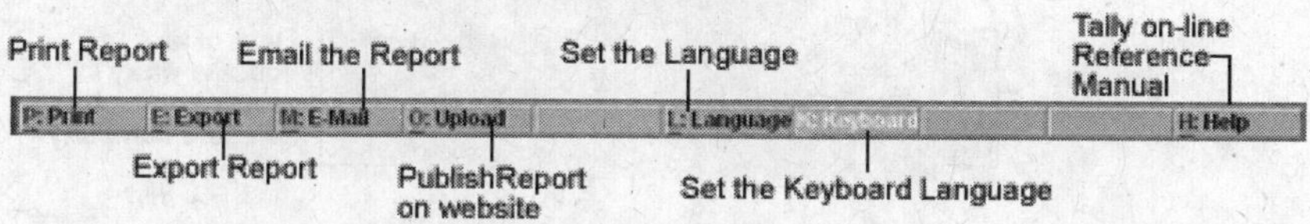

Fig 8-3: Horizontal Button Bar

This bar contains buttons for :

- Managing Reports :
  - ❋ **Print :** To print the current Report displayed on screen
  - ❋ **Export :** Export Reports and save in disk file
  - ❋ **E-mail :** E-mail the current report
  - ❋ **Upload :** To publish report on website

- Language Set Up (Refer Chapter 4)
  - ❋ **Language :** To set the Language (English/ Indic) in which you like to work
  - ❋ **Keyboard :** To set the respective Language Keyboard (English/ Indic) to use for data input
  - ❋ **Help:** Tally On-line Reference Manual

8.4 Current Status

At the left part of Gateway (Fig 8-1), you get the following information about current working status (Fig 8-4):

- **Current Period**: Shows the current period selected through *F2: Period* button (Ref 8.4.1).
- **Current Date**: Shows the current date set through *F2: Date* button (Ref 8.4.1).
- **Selected Companies**: Shows all the Companies selected (Ref 8.4.3).
- **Active Company**: Shows the company you are currently working with (the last selected company) (Ref 8.4.4).

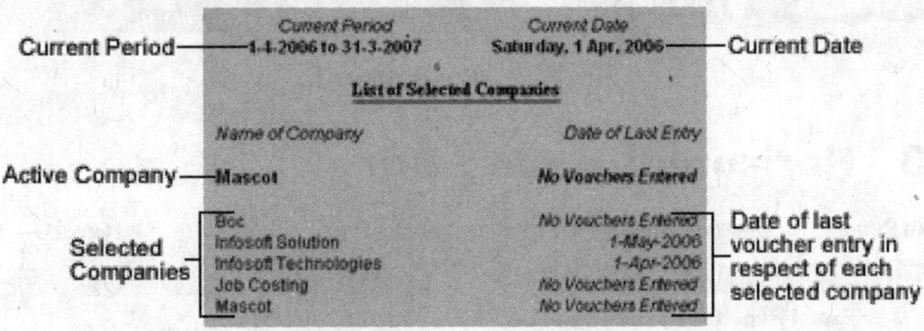

Fig 8-4: Current Status

8.4.1 Current Period

To set the Current Period, Click *F2: Period* button or press Alt+F2 and enter the Start & End Date to specify the Current Period (Fig 8-5). You may enter voucher within the current Period only. So change it accordingly to prevent wrong entry of Voucher Date..

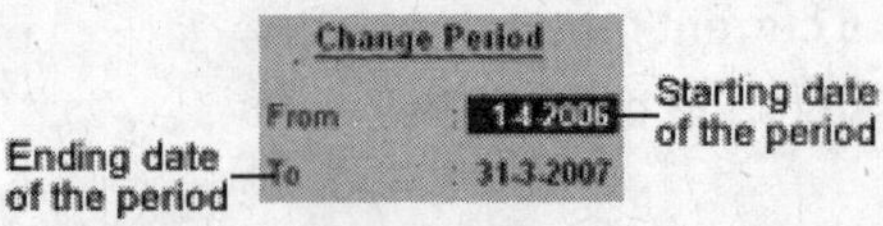

Fig 8-5: Current Period entry

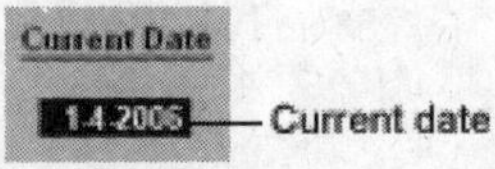

Fig 8-6: Current Date entry

8.4.2 Current Date

The Date you worked last is displayed at Current Date. It is carried as Voucher Date. To change it, Click *F2: Date* button (or press F2) and enter the Date (the next Date is carried as default), as shown in Fig 8-6. The current Date is within the Current Period currently set, as shown in Fig 8-5

8.4.3 Selected Companies

It shows the Name of all currently Selected Companies in alphabetical order with *Date of last voucher* entered is shown for reference (Fig 8-7).

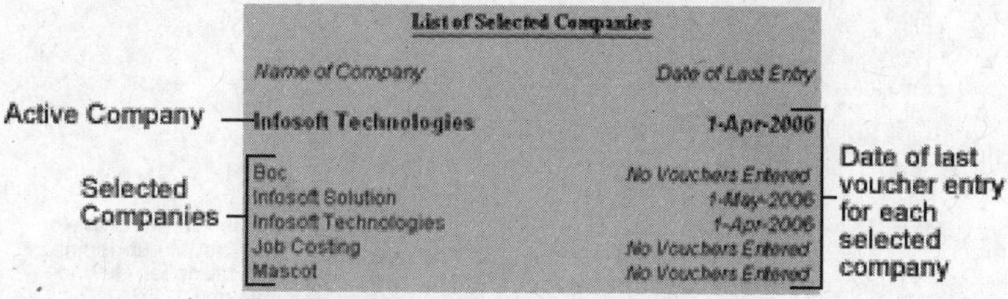

Fig 8-7: Selected Companies

8.4.4 Active Company

Active Company is the last selected Company (which you are currently working with) shown at top (in bold face) in the list of Companies (Fig 8-7). Names of other selected Companies appear next in the list, shown in regular font.

8.5 Tally Menu

At right part of the Gateway screen, the *Gateway of Tally* Menu (referred as *Tally Main menu*) appears (Fig 8.8) showing the list of Menu Options (called *Menu Items*). You have to select the respective Menu Item to invoke a task or get to a subordinate Menu. You may have to drill down several levels of subordinate Menu till you reach the menu option to invoke the desired task.

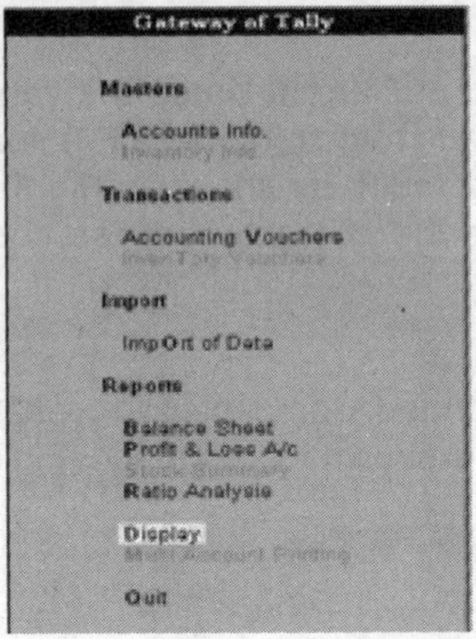

Fig 8-8: Tally Main Menu

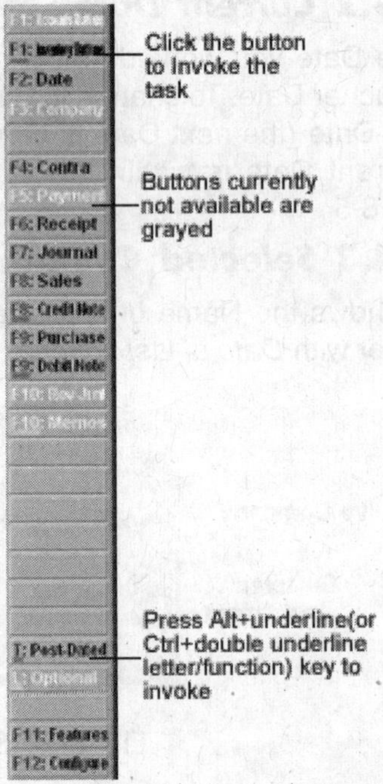

Fig 8-9: Vertical Button Bar

8.5.1 Selection of a Menu Item

You can select an option in Tally Menu in any of the following ways:

Using Keyboard

- Press the highlighted character from keyboard. For example, to select **B**alance Sheet, press B (the highlighted character). This is the fastest way of selection (using keyboard)
- Move cursor on the option (with **Up/Dn arrow** key) and press ↵.

Using Mouse

- Double click on the option by the mouse

8.5.2 Moving to Upper Menu

Select *Quit* (or Press *Esc* key) or click on the rightmost Cross button (Fig 8-10) at any Sub Menu to return to the immediate upper level menu. This way you may ultimately reach the Tally Main Menu (Ref 8.10, Exiting from Tally Main Menu).

Fig 8-10: Cross button to move to upper menu

8.6 Vertical Button Bar

At rightmost part of the Gateway (Fig 8-1), the Vertical Button Bar (Fig 8-9) shows several buttons (the buttons vary according to screen in work area). These Buttons provide quick and direct access to various options & tasks.

Depending on options currently set, some buttons may be inactive (the inactive buttons are dimmed).

8.6.1 Invoking a task through Button

You may invoke a Horizontal (Ref 8.3) or Vertical button in 3 ways:

- **By Mouse**: Click the button at the button bar.
- **By Function Key**: Some buttons are named by Function keys (F1 to F12), Press the Function key to invoke (e.g. to invoke F1: select company button, Press F1 function key).
- **By Hotkey**: Some buttons have a Character or Function key with single or double underline. Press the character / Function key in conjunction with Alt (for single underline) or with Ctrl key (for double underline), as explained below (Fig 8-11).

Button	*Function Key / Hotkey*
F3: Cmp Info	**Function Key**: With single underline Press the Function key (e.g. Press F3 Function Key) while holding Alt key.
H: Help	**Single underline letter**: Press Alt Key & Character/ with single underline (e.g Alt+H).
F8: Credit Note	**Function Key with double underline**: Press the function key (e.g. Press F8 Key) while holding Ctrl Key
V: As Voucher	**Double underline letter**: Press Ctrl Key & Character/double underlined (e.g Ctrl+V).

Fig 8-11: Invoking Buttons

8.7 Work Area

When you perform any task (after finally selecting a menu option), the respective screen covers the Current Status & Tally Menu (referred as Work Area), While the Product Info, Button Bar & Calculator Area always remain static and visible all through your work with Tally, at any point of time, either the Work Area or the Calculator remains active. To switch to Work Area, press Ctrl+M. To switch to Calculator, press Ctrl+N- these combination allows to toggle between work area and Tally Calculator.

8.8 Tally Calculator

While working with Tally, you may make arithmetical calculation and also paste the result in any numerical input field.

8.8.1 Making a Calculation through Tally Calculator

To activate *Calculator*, click on the Calculator Band (or Press Ctrl+N). The Band is highlighted and you get the cursor at Calculator Area to type the arithmetic expression .

- **Arithmetic Expression** : Type the arithmetic expression and press <enter>. You may use +, -, * and / for addition, subtraction, multiplication & Division and properly paired parenthesis '( )'.
- **Arithmetic Result** : The result of the arithmetic expression is shown in the next line. Tally Calculator follows BDMAS (Bracket, Division, Multiplication, Addition, Subtraction) rule for execution sequence.

If there is any mistake in typing the arithmetic expression, Tally will show Error! Message at the result line (Fig 8-13)

The Arithmetic Expressions and the results of successive calculations will remain in the Calculator Area till you Exit from Tally. You may scroll them through Up & Dn arrow Keys.

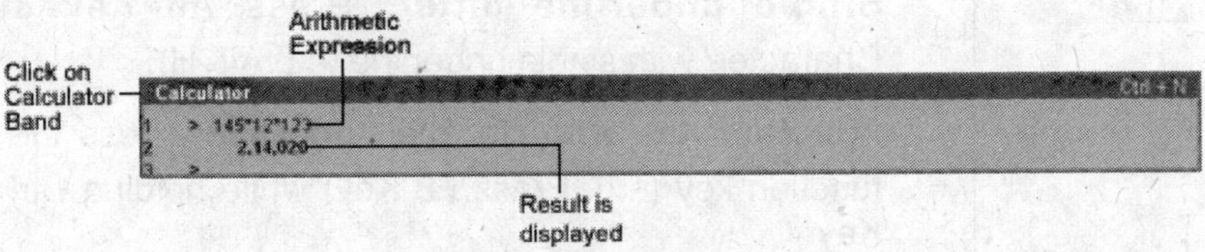

Fig 8-12: Tally Calculator

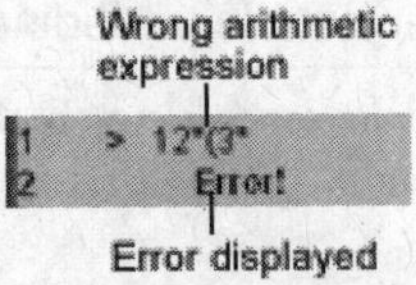

Fig : 8-13 Tally Calculator expression Error

To get back to the working area, Click on Gateway of Tally Band (or press Ctrl+M). The work area gets activated and the calculator gets deactivated.

8.8.2 Pasting Calculated value at Numeric field

To paste the result of an arithmetic calculation at Numeric input field (like Amount in Voucher) without having to re-type it :

1. At Numeric Input Field, press Alt+C to invoke the *Active Value Calculator* (Fig 8-14).
2. At Calculator Area, type the Arithmetic Expression (like 130+260+500). The result will be shown in next Result line (Fig 8-15).

The result will also be pasted in the numeric field from where the Calculator was invoked (Alt+C) was pressed.

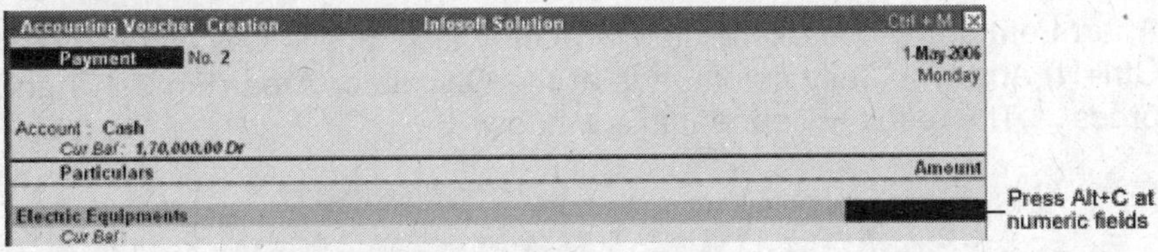

Fig 8-14: Invoking the Auto Value Calculator at numeric input field

This facility is useful when you do not have the figure to be input readily computed. For example, you have several slips for Conveyance Expenses for which you like to enter one voucher. Instead of using paper, you may directly add up the values in calculator and paste the result. This is faster and eliminates typing error.

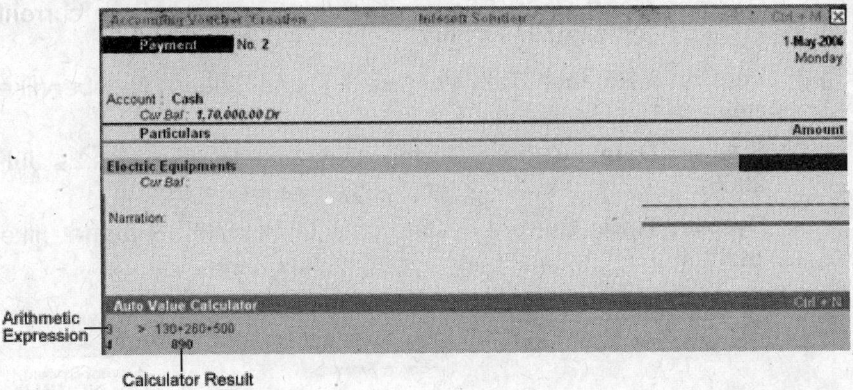

Fig 8-15: Tally Auto Value Calculator

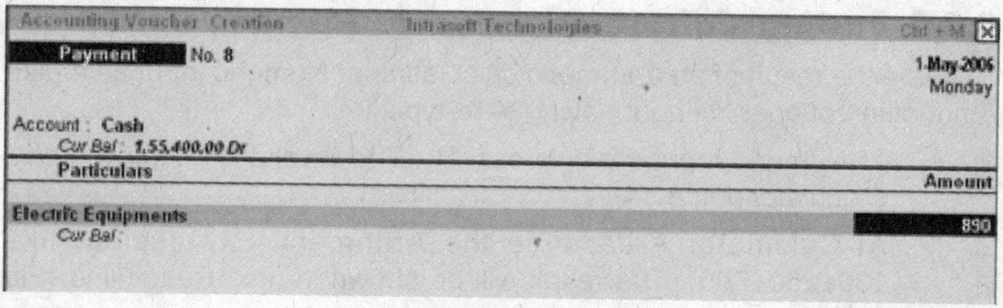

Fig 8-16: Tally Calculator

8.8.3 *Executing Tally Commands*

Apart from arithmetic expression, you may also invoke Calculator (press Ctrl+N) and type Tally commands at the Calculator Area (Fig 8-17) and press ↵. The result will appear in a window.

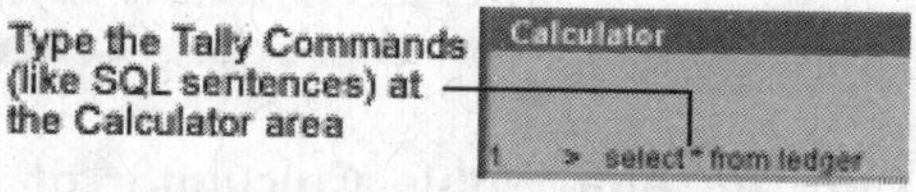

Fig 8-17: Tally Commands entry

8.9 Footer Line

Below the Calculator area, the current screen position in respect of the Tally Main Menu hierarchy from Gateway of Tally and other current info, as described below are shown in a line, called the footer line :

- **Current Menu Path**: Shows the complete Path of the current screen from Gateway of Tally
- **Version & Release**: Tally Ver (like 8.1) and Release Number (like Release 1).
- **System Date**: Current System Day & Date (like Mon,24 Jul, 2006).
- **System Time**: Current system time in HH:MM:SS format (like 14:47:45).

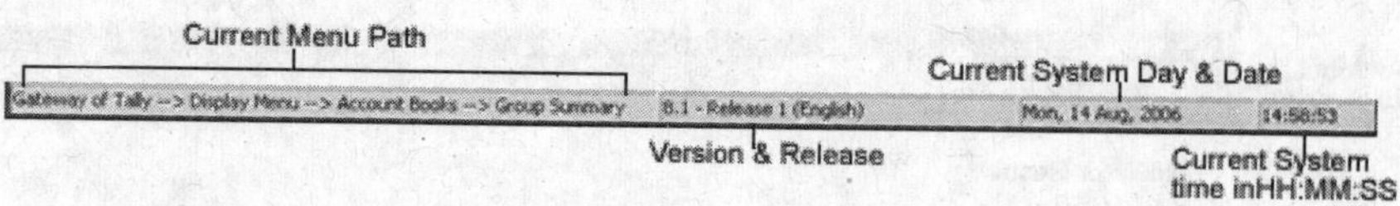

Fig 8-18: Footer Line

Footer line is the last line of Tally screen.

8.10 Windows Task Bar

Tally normally takes up the whole screen area even hiding the Windows task bar. To get bottom line (while Tally screen takes up the rest of the screen area), drag the Tally screen handle (top of the Tally screen) and move up a little. The task bar at the Windows bottom line will appear from behind (Fig 8.19). Now release the handle.

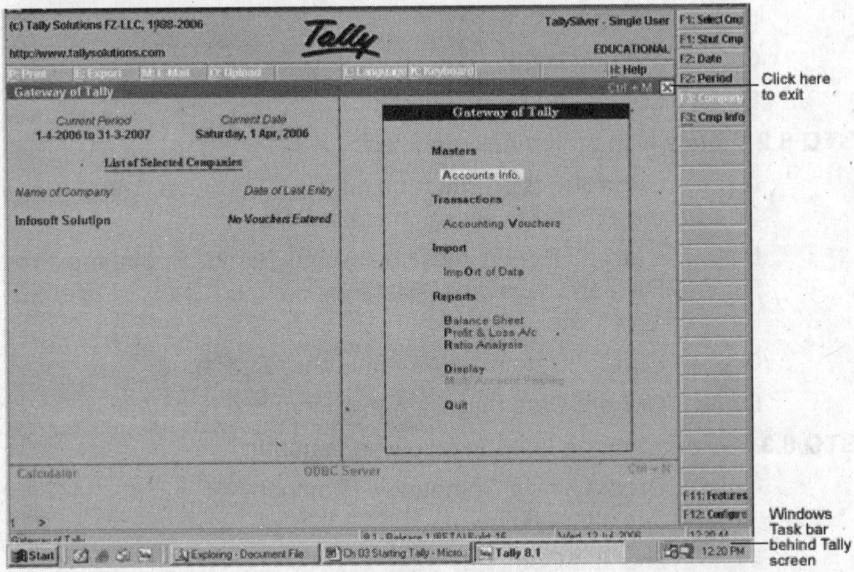

Fig 8-19: Windows Task Bar below the Tally Screen

8.10 Exiting from Tally

At Tally Main Menu bar, click on the rightmost Cross button (Fig 8-19) or select *Quit* or Press Esc key, to exit from Tally. A confirmation (Fig 8-20) is sought. Press *Y* or click at *Yes* button (Fig 8-20) to exit from Tally (or press *N* to continue to work with Tally).

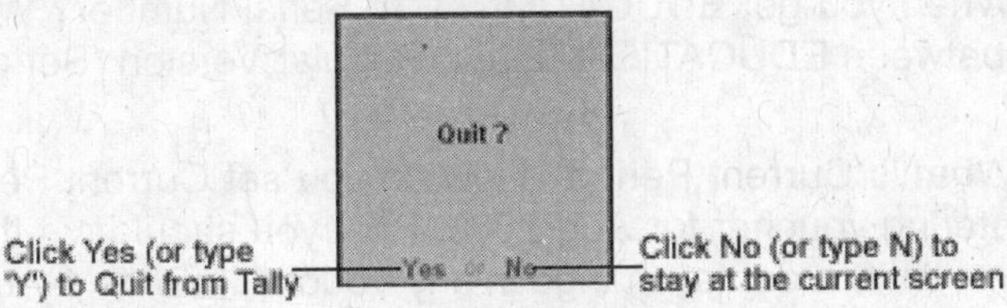

Fig 8-20: Confirmation option to Exit Tally

Self Test Questions

STQ 8.1: You have installed Tally 8.1 Rel 1 on 18-Aug-2006. You have created a Company for the FY 1-4-2006 to 31-3-2007 and entered voucher upto 19th June 2006. What date you will see at the right corner the Footer of the Gateway screen when you load Tally on 20th June 2006:

A. 12th May 2006

B. 18th May 2006

C. 19th Jun 2006

D. 20th Jun 2006.

STQ 8.2 State which statement is correct:

A. Current Period must be within 12 months Starting from the *Financial Year Start from* Date

B. Current Period must be within Books Beginning From Date and 12 months Starting from the *Financial Year Start from* Date

C. Current Date must be within Current Period.

D. Current Date may be within Financial Accounting Period

STQ 8.3 You perform the tasks in following sequence

- Create 5 new Companies (Company #1, #2, #3, #4 & #5), one after another.
- shut the Company #2
- shut the Company #3
- select Company #2

Now:

- Which are the *Companies on Disk*
- Which is the *Active Companies*
- Which are the *Selected Companies*

STQ 8.4: When you get EDUCATIONAL at Serial Number? What is the difference between EDUCATIONAL and Regular Version (Serial Number displayed)?

STQ 8.5: What is Current Period? How do you set Current Period? You are now entering voucher for Aug 2006. How you should set the current period to prevent accidental change in any Voucher prior to 1-Aug-2006.

STQ 8.6: What is *Active Company*? What is the difference between *Active Company*, *Selected Company* & *Company on Disk*?

STQ 8.7: How you exit from Tally.Gateway of Tally

Chart of Accounts

9

To get accounting reports in organized manner conforming to commonly accepted accounting principles, transactions of similar nature are collated and balanced into entities called *Ledger Accounts*. These Ledger Accounts are further organized into hierarchical levels called *Account Groups*. Account Groups are used to get summarised figures while Ledger accounts give the details of individual transactions.

9.1 Account Groups & Ledgers

Chart of Accounts represents the hierarchical view of organization of Account Groups & Ledger Accounts.

- **Ledger Accounts**: Ledger Accounts represent the assorted, summarized and balanced transactions of similar nature. For example, the ledger account *Conveyance* represents the set of transactions related to Conveyance expenses and their summarized net figure. All Accounting transactions are linked to Ledger Accounts.
- **Account Groups**: Account Groups are just a convenient method of organizing the large population of Ledger Accounts into a tree-structured hierarchical view for better understanding and interpretation.

As shown in Chapter 6, the accounting entities (Account Groups & Ledger Accounts) are classified into:

- Liabilities (also includes Capital)
- Assets
- Income
- Expenses

We will now see how Tally classifies and organizes these into Groups.

9.2 Hierarchy of Account Groups & Ledgers

In Tally, you may organise Accounts Ledgers and Groups in hierarchical way. There is no limit on depth of nesting. Any number of Group/sub Groups and number of Ledger Accounts may be placed under a Group/sub-group.

Fig 9-1 shows a typical example of Account Groups & Ledgers (Account Groups are shown Bold; Account Ledger Names are shown in Italics).

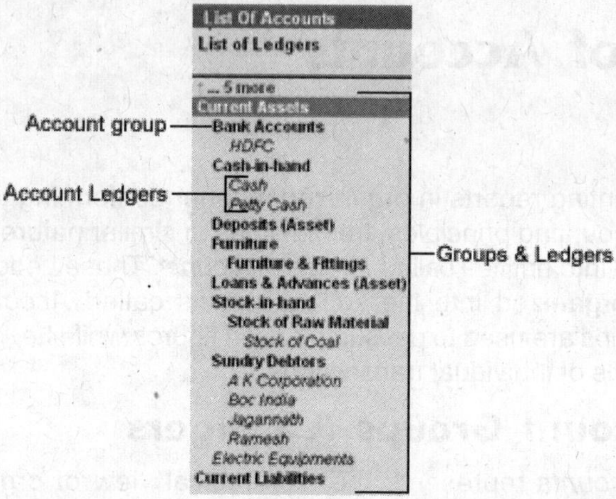

Fig 9-1: Hierarchy of Accounts Groups & Ledgers

You get organised reports with control totals at each level. Only Ledger Accounts are transacted in Vouchers. Account Groups do not participate in any voucher (they are used to organise the Ledger Accounts). You Debit or Credit a Ledger in any Voucher (but not any Group).

9.3 Reserved Account Groups

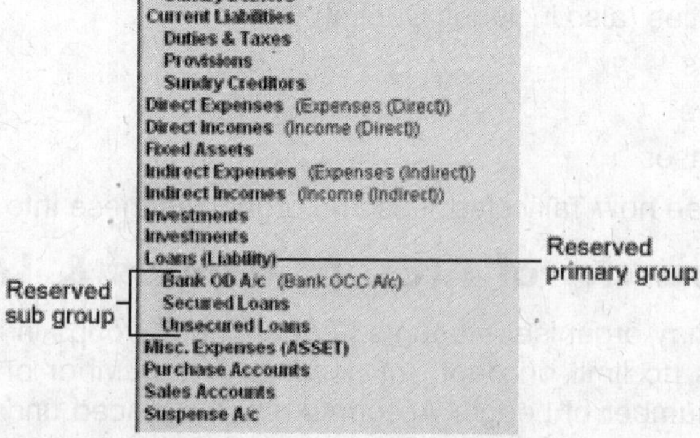

Fig 9-2: List of Reserved Groups

As soon as you create a Company, Tally auto creates 28 pre-defined Account Groups called Reserved Groups (these Groups can not be deleted) to maintain consistency and integrity of the accounting system representing Assets, Liabilities, Income and Expenditure (Fig 9-2). Of these 28 Reserved Account Groups, 15 are top level Primary Groups (the rest 13 are Sub Groups of one of these 15 Primary Groups).

Fig 9-3 shows the Reserved Groups & sub groups of Liabilities & Fig 9-4 shows the Reserved Groups & sub groups of Assets.

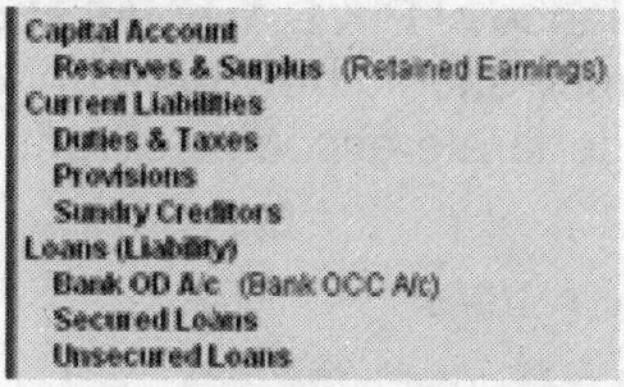

Fig 9-3: Reserved Account Groups of Liabilities

Fig 9-4: Reserved Account Groups of Assets

Fig 9-5 shows the Reserved Account Groups of Income & Fig 9-6 shows the Reserved Account Groups of Expenses.

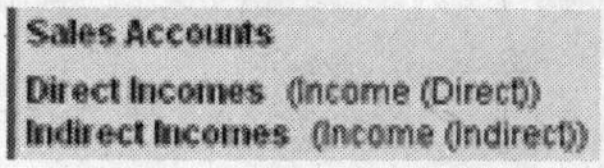

Fig 9-5: Reserved Account Groups of Income

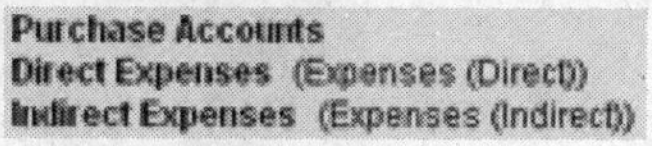

Fig 9-6: Reserved Account Groups of Expenses

9.4 Account Groups of Balance Sheet

We now describe the Accounts Groups that appear in Balance Sheet.

9.4.1 Account Groups of Liabilities

The Groups of Liabilities of Balance Sheet are shown below:

9.4.1.1 Account Group - Capital

This is a primary Group that contains the Capital and Reserves & Surplus of the Company (Fig 9-7).

- **9.4.1.1.1 Account Group - Capital Account**: Ledger Accounts for Owners Capital may be placed under Capital Group (or its sub-group). Common example of Ledger Accounts under Capital Account group is Share (or Equity) Capital, Partners' Capital Accounts, Proprietors Capital Account. Members Capital A/c etc.

Separate Ledgers may be created for Equity Capital, Preference Capital A/c etc.

- **9.4.1.1.2 Account Group - Reserves & Surplus [Retained Earnings]**: It's a child-group to Capital Account. All Reserve Accounts (referred as Retained Earnings) are placed under this group. Common examples are: General Reserve, Capital Reserve, Investment Allowance Reserve, Share Premium Account etc.

In case of Companies limited by shares (Limited & Private Limited Companies), though normally Credit Balance of P & L Account should go into Reserves & Surplus and Debit Balance should be shown under Misc Expenses (Assets), Tally shows under separate account – Profit & Loss account.

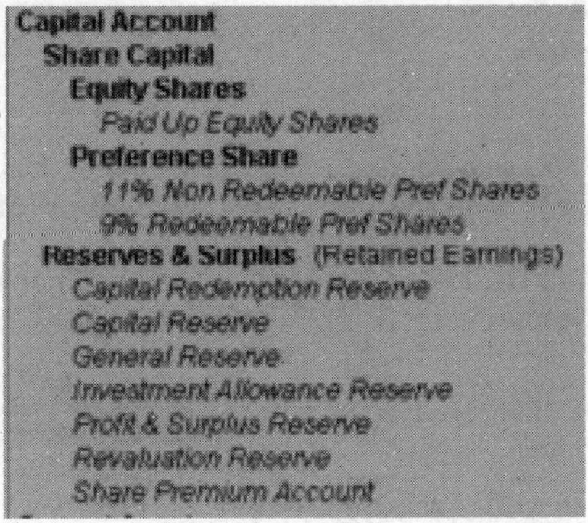

Fig 9-7: Groups & Ledgers of Capital Account

9.4.1.2 Account Group - Loans (Liabilities)

All loans taken by Company should be placed here. Tally creates 3 reserved sub-groups (Fig 9-3).

- **9.4.1.2.1 Account Group - Bank OD Accounts [Bank OCC A/c]**: While Current Bank A/c should be placed under Current Assets (explained later), Bank Overdraft and Cash/Credit Accounts availed under Hypothecation, Bill Discounting etc. operated on a day-to-day basis should be placed under this group. Though these bank accounts may be a kind of secured loans, to allow transactions in Payment, Receipt and Contra Vouchers like normal Bank Accounts (although normally these are Secured Loan), the ledger accounts under this group participate in the Vouchers in same manner like ledgers placed under Bank Accounts (under Current Assets), as explained later.

- **9.4.1.2.2 Account Group - Secured Loans**: Debentures, Term Loans (Medium/Long term), Secured Loans taken from Banks, Financial Institutes etc. against security (like mortgage/ hypothecation, pledge etc) should be placed under this group.
- **9.4.1.2.3 Account Group - Unsecured Loans**: Loans from outside Parties, Directors, Friends and Relatives (without any collateral security), Deposits etc, should be placed under this group.

9.4.1.3 Account Group - Current Liabilities

This group normally constitutes a large number of Ledger Accounts and Sub Groups and is subdivided into 3 sub-groups: Duties & Taxes, Provisions and Sundry Creditors.

- **9.4.1.3.1 Account Group - Duties and Taxes**: This sub-group is for all Excise, Sales and other Trade Taxes. This head normally constitutes all the Duties & Taxes that you collect or pay through Sales & Purchase transactions, whose balance will appear in Balance Sheet. Examples are: Sales Tax (e.g., WBST, CST), Excise Duty, Marketing Fee, Purchase Tax etc.
- **9.4.1.3.2 Account Group - Provisions**: It is a place for all sorts of Provisions (like Provision for Bad Debts etc). Place similar Provisions as applicable.
- **9.4.1.3.3 Account Group - Sundry Creditors**: Place the ledger accounts of all Trade Creditors / suppliers (even if any ledger account has Debit Balance at some point of time due to advance payment etc). If you sell to or purchase from same party, create only one ledger account and place under Sundry Debtors or Sundry Creditors Group (as convenient).

9.4.1.3.4 Account Group - Current Liabilities: Place all other liability accounts (which are not candidates of any the above 3 groups), like Liabilities for Expenses, Employees contribution for ESI/PF or TDS realized from Contractors/Employees, etc.

- **Current Liabilities**
  - **Advance From Customers**
    - *P Sureka & Co.*
  - **Duties & Taxes**
    - **Excise Duties**
      - *Excise Duty 10%*
      - *Excise Duty 12%*
    - **Sales Tax**
      - *Central Sales Tax*
      - *Local Sales Tax 10%*
      - *Local Sales Tax 12%*
      - *Local Sales Tax 12.5%*
      - *Local Sales Tax 15%*
      - *Local Sales Tax 5%*
      - *Surcharge Sales Tax*
    - **Valu Added Tax**
      - *Purchase VAT*
      - *Sales VAT*
  - **Liabilities for Expenses**
    - *Liabilities for Casting Charges*
    - *Liabilities for Moulding Charges*
    - *Salary Payable*
  - **Provisions**
    - *Additional Tax*
    - *Leave Encashment*
    - *Pension Scheme*
    - *Proposed Dividends*
  - **Sundry Creditors**
    - **Jubbers (Creditors)**
      - *Mahalaxmi Pvt. Ltd.*
      - *Sham Sunder Casting*
    - **Supplier (Creditors)**
      - *Abhishek Enterprise*
      - *Manoj Metal Udyou*
      - *Pramod Enterprise*
  - **Unpaid Dividends**
    - *Unpaid Dividends for Year 1999*
    - *Unpaid Dividends for Year 2000*

Fig 9-8: Groups & Ledgers of Current Liabilities

9.4.2 Account Groups of Assets

9.4.2.1 Account Group - Fixed Assets

This constitutes all the Fixed Assets like Immovable Properties, Patents, Trade Rights etc, Work-in-progress (Capital Projects) etc (Fig 9-9). Fixed Assets may have several subgroups for each type of assets if you wish to have separate Ledger Accounts for individual Asset. You may keep the figures of Original Cost and Accumulated Depreciation for Fixed Assets separately.

Fig 9-9: Groups & Ledgers of Fixed Assets

9.4.2.2 Account Group - Investments

Place here all Ledger Accounts related to Investments in Shares, Bonds, Govt. Securities and Investment in other companies (Fig 9-10).

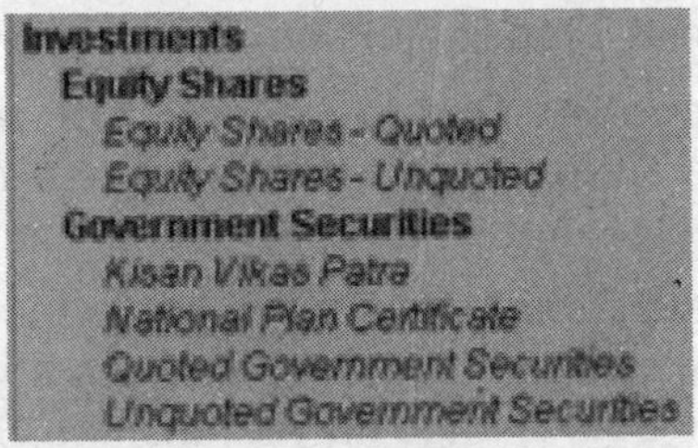

Fig 9-10: Groups & Ledgers of Investments

9.4.2.3 Account Group - Current Assets

It constitutes 6 Reserved Sub Groups: Stock-in-hand, Deposits (Assets), Loans & Advances (Assets), Cash-in-hand, Bank Accounts, Sundry Debtors (Fig 9-11).

You should place individual Ledger Account under the appropriate subgroups and avoid placing any Ledger directly under primary group, i.e., Current Assets.

- **9.4.2.3.1 Account Group - Stock-in-hand**: Create all Ledger Accounts for Closing Stock under this group. Normally, you should create separate Ledger Accounts for Raw Materials, Work-in-process and Finished Goods, as required.
- **9.4.2.3.2 Account Group - Deposits (Assets)**: Place all the Deposits made by the Company (Deposits received by the Company should be placed under Unsecured Loans) like Fixed Deposits, Security Deposits, Deposits with Electricity, Telephone dept, Deposits in other companies, Rental Deposits etc. under this Group.
- **9.4.2.3.3 Account Group - Loans and Advances (Assets)**: Place all Loans & Advances of non-trading nature given (Advances to Suppliers should be debited to the respective Supplier Ledger Account). Examples are: Advances against Salary, Loans to Employees, Advances to Fixed Assets Suppliers etc.
- **9.4.2.3.4 Account Group - Sundry Debtors**: Place all the Trade Customer Ledger Accounts (even if Opening Balance is Credit). If you sell to or purchase from same party, create only one ledger account and place under Sundry Debtors or Sundry Creditors Group. Advances received from Customers also should also be Credited to the Customer's ledger under Sundry Debtors group.
- **9.4.2.3.5 Account Group - Cash-in-Hand**: Tally creates a Cash Ledger Account (Cash-in-Hand) and places under this group. You may create more Cash accounts (e.g., Petty Cash, Cash-at-Branch, Cash-in-Transit etc) and place under this group.
- **9.4.2.3.6 Account Group - Bank Accounts**: All the Bank Accounts like Current Accounts, Savings Accounts etc. (except Cash Credit, Overdraft or Loan Accounts) should be placed here.

Tally creates 2 separate Groups for Cash & Bank Accounts. However, you may place all cash and bank accounts under same group (like Cash & Bank Accounts). To do that, change the name of the Group Bank Accounts to Cash & Bank Accounts. Change the parent of Cash ledger account to Cash & Bank Accounts. With this, you may get a combined statement of Cash & Bank vouchers with their combined balances (See Group Voucher – Ref 15.1.3). This is normally found useful for small business and Non Profit Organizations.

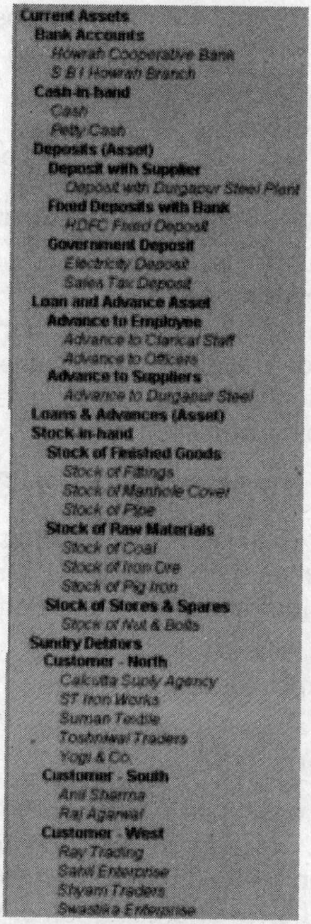

Fig 9-11: Groups & Ledgers of Current Assets

9.4.2.4 Account Group – Branch / Divisions

Place Ledgers for Branch, Division, Affiliate, Sister Concern, Subsidiary etc under this Group (Fig 9-12). It may help Inter branch reconciliation & consolidation. Tally permits Sales/Purchase transactions also (like Party Accounts).

Fig 9-12: Groups & Ledgers of Branch / Divisions

9.4.2.5 Account Group - Misc. Expenses (Asset)

For Limited Companies, Preliminary, Pre-operative and similar expenses (to the extent not written off to Profit & Loss A/cs) should fall here (Fig 9-13). Though the accumulated Loss of a Company should also fall in this category, Tally treats it as negative Profit (Nett Loss) and carries to Profit & Loss a/c.

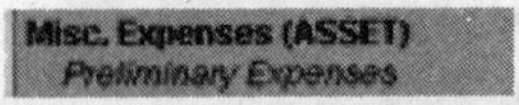

Fig 9-13: Misc. Expenses Groups & Ledger Accounts

9.4.2.6 Account Group - Suspense Account

This is a primary Group that appears in Balance Sheet. You may create a Suspense ledger to record money paid/received whose details are not yet known. Later on the transaction is posted to the appropriate account. Example: Advance paid for Travelling Expenses etc. details for which will be known upon submission of TA bills may be recorded in such ledger. As far as practicable, avoid using such Account.

9.5 Account Groups of Profit & Loss Account

These groups are further classified as Direct Income & Direct Expenses (apart from Sales & Purchase) considered for Gross Profit computation and Indirect Income & Indirect Expenses, considered for Net Profit computation.

Direct Income & Direct Expenses are considered for computation of Gross Profit / Loss.

9.5.1 Account Group - Sales

All sorts of Sales should constitute this group (Fig 9-14). You may have multiple Sales Accounts. You may create separate accounts for Sales and Sales Returns or club up Sales and Sales Returns in one Account - the net effect in Accounts however remains same. You may create different Ledgers for Sales according to Tax Liability or Products or other criterion as per your reporting requirement.

Professionals or Servicing companies who do not have Sales income but have Income from Professional Fees & Services, may alter name of the Sales group to Professional Service Charges (or some similar name) or place the Professional Service Charges or Servicing Charges under Direct Income (explained next).

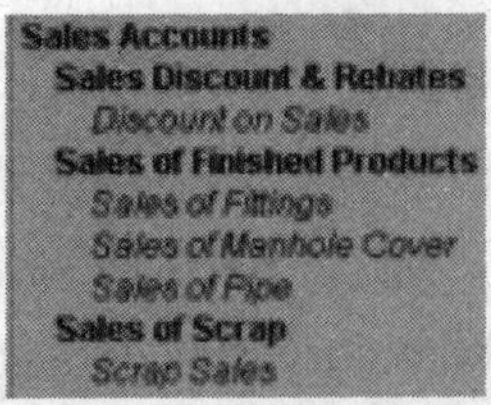

Fig 9-14: Groups & Ledgers of Sales

9.5.2 Account Group - Direct Income [Income Direct]

This Group holds Ledger Accounts for Income considered for computation of Gross Profit (Fig 9-15). Professionals may place Ledger Accounts like Professional Service Charges or Servicing Charges under this group.

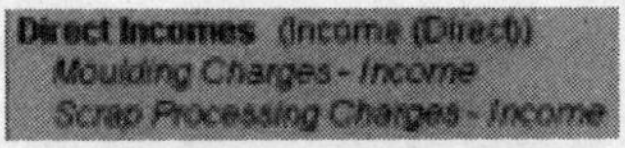

Fig 9-15: Groups & Ledgers of Income (Direct)

9.5.3 Account Group - Indirect Income [Income Indirect]

Normally, all non-major revenues like receipts on account of Rent, Interest, Commission, Dividend etc should be placed here. Ledger Accounts placed under this group are excluded for computation of Gross Profit but are considered for computation of Net Profit only.

9.5.4 Account Group - Purchase

This group holds all trade Purchases (Fig 9-16). You may create separate Accounts for Purchases and Purchases Return or club up Purchases and Purchases Returns in one account – although net effect in accounts remains same. Most often, Purchases Bills include various additional charges like Freight, Delivery Charges, Postage, Sales Tax, Excise Duty, etc., required for computing additional cost on Purchase should be placed here.

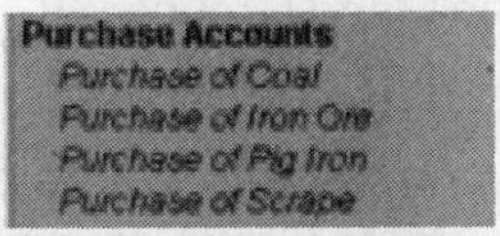

Fig 9-16: Groups & Ledgers of Purchase

9.5.5 Account Group - Direct Expenses [Expenses Direct]

Place all Ledger Accounts of Direct Expenses considered for computing Gross Profit/Loss, Example: Carriage Inwards, Wages etc (Fig 9-17).

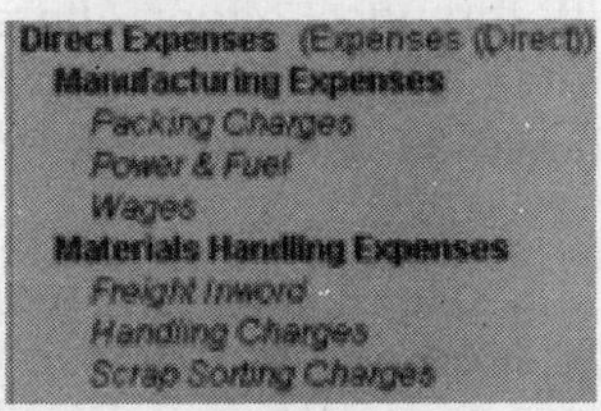

Fig 9-17: Groups & Ledgers of Direct Expenses

9.5.6 A/c Group - *Indirect Expenses [Expenses Indirect]*

All expenses considered for computation of Net Profit/Loss only (and not considered for computation of Gross Profit) should be placed here (Fig 9-18).

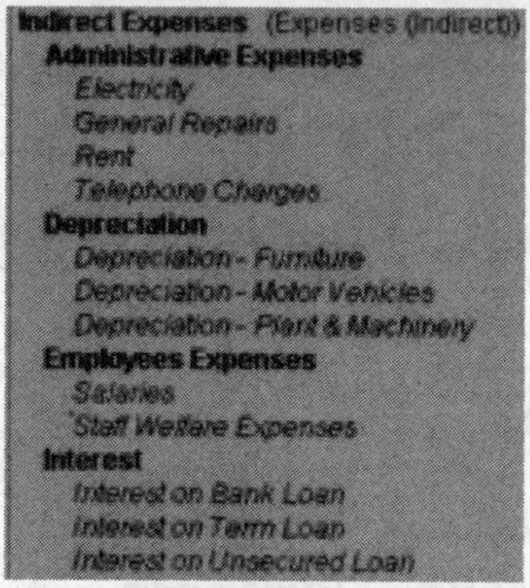

Fig 9-18: Groups & Ledgers of Indirect Expenses

Miscellaneous Expenses (Asset) is not an Expense Account – it's an Asset which appear under Balance Sheet and not in Profit & Loss Account.

9.6 Reserved Ledger Accounts

Tally automatically creates two Ledger Accounts:

- Cash (under Cash-in-Hand Group)
- Profit & Loss Account (Direct Primary Account)

Besides these 2 Ledgers, you have to create all other Ledger Accounts and place them under appropriate Group as explained above.

9.6.1 *Profit & Loss Account*

The Profit & Loss Account is a special Ledger which appears as primary Ledger in Liabilities side of the Balance Sheet and the also appears as Net Profit in the Income Side of the Profit & Loss Account

The Opening Balance of Profit & Loss Account, if any, should be entered in Opening Balance field, through Ledger Alteration option. In Balance sheet, the Opening Balance is shown as Opening Balance and the Net Current Year Profit is shown as Current Year Profit under Profit & Loss Ledger Account.

The current year profit is shown separately under Profit & Loss Ledger account. This is the only ledger account whose Opening Balance & Net transaction amount is shown separately in Balance Sheet. In P L Statement the Net Current Year Profit would be shown (excluding the Opening Balance).

The Profit & Loss Account can be transacted in Journal only. Such voucher should contain transaction with Capital Account. Never make a Journal voucher to adjust the Revenue Accounts with P & L Account as Tally automatically computes Net Profit/Loss and reflects it in the Profit & Loss account.

9.6.2 Cash Account

The Cash Account is auto created and placed under Cash-in-Hand Reserved Group.

Self Test Questions

STQ 9.1 state which is the most appropriate Group for the ledger account

(i) Depreciation on Fixed Asset

A. Fixed Assets,

B. Indirect Expenses

C. Investments

D. Reserves

(ii) Motor Cars (for sale by a Motor Car Dealer)

A. Fixed Assets,

B. Investments

C. Stock-in-Hand

D. Reserves

(iii) Motor Car (used by a Company)

A. Fixed Assets,

B. Investments

C. Stock-in-Hand

D. Duties & Taxes

(iv) HDFC Bank Cash Credit Account

A. Bank A/c,

B. Bank OCC A/c,

C. Cash in Hand

D. Secured Loans

(v) Employers Contribution to Provident Fund

A. Indirect Expenses,

B. Sundry Creditors,

C. Sundry Debtors,

D. Duties & Taxes

(vi) TDS deducted by Bank on Interest paid on Bank Fixed Deposite

A. Indirecet Expenses,

B. Sundry Creditors,

C. Loans & Advance,

D. Duties & Taxes

(vii) TDS deducted by you on Interest paid on Loans Taken

A. Indirect Expenses,

B. Current Liabilities,

C. Loans & Advance

D. Duties & Taxes

(viii) Advance paid to an employee for purchase of Stores Item for the Company

A. Indirect Expenses,

B. Direct Expenses

C. Loans & Advances (Asset)

D. Suspense a/c (Liabilities)

(ix) Sales VAT (realized in Sales Bills, to be deposited with government)

A. Indirect Income,

B. Direct Income,

C. Loans & Advances(Asset),

D. Duties & Taxes

(x) Purchase VAT (paid in Purchase Bills, to be adjusted against Sales VAT payable to Government)

A. Indirect Expenses,

B. Direct Expenses,

C. Current Liabilities,

D. Duties & Taxes

(xi) Provision for Bad Debts

A. Provision

B. Indirect Expenses,
C. Current Liabilities,
D. Capital

(xii) Bad Debts Written Off
A. Provision
B. Indirect Expenses,
C. Current Liabilities,
D. Capital

(xiii) A Mohan & Co (Supplier of Goods)
A. Sundry Debtor,
B. Sundry Creditor,
C. Sales,
D. Investments

(xiv) Premier Trading (Customer)
A. Sundry Debtor,
B. Sundry Creditor,
C. Purchase,
D. Investments

(xv) Redeemable Preference Shares
A. Capital,
B. Secured Loan,
C. Unsecured Loan,
D. Reserve & Surplus

(xvi) Shares Premium
A. Capital,
B. Secured Loan,
C. Unsecured Loan,
D. Reserve & Surplus

(xvii) Conveyance Expenses
A. Direct Expenses,
B. Indirect Expenses,
C. Loans & Advances,
D. Misc Expenses (Assets)

STQ 9.2: Write down all the Reserved Groups and place following Ledger Accounts under the proper Reserve Group:

(a) Depreciation on Fixed Asset

(b) Motor Cars (for sale by a Motor Card Dealer)

(c) Motor Car (used by a Company)

(d) HDFC Bank Cash Credit Account

(e) Employers Contribution to Provident Fund

(f) Provision for Bad Debts

(g) A Mohan & Co (Supplier of Goods)

(h) Premier Trading (Customer)

(i) Redeemable Preference Shares

(j) Shares Premium

(k) Conveyance Expenses

(l) Legal Expenses Payable to Lawyer (for previous year)

10

Account Masters

Having planned the Chart of Accounts (Account Groups and Ledgers), it is time to create them.

In this Chapter, we discuss about creation of Account Group & Ledger Accounts and the related Configuration options.

10.1 Accounts Info Menu

Select *Accounts Info* at Tally Main Menu to get *Accounts Info* Menu (Fig 10.1), which contains options for all Accounts Masters.

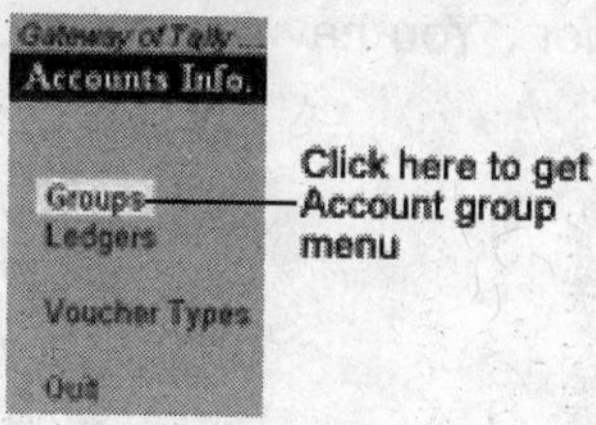

Fig 10-1: Accounts Info menu

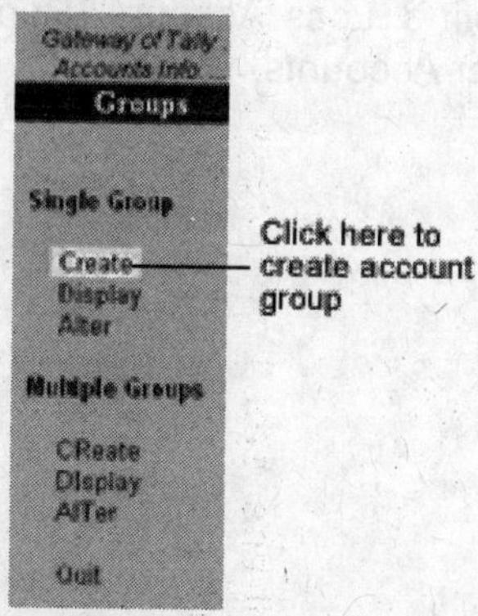

Fig 10-2: Account Group Menu

10.2 Account Groups Creation

You have seen Tally creates all the important Account Groups (*Reserved Groups*). However, you may create a new Group as a child Group of any of the existing Group.

At Accounts Info menu (Fig 10-1), select *Groups* to get Account Groups Menu. (Fig 10-2).

At Groups Menu, select *Create* under *Single Group* (Fig 10-2) to get Account Groups creation screen. Now enter as follows (Fig 10-3).

- **Account Group Name:** At *Name* field, enter unique Account Group Name. Such a name by which any account group is not existing.
- **Parent Group:** At *Under* field, select the Parent Group from List of Groups. The new Group would be placed under the selected parent group and will inherit its properties.

Type Yes to save (or press Ctrl+A to save without asking for confirmation).

You cannot leave any of the above fields blank

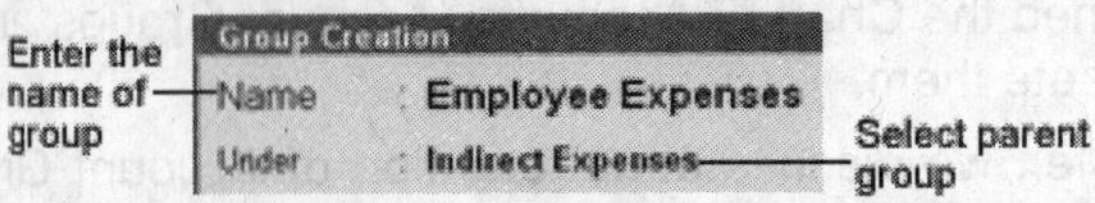

Fig 10.3: Account Group Creation

10.3 Account Ledgers Creation

Tally automatically creates 2 Ledgers, Cash (under Cash-in-hand Group) & Profit & Loss Account (Primary ledger). You have to create all other Ledger Accounts.

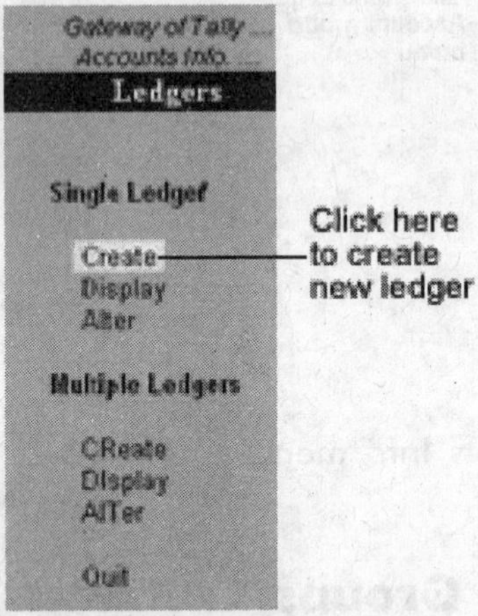

Fig. 10.4: Ledger Menu

At Gateway, select Accounts Info to get Accounts Info menu (Fig 10-1). At Accounts Info menu, select *Ledgers* to get *Ledger* Menu (Fig 10-4).

At Ledger Menu (Fig 10-4), select *Create* under *Single Ledger* to get Ledger creation screen (Fig 10-5). Now enter as follows:

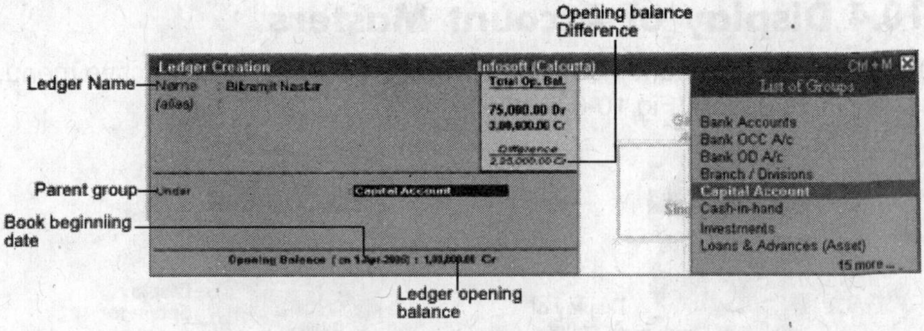

Fig 10-5: Ledger Account Creation

- **Ledger Name:** At *Name* field, enter a unique *Name* of the Ledger.
- **Parent Group:** At *Under* field, select the Parent Group of the Ledger from *List of Groups.*
- **Account Ledger Opening Balance:** At *Opening Balance* field, enter Ledger Opening Balance as at the *Books Beginning From* date (the date is displayed for instant reference - Fig 10-5).

If *Financial Year From* and *Books Beginning From* dates are same, you may not need to enter Opening Balance for Revenue Accounts (as the Opening Balance for such account is normally zero). Tally proposes Dr or Cr at Opening balance field, according to the primary Group (Fig 10-5) of the ledger (Dr for Assets and Expenses, Cr for Liabilities & Income), which you may change if necessary.

10.3.1 Opening Balance Difference

As you create Ledger, Tally displays the current *Total of Debit* and *Credit Balances* for ledgers created and *Difference* (difference of Total Debits & Credits of Opening Balance all ledger accounts so far entered) under *Difference* at right corner for information (Fig 10-5). When Opening Balance entry of all ledgers is complete & correct, the Difference Figure will be zero. The Opening Balance difference, if any, will be reported in primary Trial Balance (Ref 13.1) & in primary Balance Sheet (Ref 19.1.1).

10.3.2 Creation of Parent Group during Group/ Ledger Entry

During Account Group (Ref 10.2) or Account Ledger (Ref 10.3) entry, if you find the Parent Group not existing, press Alt+C at *Under* field (Fig 10-5) to get Account Group creation screen. Create the Parent Group as explained and then select it at *Under* field in Group / Ledger entry as usual.

10.4 Display of Account Masters

To Display any Account Master, select *Display* from the respective menu, under single option (Fig 10-6 & 10-7).

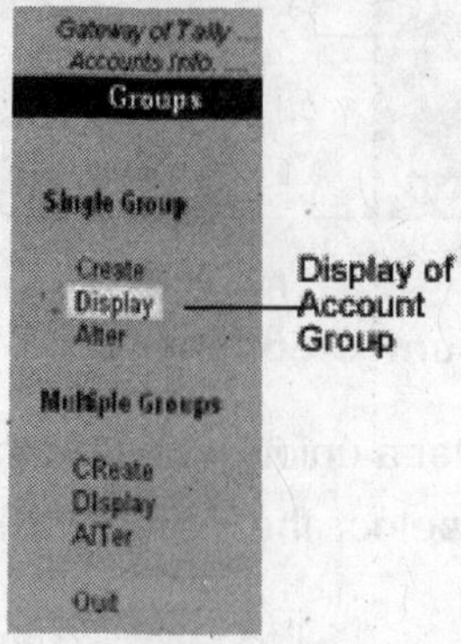

Fig 10.6: Display option for Account Group

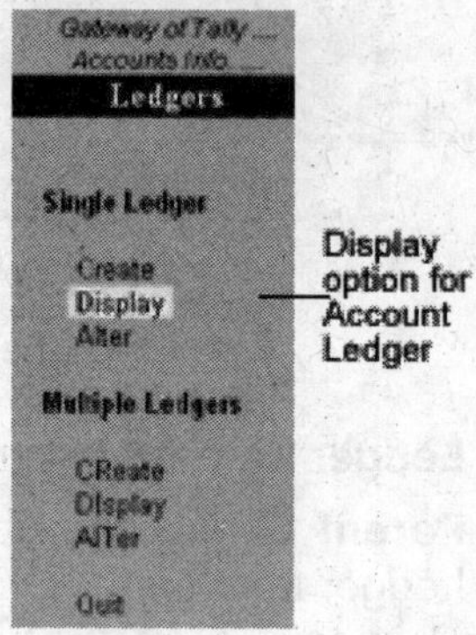

Fig 10.7: Display option for Account Ledger

- **Display of Group**: Select *Accounts Info* > Groups > Display *(Fig 10-6) and select the Account Group* to view (Fig 10-11).
- **Display of Ledger**: Select *Accounts Info > Ledgers >* Display *(Fig 10-7) and select the Account Ledger* to view (Fig 10-13).

In Display, you may view the record, but cannot make any modification (the cursor is invisible).

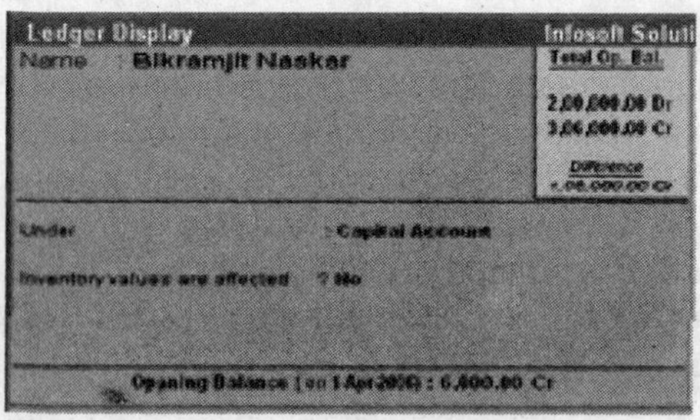

Fig 10.8: Account Ledger Display

10.5 Alteration / Deletion of Account Masters

To *Alter* any particulars in any Master (or to *Delete* the Master record), select *Alter* from the respective menu (Fig 10-9 & 10-10).

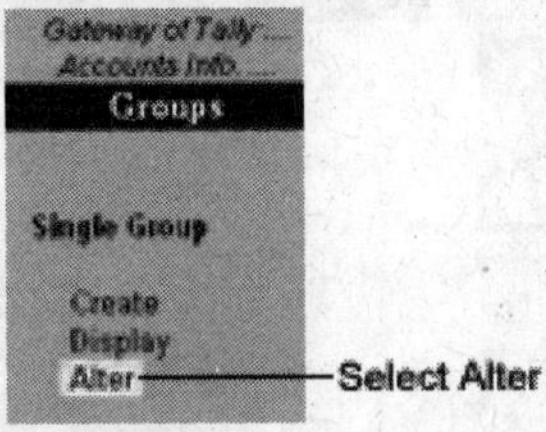

Fig 10.9:Account Group alteration

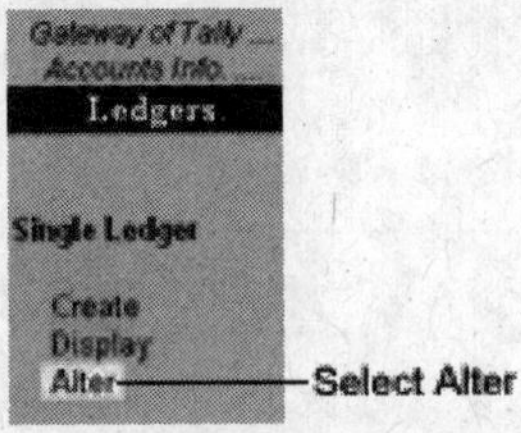

Fig 10.10: Account Ledger alteration

10.5.1 Alteration of Account Master

Alteration / Deletion of Account Group: Select Accounts *Info* > Groups > Alter *(Fig 10-9) and select the Account Group* (*Fig 10-11)* to get it in Alteration mode (Fig 10-12).

Alteration / Deletion of Account Ledger: Select *Info > Ledgers >* Alter *(Fig 10-10) and select the Account Ledger (Fig 10-13)* to get the Account Ledger in Alteration mode (Fig 10-14).

The respective Group (Fig 10-12) or the Ledger (Fig 10-14) is displayed. Now modify as desired.

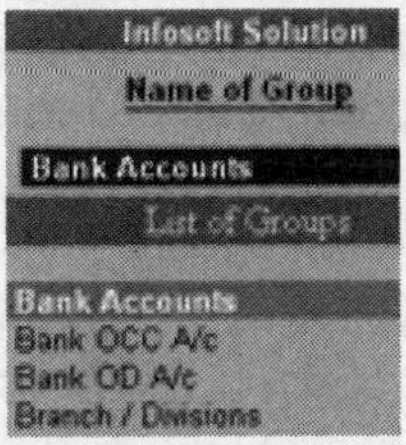

Fig 10.11: Selection of Account Group from list

Fig 10.12: Alteration of selected Account Group

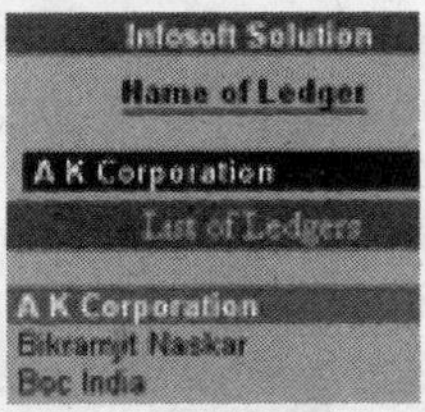

Fig 10.13: Selection of Account Ledger from list

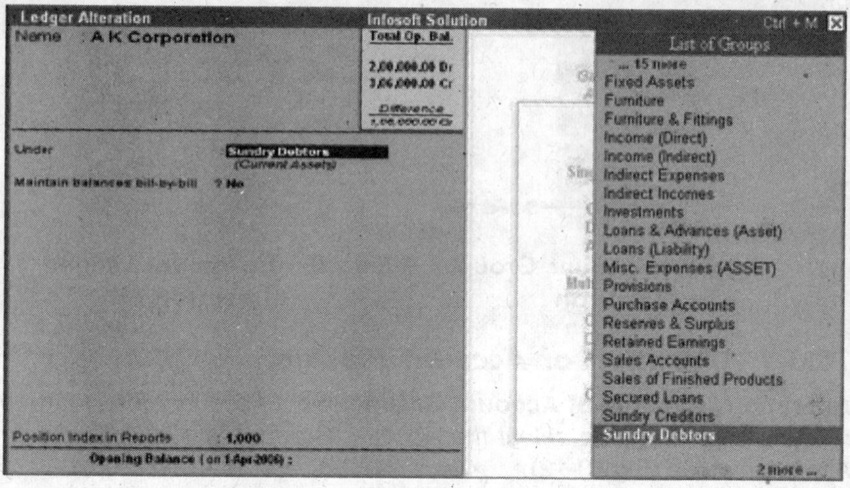

Fig 10-14: Alteration of Account Ledger

10.5.1.1 Alteration of Account Masters during entry

While creating Account Groups, Account Ledgers, to alter another record (Account Group/ Account Master) during entry, press PgUp (to get previous record) or Pg Dn (to get next record) without leaving the current entry screen. Make necessary alteration in the desired record and press Ctrl+A to save the changes in that record. You will come back to the previous entry screen you left to continue new entries.

This way you may scroll through entire List of Master Records. On reaching the dead-end of List, you will get back to *Creation* mode getting a blank entry form to *Create* a new Master Record as shown in Fig 10-3 (Account Group) & Fig 10-5 (Account Ledger).

10.5.1.2 Alteration of Parent Group

To change the Parent Group at *Under* field of any Group or Ledger, select the (new) Parent Group from the list (Fig 10-15). If the parent Group does not exist, press *Alt+C*, at under field, to get the Account Group entry screen. Now create the parent Account Group and select it at *Under* field (Fig 10-3). You cannot change the parent of Reserved Group (the cursor will not move to the Parent Group).

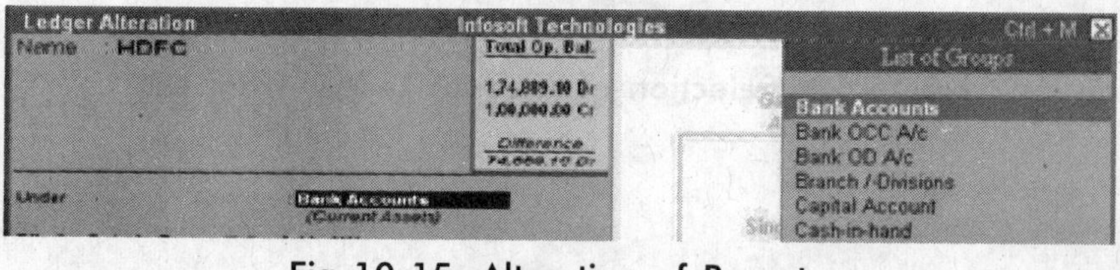

Fig 10-15: Alteration of Parent

Fig 10-16 shows the Ledger with changed Parent Group.

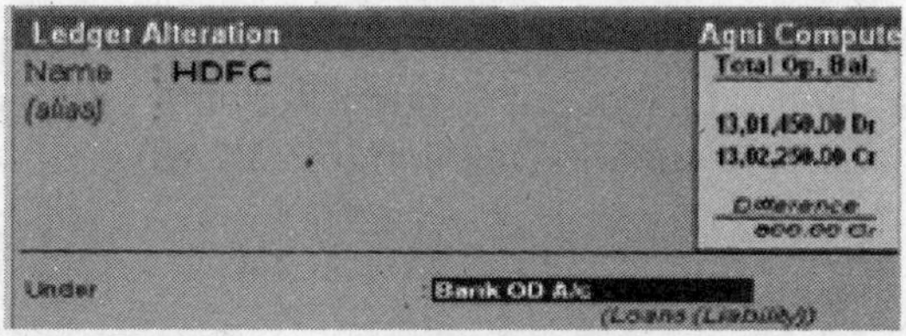

Fig 10-16: Ledger Account after change of Parent

10.5.1.3 Entry of Ledger Opening Balance in Alteration mode

As explained, you may enter Opening Balance of the ledger, if any, during Ledger Creation as shown in Fig 10-5. However, sometimes the Ledger Opening Balance is not known at the time of creation. In such case, you may leave zero at Opening Balance during creation of Ledger Account. Later on, you may enter the Opening Balance of the respective Ledger through *Alter* mode (Fig 10-14).

10.5.1.4 Opening Balance Entry of Cash & P L Account

Cash and *Profit & Loss Account* ledgers are auto created during Company creation. To enter Opening Balance for these ledgers, select the ledgers in *Alteration* mode (Ref 10.5) and enter Opening Balance as explained (Fig 10-17).

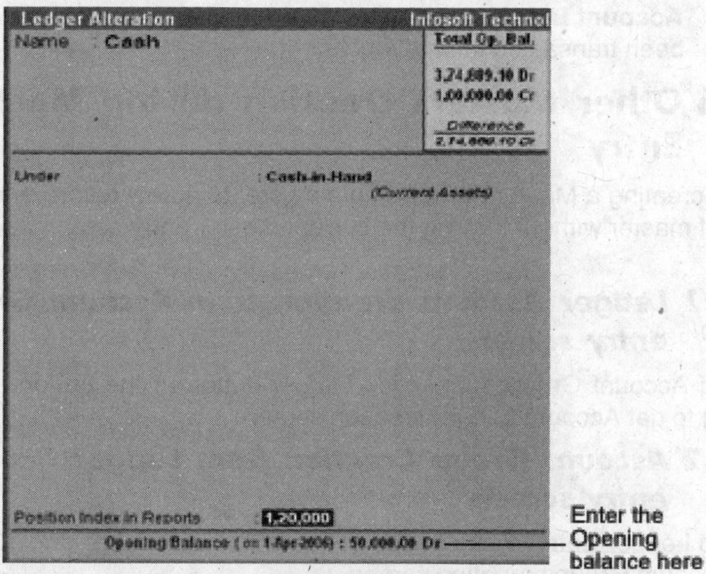

Fig 10-17: Entry of Cash Opening Balance

10.5.2 Deletion of Account Master Records

While in Alteration mode (Ref 10.5), press Alt+D to Delete the the currently selected Master Record (Account Group / Account Ledger) and press **Y** at *Delete? Yes or No*, to confirm Deletion (Fig 10-18).

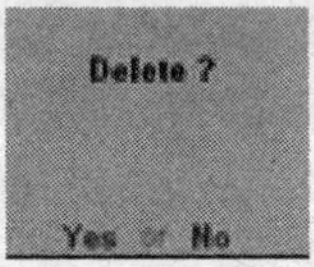

Fig 10-18: Confirmation of Deletion of Account Master

However, deletion is not permitted when you attempt to Delete a master record in the following cases:

10.5.2.1 Deletion of Reserved Masters Records: Reserved Account Groups) & Reserved Account Ledgers can not be Deleted (even if the name is altered).

10.5.2.2 Deletion of Linked Masters Records : An Account Master cannot be deleted if it has been referred in any other entity, like:

- **Account Group:** An Account Group cannot be deleted if it has been specified as Parent (selected at Under field) of any Ledger Account or Account Group.
- **Account Ledger :** An Account Ledger cannot be deleted if it has been transacted in any Voucher.

10.6 Other Masters creation during Masters Entry

While creating a Master record, you may create a new record of another type of master without leaving the current master entry screen as explain below.

10.6.1 Ledger Account Creation from Account Group entry screen

During Account Group entry, click *Ledger* button at the button bar (Fig 10-19) to get Account Ledger creation screen.

10.6.2 Account Group Creation from Ledger Account entry screen

During Ledger Entry, click *Groups* button at the button bar (Fig 10-20) to get Account Groups creation screen.

Fig 10-19: Ledger Creation during Groups entry

Fig 10-20: Group Creation during Ledger entry

10.7 Closing Stock Value entry

Unlike manual books, you do not need to enter Journal Voucher for Closing Stock in Tally. Instead, you enter the value in the respective ledger account of Closing stock.

Select the Closing Stock ledger (under *Stock-in-Hand* Group) in Alteration mode (Ref 10.5). You get a field Closing Balance where you enter the Date and Closing Stock Value for the respective Date (Fig 10-21). Having entered the value, it will be shown in Profit & Loss Account (Ref 19.2) and also in Balance Sheet (Ref 19.1). You may enter Closing Stock value for several Dates.

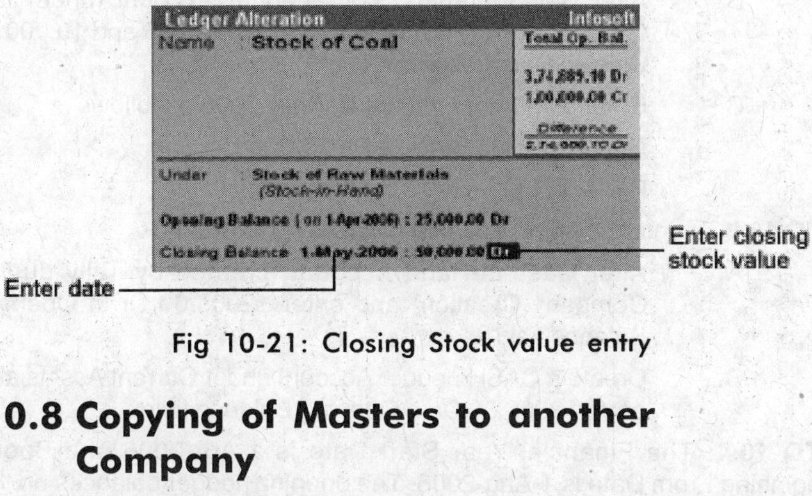

Fig 10-21: Closing Stock value entry

10.8 Copying of Masters to another Company

To copy a master record from one Tally company to another Company, select the Master (Account Group or Account Ledger) in Source Company in Alteration mode (Ref 10.5.1). Click *F3: Company* and select the destination Company. Press Ctrl+A to copy & save the Master in Destination Company. For this, you must select both the companies (source & destination) first

If the Parent Group (at *Under* field) of the copied master does not exist at destination Company, you would be prompted to create a parent for Group.

Self Test Questions

Select the correct option

STQ 10.1: To create a new Parent Account Group during a new Ledger Account creation, press :

A. Ctl+C at Name field

B. Alt+C at Name field

C. Alt+C at Under field

D. Ctl+C at Under field

STQ 10.2: To enter Raw Materials Stock value Rs 10,000 as on 30-4-2006 (for FY 1-4-2006 to 31-3-2007) :

A. Alter Raw Materials Stock Ledger Account (under the Group Stock-in-Hand) and enter 10,000 at Opening Balance

B. Alter Raw Materials Stock Ledger Account (under the Group Stock-in-Hand) and enter 30-4-2006 and 10,000 at Closing Balance field

C. Enter a Journal Voucher Dt 30-4-2006 as follows :

Raw Materials Stock - Rs 10,000 Dr

P L Account – Rs 10,000 Cr

STQ 10.3 To enter Opening Balance of Cash Rs 12005.00 :

A. Alter Cash-in-Hand Account (created by Tally during Company Creation) and enter 12005.00 Dr in Opening Balance field

B. Create a CASH Ledger Account under Current Assets and enter 12005.00 Dr in Opening Balance field

STQ 10.4: The Financial Year Start Date is 1-Apr-2006 and Books Beginning From Date is 1-Aug-2006. The opening ledger balances on the respective dates are as follows :

Ledger Account	*Opening Balance as on 1-Apr-2006*	*Opening Balance as on 1-Aug-2006*
Conveyance Expenses	0.00	12000.00 Dr
Sales	0.00	350000.00 Cr
K K & Co (Customer)	12035.37 Dr	61034.45 Dr
Cash	15030.00 Dr	18034.00 Dr

Which figure you should enter in Opening balance for the Ledger Accounts. Explain for each of the above accounts.

STQ 10.5: How you can create a new Account Group master during a new Account Ledger master creation and select it as the parent Group for the new Ledger Account being created.

STQ 10.6: How to Delete Ledger Account master.

- Can a Ledger Account be deleted if the Account has opening balance ?
- Can a Ledger Account be deleted if it is referred in any voucher

STQ 10.7: Explain how to create the following Ledger accounts under the Group Stock-in-Hand and enter the Closing Stock :

Account Name	*Stock as on 30-Jun-2006*	*Stock as on 30-Sep-2006*
Raw Materials Stock	1,70,000	1,40,000
Finished Products Stock	1,50,000	1,70,000

STQ 10.8: How you enter the Opening Balance of Cash-in-Hand Account. Is the process different from Opening Balance entry of other Ledger Accounts.

STQ 10.9: How to get the number of Master records for each type of Master. Does the number include the Reserved Master records created by Tally.

Voucher Entry

11

11.1 Accounts Voucher

Voucher is the primary document in which the complete details of accounting transaction are recorded, e.g :

- Payment of Salary to Employees
- Withdrawal of Cash from Bank Account

You make an accounts voucher whenever there is a transaction affecting accounts, even when no money transaction is involved, like:

- Credit Sale
- Provision of Depreciation for Fixed Assets
- Appropriation of Profit to Partner's Capital Accounts

11.2 Tally Accounts Voucher Types

As per classic accounting principle, all accounting transactions may be entered in Journal Voucher. In fact, in old days, people used only Journal *Day Book* to record all transactions, cash or non-cash. But for sake of convenience, accounting communities now use several Voucher Types, according to nature of transactions.

The following are the basic voucher types, considered essential by all kinds of business, irrespective of its nature, size or book keeping methods.

- **Contra**: To record transfer of funds between Cash & Bank Accounts.
- **Receipt**: To record receipts of money by cash, cheque, bank transfers, etc.
- **Payment**: To record payments of money by cash, cheque, bank transfers, etc.
- **Journal**: To record all Non Cash transactions (all accounting transactions not involving any cash or bank ledger).

  Further, Journal Vouchers relating to Customers & Suppliers are further classified for convenience of book keeping. These are discussed in later chapters.

- **Sales**: To record all sorts of Sale. In Tally, Cash Sales may also be recorded through Receipt Voucher & Credit Sales may also be recorded through Normal Journal Voucher.
- **Purchase**: To record all sorts of Purchase. In Tally, Cash Purchase may also be entered as Receipt Voucher & Credit Purchase may also be recorded through Normal Journal Voucher.
- **Debit Note & Credit Note**: Transactions with Customer & Supplier other than Sales or Purchase. In Tally, these transactions may also be recorded through Normal Journal Voucher.
- **Normal Journal Vouchers** : Any other Journal Voucher which do not contain transaction with Customer / Supplier.

11.3 Voucher Entry

You record a transaction through a voucher entry. To enter Accounts Voucher, select *Accounting Voucher* (or type V) at Tally Main Menu.

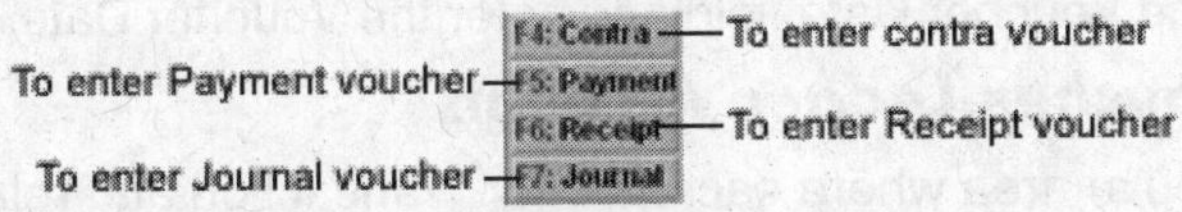

Fig 11-1: Voucher Type buttons at Vertical Button Bar at Accounts Voucher Entry screen

At the Vertical Button bar in the Voucher entry screen, you get a button for each of the voucher type (Fig 11-1). Click the appropriate button (or press the respective Function Key, e.g F7 for Journal) to get the respective type of voucher entry screen (like Fig 11-2).

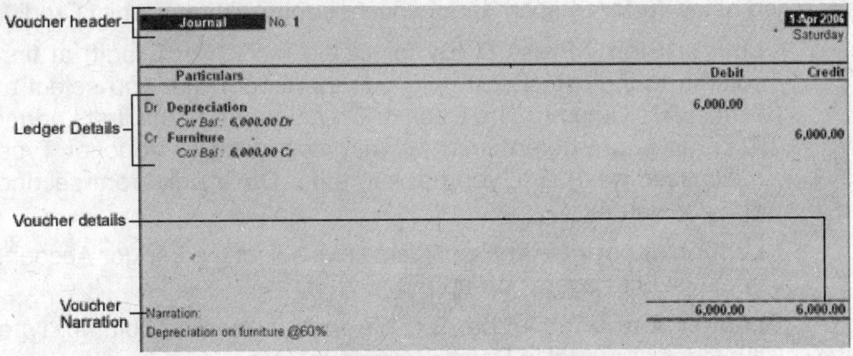

Fig 11-2: Accounts Voucher Entry screen

For convenience, Tally provides a standard interface and operational process common to all voucher types. We first discuss these common elements of voucher and then discuss the specific details in respect of each voucher types, separately.

11.3.1 Voucher Header

At Voucher Header, enter the following (Fig 11-2).

- **Voucher Number**: By default, Tally displays voucher number, serially generated in chronological order, for each Voucher type. For example, if the last voucher number was 5, the next voucher number will be 6. However, if you enter a back dated voucher, or delete a voucher, Tally will rearrange the voucher numbers in sequence of Date (Ref 11.9).
- **Voucher Date**: By default, the Current Date (Ref 8.4.2) is carried at this field to denote the Date of Voucher. To change Date, press *F2: Date* button and enter the Voucher Date (Fig 11-2). Day of the voucher (e.g., Saturday) is displayed just below the Voucher Date (Fig 11-2). This helps to trap if any voucher is being entered on weekly holiday. You may also press Backspace to get back to the Voucher Date field and enter the Voucher Date.

11.3.2 Voucher Ledger Accounts

This is a tabular area where each Ledger Transaction and related data is entered (Fig 11-2).

In Chapter 6 we have explained the effect of transaction (increase / decrease in Liabilities, Assets, Income or Expenses). Accountants have classified the nature of transactions into *Debits* & *Credits*. Normally Debit represents Increase in Assets / Expenses (or Decrease in Liabilities / Income) and Credit represents Increase in Liabilities / Income (or Decrease in Assets / Expenses). This is indicated in the Ledger Sign column, as explained below (refer Chapter 12 for voucher entry without Debit / Credit).

- **Ledger Sign** *:* Press D (By for Debit) or C (for Credit) at first column to indicate Debit or Credit the ledger that you select at *Particulars* Column. The Debit or Credit nature of the first Ledger Account is pre-determined by Tally according to Voucher Type (discussed next). So, you have to enter Dr/Cr only from second entry onwards.
- **Ledger Account** : At *Particulars* field, select the Ledger Account from List of Ledgers pop-up
- **Ledger Amount** : As per Dr / Cr entry in the first column, type the ledger Amount in Debit or Credit column.

- **Terminating Ledger Entries**: You may enter many Debit and Credit entries in a single voucher. The Ledger entries will be terminated (showing the total of Debit & Credit under both the columns) as soon as the total of *Debit* and *Credit amount* is equal.

11.3.2.1 Carrying First Ledger Accounts from previous voucher

To auto select the first ledger account of previous voucher (of same voucher type), press Ctrl+R at particular column (useful to enter consecutive vouchers with same Ledgers). On selecting first Ledger, Tally proposes the other Ledger Accounts participated in previous voucher to speed up data entry.

For example, you are entering several Conveyance Vouchers consecutively. In the first ledger account, you enter Conveyance Account. You enter other details and save the voucher.

In the next voucher, to select the Conveyance Account quickly, just press Ctrl+R (at particulars field). The Conveyance Account will get auto selected and other ledgers (similar to previous voucher) will be proposed you may however select any other ledger to transact.

11.3.3 Voucher Narration

At *Narration* field, enter Voucher Narration (Fig 11-2), describing the voucher transactions briefly but writing the essential details for future reference.

To quickly rectify / insert words while entering Narration, use the following keys:

- **Home**: To reach beginning of the Narration.
- **End**: To reach end of the Narration.
- **Left & Right Arrow**: To move one character each time in the direction.
- **Cntl+ Left or Right Arrow**: To jump one word at a time Left or Right.
- **Insert**: To insert any text within the Narration, press Insert button. It is a toggle to move between Insert Mode (cursor is blinking line – letters are inserted at the cursor position) and *Overwrite* (cursor is blinking block- letters at the cursor position are overwritten) mode.

11.3.3.1 Copying Voucher Narration

To speed up data entry, you may copy Narration from another voucher using following key combination at Narration field:

- **To Repeat the Narration entered in the preceding voucher**: Press Ctrl+R. This is useful when you enter voucher of similar nature consecutively.

- **To Repeat the Narration entered in the previous voucher involving the same first Ledger account**: Press Alt+R. This is quite useful as the Narration of a voucher is normally related to the ledger account (e.g, Narration of Conveyance Expenses will be similar). So, in Payment Voucher debiting Conveyance Expenses, press Alt+R at Narration field, the Narration of Previous Voucher with Conveyance Expense as *First Ledger* account, will be copied.

After getting the Narration copied, you may alter the Narration as desired. This helps you to enter Narration faster and make the Narration text consistent in all vouchers of similar nature of transactions.

11.3.3.2 Cheque Number Entry in Voucher

When any Bank Account (ledger placed under Bank Accounts or Bank OCC Groups) is transacted in the Voucher (except for Cash Deposit in Contra Voucher), Tally prompts *Ch. No* at Narration field (Fig 11-3). Enter Cheque Number and Voucher Narration next to Cheque Number in the same line (Fig 11-3). Don't press <enter> or <Tab> after cheque number before writing the Narration. Press <enter> after writing Narration (or press Ctrl+A to save directly). In case of Receipt Voucher, it is recommended to write the Cheque Date and Drawee Bank Name in Narration to keep full record of the cheque received.

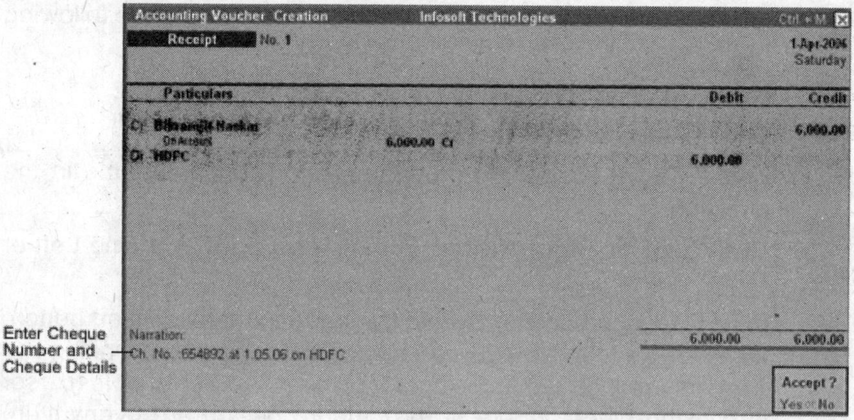

Fig 11-3: Entry of Cheque Number & cheque Details in Voucher

11.4 Voucher Modification during Entry

To alter data in any field before saving the voucher, click on the field or use the following keys:

- To move the cursor to previous field, press *Backspace* or *Up Arrow* key.
- To move to the next field, press ↵.

Now modify the data at the desired field

11.5 Saving the Voucher

After complete entry of the voucher, press ↵ or type Yes at Accept*? Yes or No* (Fig 11-4), to save the voucher (or press Ctrl+A to save instantly without getting the message). The current voucher will be saved.

Fig 11-4: Saving a Voucher

11.6 Terminating Voucher Entry Task

After saving the current voucher, a blank Voucher entry screen would appear to continue voucher entry. To terminate voucher entry, press Esc and press 'Y' at *Quit? Yes or No*. to quit (Fig 11-5). To enter any other type of Voucher, click the respective button (F4 to F7) for the Voucher Type.

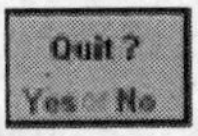

Fig 11-5: Quitting Voucher Entry screen

11.7 Accounts Voucher Entry

Now we describe the nature of transaction for each Voucher Type. To trap mistakes, Tally follows certain rules for certain voucher types. These rules (explained at each Voucher Type) are validated during voucher entry and any violation is trapped immediately. This helps to minimise errors in voucher entry.

11.7.1 Contra Voucher

Contra Voucher is used for *Fund Transfer* between Cash & Bank Accounts (Ledgers placed under Groups: Cash-in-hand, Bank Accounts and Bank OCC) only (where no actual money is paid or received).

Example: Following transactions should be entered in Contra voucher:

- **Cash deposited into Bank**: Cash Outflow, equal Inflow at Bank Account (Fig 11-6).

- **Cash withdrawn from Bank**: Outflow from Bank Account, equal Cash Inflow (Fig 11-7).
- **Money transferred from one Bank account to another Bank account**: Outflow from One Bank Account, equal Inflow to another Bank Account (Fig 11-8).
- **Cash deposited to Multiple Bank Account** : Outflow from One Cash Account, equal Inflow to various Bank Accounts (Fig. 11.9).

Press F4 function key (or click *F4: Contra* button) at the Voucher Entry Screen to enter a Contra Voucher

Voucher Rules: The entries in Contra Voucher follow the rule shown below:

Particulars	*Debit*	*Credit*
Cr Source of Funds		(Amount)
Dr Destination of Funds	(Amount)	

Entry Rules: The first entry is always credit. From 2nd entry onwards you may Debit or Credit a ledger under Cash, Bank Accounts and Bank OCC Group only.

Examples of Contra Vouchers

1. Rs. 5000 Cash withdrawn from HDFC. So the entry would be:

Cr HDFC		6000
Dr Cash	6000	

2. Cash Deposited Rs. 3000 to HDFC and Rs. 4000 to Vijaya Bank.

❋ You may make two separate vouchers

1st Voucher	Cr Cash		3000
	Dr HDFC	3000	
2nd Voucher	Cr Cash		4000
	Dr Vijaya Bank	4000	

❋ Or make one combined voucher

Cr Cash		7000
Dr HDFC	3000	
Dr Vijaya Bank	4000	

We recommend 2 separate vouchers as source documents (Pay-in-slips) are different.

Fig 11-6 to 11-9 shows various types of Contra Voucher transactions.

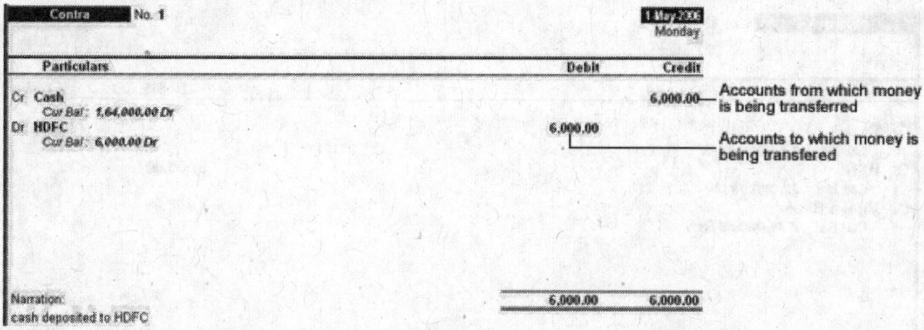

Fig 11-6: Contra Voucher Entry - Cash Deposited to Bank account

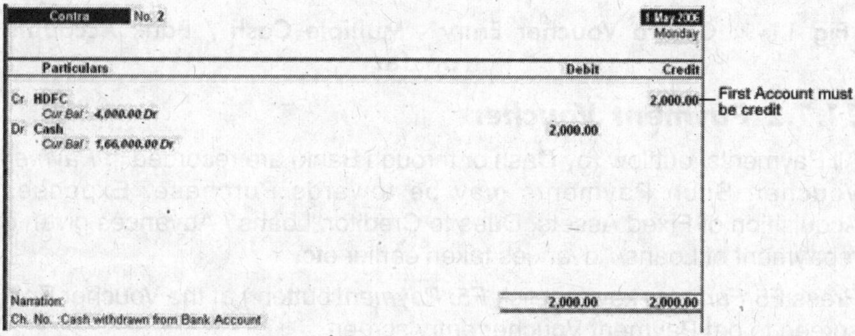

Fig 11-7: Contra Voucher Entry - Cash withdrawn from Bank Account

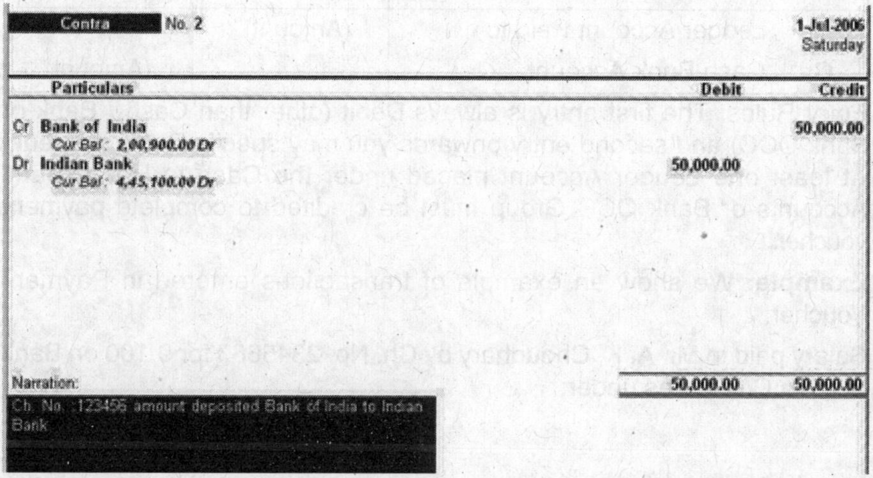

Fig 11-8: Contra Voucher Entry - Inter Bank Account Transfer

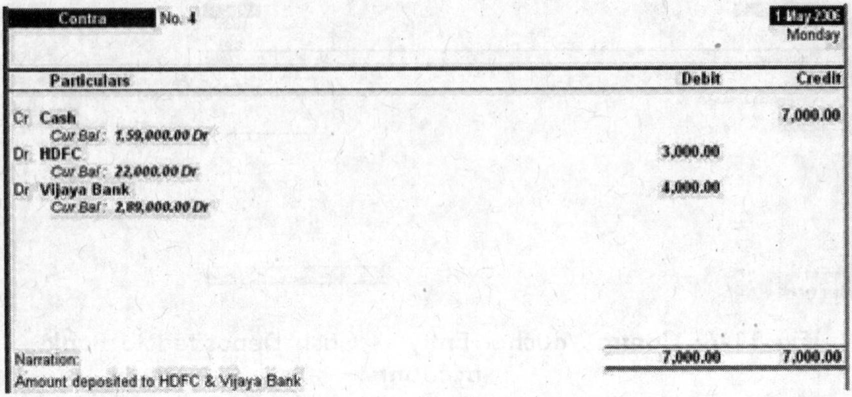

Fig 11-9: Contra Voucher Entry - Multiple Cash / Bank Accounts transfer

11.7.2 Payment Voucher

All Payments/ outflow (by Cash or through Bank) are recorded in *Payment* Voucher. Such Payments may be towards Purchase, Expenses, Acquisition of Fixed Assets, Dues to Creditor, Loans / Advances given or repayment of Loans/Advances taken earlier etc.

Press F5 *Function* key (or click *F5: Payment* button) at the Voucher Entry screen to get Payment Voucher entry screen.

Voucher Rules: Payment Voucher follows the rules as stated below:

Particulars	*Debit*	*Credit*
Dr Ledger Account Paid to	(Amount)	
Cr Cash/Bank Account		(Amount)

Entry Rules: The first entry is always Debit (other than Cash / Bank or Bank OCC) and second entry onwards you may specify Debit or Credit. At least one Ledger Account placed under the Cash in Hand, Bank Accounts or Bank OCC Group must be credited to complete payment voucher.

Example: We show an example of transactions entered in Payment Voucher:

Salary paid to Mr. A. K. Choudhary by Ch. No. 2345667 for 9,100 on Bank of India C/C A/c as under:

Salary	9000	
Dearness Allowance	1500	
		10500
Deductions		
Contribution for E. S. I	1050	
Contribution for P. F	150	
Income Tax	200	
		1400
Net Amount Paid by cheque on HDFC Bank		9100

The transaction in Payment Voucher would be entered as under

Dr Salary	9000	
Dr Dearness Allowance	1500	
Cr Contribution for P. F		1050
Cr Contribution for E.S.I.		150
Cr Income Tax		200
Cr HDFC		9100

Narration: Ch. No. 563987 paid for Staff Salary.

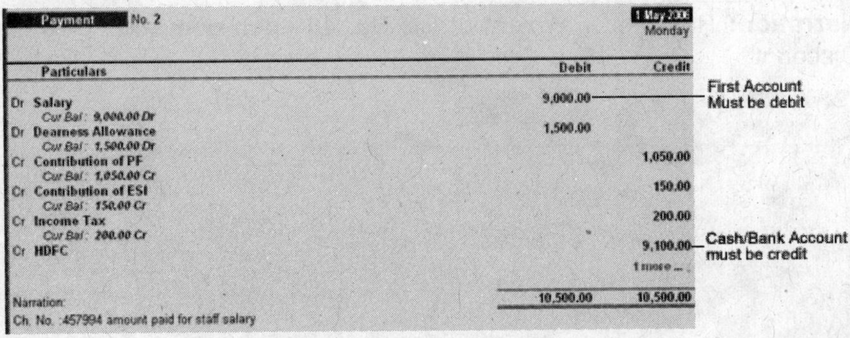

Fig 11-10: Payment Voucher Entry

11.7.3 Receipt Voucher

All *Inflow* of money (in Cash or through Bank) is recorded through Receipt Voucher. Such receipts may be towards any Income, from Debtors, Loans/ Advances taken or Refund of Loans/Advances given earlier etc.

Press F6 function key (or click *F6: Receipt* button– Fig 11-1) at the Voucher Entry scre... to get Receipt Voucher entry screen (Fig 11-11).

Voucher Rules: Payment Voucher follows the rules as stated below:

Particulars	*Debit*	*Credit*
Cr Ledger Account Recd From		(Amount)
Dr Cash/Bank Account	(Amount)	

Entry Rules: The first entry is always Credit (other than Cash/ Bank/ Bank OCC) and second entry onwards you may specify Debit or Credit. At least one Ledger account placed under the Cash in Hand, Bank Accounts or Bank OCC Group must be Debited to completed a receipt voucher.

Example of transactions entered in Receipt voucher:

Rama Trading Co. to whom goods were sold earlier on Credit, paid Rs. 4,000.00 In cash, upon deduction of Cash Discount for 500.00 against Bill No. 45 for 4,500.00.

Bill Amount	4,500
Less: Cash Discount	500
Paid by Cash	4,000

The transaction in Receipt Voucher would be as under (Fig 11-11).

Cr Rama Trading Co	4,500
Dr Cash Discount	500
Dr Cash	4000

Narration: Received Payment of Bill No. 45 upon deduction of Cash Discount.

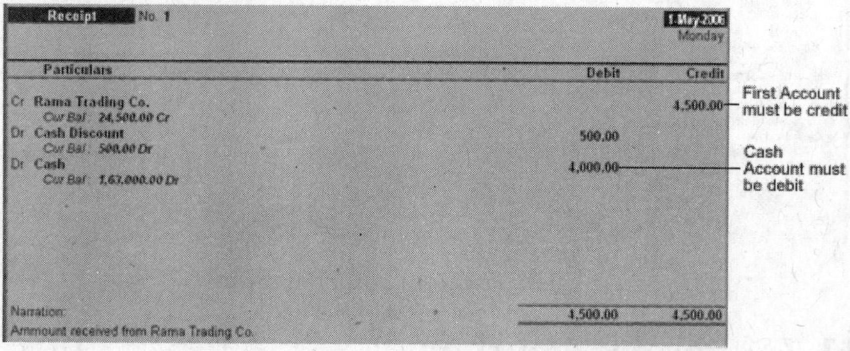

Fig 11-11: Receipt Voucher Entry

As explained, Tally validates the Ledger Account according to Voucher Types. If any ledger account has been placed under wrong group, sometimes, Tally may not show a ledger account (though it is existing) in the selection list and you may get 'Duplicate Name' message when you attempt to create it again (in such case, rectify the parent Group of the ledger through Alter option).

11.7.4 Journal Voucher

Journal is an *Adjustment* Voucher, normally used for non cash transactions for adjustment between Ledger Accounts.

Press F7 function key (or click *F7: Journal* button – Fig 11-1) to get Journal Voucher entry screen (Fig 11-12).

Entry Rules: In a Journal Voucher, only Non Cash/Bank Accounts (Ledger Accounts other than Cash, Bank or Bank OCC) may be transacted. The First entry must be Debit (Fig 11-12).

Example of a Journal Voucher:

Particulars	*Debit*	*Credit*
Dr Depreciation	(Amount)	
Cr Machinery		(Amount)
Cr Furniture & Fixtures		(Amount)
Cr Motor Car		(Amount)

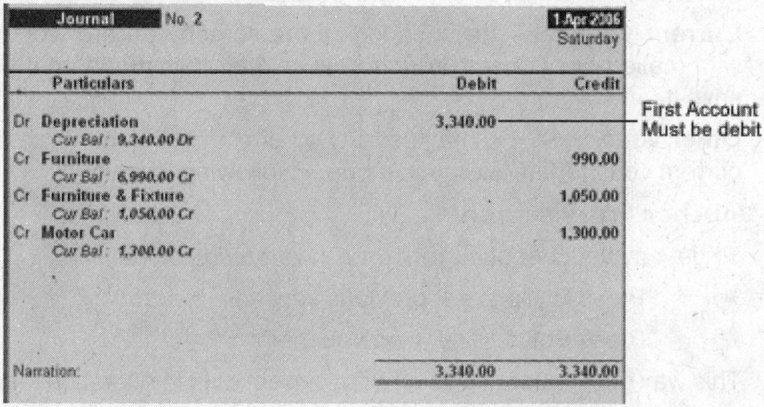

Fig 11-12: Journal Voucher Entry

11.7.5 Sales & Purchase Voucher

You may enter Sales, Purchase, Debit Note & Credit Note through Journal Voucher. However, Tally has provided separate voucher types for these transactions, which are explained in Chapter 26.

Entry Rules : The entry rules for such vouchers are summarized below:

- **Sales Voucher :** The First entry is Debit (Sundry Debtors/ Creditors, Cash / Bank / Bank OCC, Branch & Divisions). The second entry is Credit (Sales). Third entry onward may be Sales, any revenue account (except Purchase) / Duties & Taxes.
- **Purchase Voucher :** The First entry is Credit (Sundry Debtors/ Creditors, Cash / Bank / Bank OCC, Branch & Divisions). The second entry is Debit (Purchase). Third entry onward may be Purchase, any revenue account (except Sales) / Duties & Taxes.
- **Debit Note :** The First entry is Debit (Sundry Debtors/ Creditors, Cash / Bank / Bank OCC, Branch & Divisions). The second entry is Credit (any revenue account / duties & taxes). Third entry onward may be any revenue account / Duties & Taxes.
- **Credit Note :** The First entry is Credit (Sundry Debtors/ Creditors, Cash / Bank / Bank OCC, Branch & Divisions). The second entry is Debit (any revenue account / duties & taxes). Third entry onward may be any revenue account / Duties & Taxes.

11.8 Voucher in Alteration Mode

To perform Voucher Alteration, Deletion & Cancellation, you have to get the Voucher in Alteration Mode in following ways :

- **Current Voucher**: The voucher on the screen you are working with (called the *Current Voucher*) is in *Alteration* mode until you save it.
- **Other Vouchers**: You may get any other voucher (other than the current voucher) in Alteration mode, in following 2 ways:

From Voucher Entry screen

- To get any voucher of current date in *Alteration* mode:
  - ❋ Press PgUp to get previous voucher
  - ❋ Press PgDn to get next voucher

  This way get the desired voucher of current date in Alteration mode
- To get a voucher of any other date:
  - ❋ Press F2 and change the *Current Date* (Fig 8-6)
  - ❋ Now scroll through vouchers of the day by pressing PgUp / PgDn as explained above to get the voucher in Alteration mode in the screen.

From Display

You may also get a voucher in Alteration mode by drilling down from Display.

11.8.1 Voucher Alteration, Deletion & Cancellation

In Voucher Alteration mode (as explained above), you may perform the following operation on the voucher:

- **Voucher Deletion**: Press Alt+D, and click *Yes* at *Delete? Yes or No* to confirm Deletion (Fig 11-13).The deleted Voucher is permanently removed. You cannot get back the deleted voucher.
- **Voucher Cancellation**: Press Alt+X, and click *Yes* at *Cancel? Yes or No* to confirm Cancellation (Fig 11-14). The Cancelled Voucher remains but the voucher becomes zero valued. The Cancelled voucher is shown as zero valued vouchers in Day Book retaining the voucher number.
- **Voucher Alteration**: Move the cursor to the desired field (or click at the field) and modify as desired (in the same way as you have entered the data earlier). Press Ctrl+A or click *Yes* at *Save? Yes or No* to save the voucher.

Finally press Esc to return to previous level.

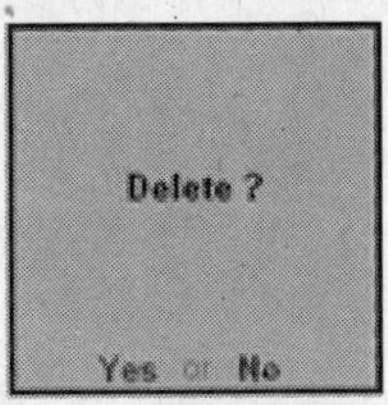

Fig 11-13: Confirmation for Voucher Deletion

Fig 11-14: Confirmation for Voucher Cancellation

11.9 Auto Renumbering of Voucher

For all Auto generated Voucher Number, when you Delete or Insert a back dated Voucher (or even modify the Date of a back dated voucher), all the voucher number of subsequent dates will automatically get renumbered chronologically.

So, if you have already printed the vouchers (Ref Chapter 13), DO NOT Insert or Delete (rather Cancel a Voucher), else your vouchers will get renumbered.

11.10 Conversion of Voucher Type

You may convert a voucher from one type to another in the following way (useful when you entered a voucher in wrong voucher type)

- Select the voucher in Alteration mode.

- Click the appropriate Voucher Type button on the Button Bar (and select the voucher type, if multiple voucher types are listed), press **Ctrl+A** to save the Voucher.
- If some entries offend the voucher type to which you like convert to, you would be prompted to select appropriate Ledger from List of Ledgers.

11.11 Accounts Statistics

To get the number of Account Masters of each Type and Vouchers in respect of each Voucher Type (Fig 11-15), select Display > Statement of Accounts > Statistics.

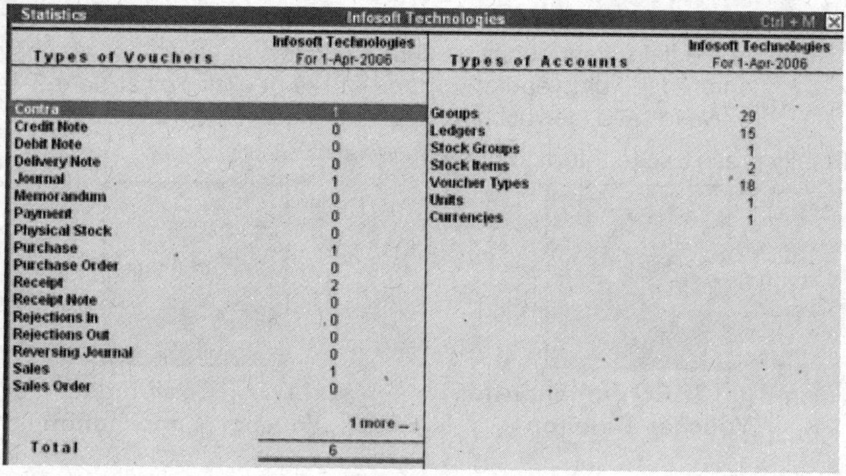

Fig 11-15: Voucher Statistics

In the left pane, you get the number of vouchers for each Voucher Type and in the right pane, you get the number of Masters of each Type (Fig 11-15).

Self Test Questions

Check the correct option

STQ 11.1: In Contra Voucher:

A. First account must be a Cash Account

B. First account must be a Bank Account

C. All Accounts must be either Cash, Bank or Bank OCC Account

D. One of the Account must be a Cash Account

STQ 11.2: In Receipt Voucher :

A. First account must be a Cash Account

B. First account must be a Bank Account

C. First Account cannot be Cash, Bank or Bank OCC Account

STQ 11.3: In Payment Voucher :

A. First account must be a Cash Account

B. First account must be a Bank Account

C. First Account cannot be Cash, Bank or Bank OCC Account

STQ 11.4:

A. In Receipt Voucher, Cash, Bank / Bank OCC must be Debited

B. In Receipt Voucher, Cash, Bank / Bank OCC must be Credited

C. In Payment Voucher, Cash, Bank / Bank OCC must be Debited

STQ 11.5:

A. In Receipt Voucher, First Account must be a non Cash / Bank Credit Account

B. In Receipt Voucher, First Account must be a non Cash / Bank Debit Account

C. In Receipt Voucher, First Account must be a Cash / Bank Debit Account

D. In Receipt Voucher, First Account must be a Cash / Bank Credit Account

STQ 11.6:

A. In Payment Voucher, First Account must be a non Cash / Bank Credit Account

B. In Payment Voucher, First Account must be a non Cash / Bank Debit Account

C. In Payment Voucher, First Account must be a Cash / Bank Debit Account

D. In Payment Voucher, First Account must be a Cash / Bank Credit Account

STQ 11.7: State the Type of Voucher (Contra / Receipt/ Payment/ Journal) and the ledger account Debit & Credit for each of the following Transactions

Example: Rs 120 paid in Cash for Conveyance Expenses

Voucher Type	*A/c Name*	*DEBIT*	*CREDIT*
Payment	Conveyance	120	
	Cash		120

(a) Cash Withdrawn from HDFC cash Credit A/c (under Bank OCC)

(b) A cheque for Rs 1000 drawn on HDFC Cash Credit A/c deposited into Syndicate Bank Current A/c

(c) Sales made to a customer for Rs 120 in cash

(d) Sales made to a customer for Rs 120 through Credit Card

(e) Salary Paid in Cash as follows:

Gross Salary	3500
Less PF (deduction)	350
Net Amount Paid	3150

(f) Depreciation @10% provided on Furniture valued Rs.25000

STQ 11.8: How you can carry the first ledger account of the previous voucher automatically while entering a new voucher.

STQ 11.9: How you can copy the voucher narration of previous voucher entered.

STQ 11.10: How you can copy the voucher narration of previous voucher with same first ledger account

STQ 11.11: How to delete a voucher

STQ 11.12: How to cancel a voucher

STQ 11.13: How can get the statistics (number of vouchers entered) of all types of vouchers. Does this number include Cancelled Vouchers also?

Single Mode Voucher Entry

12

As you have seen in previous chapter, you have to specify Debit/ Credit sign before you select Ledger Accounts in voucher entry. For centuries, these two seemingly simple terms have baffled naïve accountants.

So if Debits & Credits haunt you, you may enter *Payment, Receipt & Contra* Voucher in Single Mode Entry, without specifying Debit or Credit. Tally, with its built-in intelligence, will automatically recognise Debits & Credits according to voucher types, ledger position and amount sign. The entry process is simple and intuitive.

> Do not confuse Single & Double entry mode with Single (Cash Accounting) & Double (Mercantile) entry accounting system. Tally just provides two types of voucher entry forms for convenience, internally the data is stored in same way. You get same results whether you enter voucher in single or double mode.

12.1 Configuration for Single Mode Voucher

Click *F12: Configuration* at Gateway and select Voucher Entry at Configuration menu. Set *Yes* at *Use Single mode for Payment/Receipt/ Contra* to get single entry mode for Payment, Receipt & Contra vouchers (Fig 12-1).

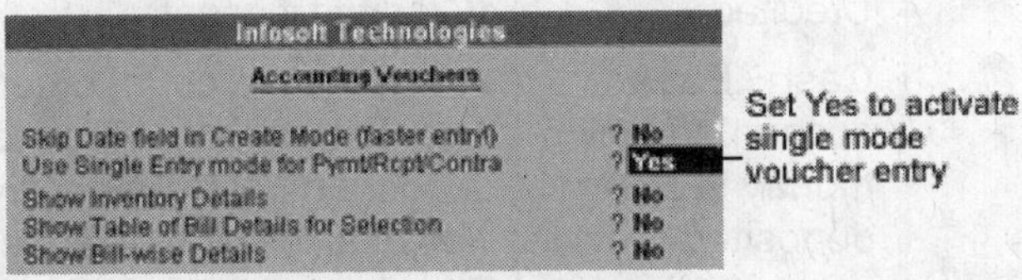

Fig 12-1: Single Mode Voucher entry option set up

12.2 Single Mode Voucher Entry rules

In Single Entry mode, you select one Cash / Bank ledger account in Header (referred as *Header Account)* without any amount. The debit/ credit nature of Header Account is determined by the voucher type and the amount for the Header ledger account is computed as balancing amount of all other ledgers entered in the Line area. The current balance of the Cash / Bank Ledger account is displayed against the Cash Bank Ledger Name.

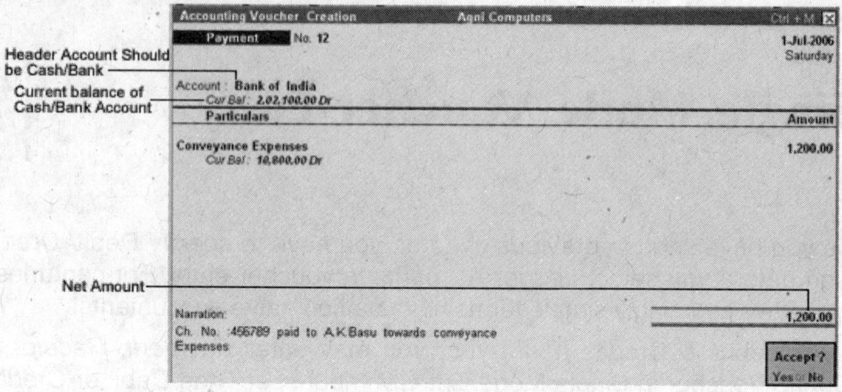

Fig 12-2: Components of single mode voucher

In Line area, enter the other ledger accounts (one or more) and the amount (negative amount for deductions) for each ledger account (referred as *Line Accounts*). The Debit/ Credit nature is determined by the Voucher Type and the amount sign.

The rules of entry of contra, payment & receipt voucher in single entry mode are as under:

Voucher Type	*Header Account*	*Line Accounts*
Payment	Cash / Bank account from which money is being paid. This account is Credited	Any ledger account other than cash / bank, bank occ. First ledger account must have positive figure. Net of all entries must be positive. These accounts are Debited (Credited if negative).
Receipt	Cash / Bank account to which money is being deposited. This account is Debited	Any ledger account other than cash / bank, bank occ.. First ledger account must have positive figure. Net of all entries must be positive. These accounts are Credited (Debited if negative).
Contra	Cash / Bank Account to which money is being transferred. This Account is Debited.	Any other Cash / Bank/ Bank OCC account from which money is being transferred. This account is Credited.

Fig 12-2 shows Conveyance A/c Dr – 1200, Advance A/c Cr 100 & Bank of India A/c Cr 1100.

12.2.1 Single Mode Contra Voucher Entry

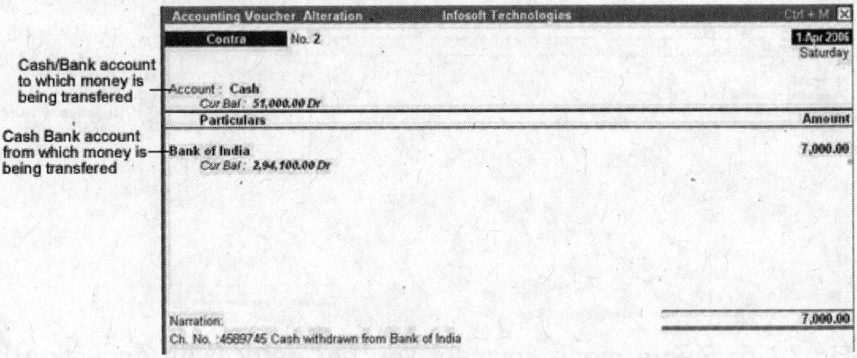

Fig 12-3: Single Mode Contra voucher entry

Fig 12-3 shows Single Mode Contra Voucher, Cash A/c Dr – 7000, Bank of India A/c Cr 7000.

12.2.2 Single Mode Payment Voucher Entry

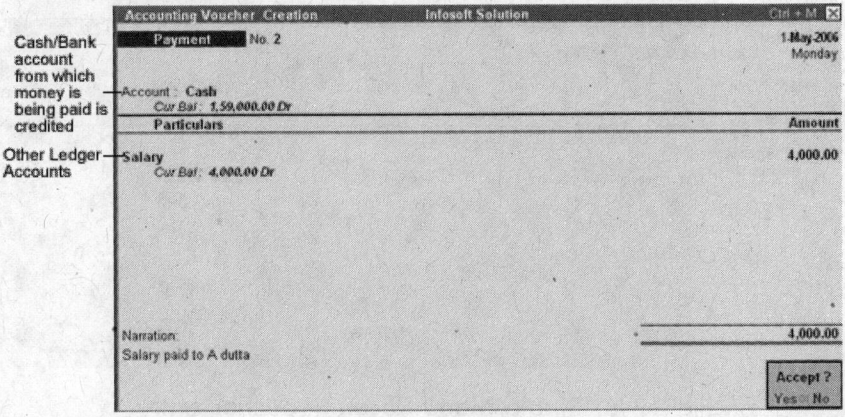

Fig 12-4: Single Mode payment voucher entry

Fig 12-4 shows a Single Mode Payment Voucher. Salaries A/c Dr 4000, Cash A/c Cr – 4000.

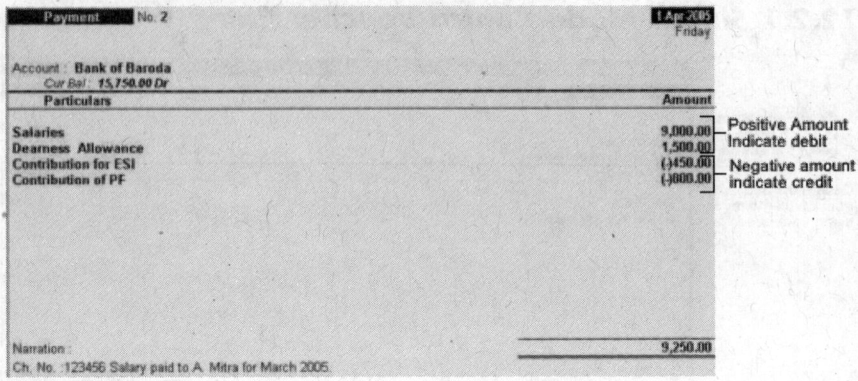

Fig 12-5: Single mode Payment voucher entry (with deductions)

12-5 shows Single Mode Payment Voucher entry with deductions (as negative amount). Salaries A/c Dr 9000, Dearness A/c Dr 1500, Contribution to ESI A/c Cr 450, Contribution to PF A/c Cr 800, Bank of Baroda Cr 9250.

12.2.3 Single Mode Receipt Voucher Entry

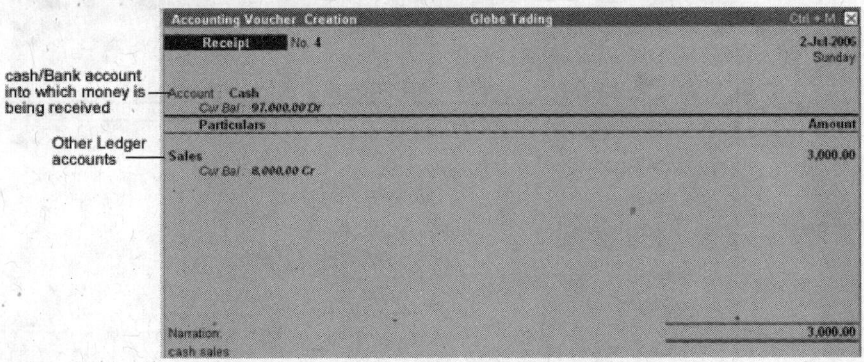

Fig 12-6: Single Mode Receipt voucher entry

Fig 12-6 shows a Single Mode Receipt Voucher entry. Cash Sales A/c Cr 3000 & Cash A/c Dr 3000

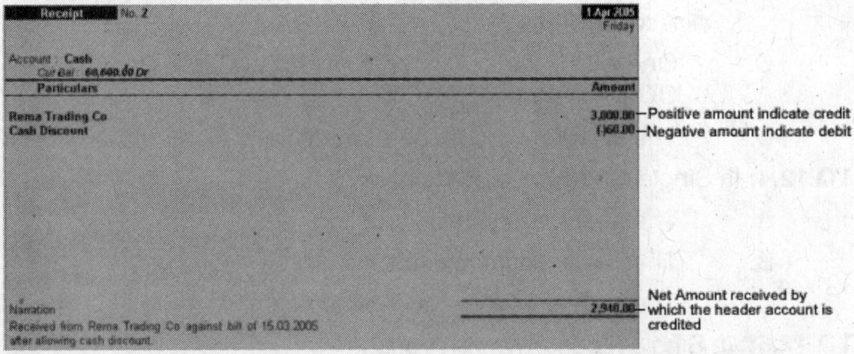

Fig 12-7: Single Mode Receipt voucher entry (with deductions)

Fig 12-7 shows Single Mode Receipt Voucher entry with deductions (as negative amount). Rama Trading A/c Cr 3000, Cash Discount A/c Dr 60 & Cash A/c Dr 2940

Self Test Questions

Select the correct options

STQ 12.1 In Contra Voucher entry in Single Mode

A. The Header account must be a Cash Account

B. The Header account must be a Bank Account

C. The Header Account must be either Cash, Bank or Bank OCC Account from which money is transferred out

D. The Header Account must be Cash, Bank or Bank OCC Account to which money is transferred in.

STQ 12.2: In Payment Voucher in Single Mode:

A. The Header Account must be Cash, Bank / Bank OCC Account

B. The Header Account cannot be Cash, Bank / Bank OCC Account

C. One of the Line Accounts must be Cash, Bank / Bank OCC Account

D. The Header Account gets Debited

STQ 12.3: In Receipt Voucher in Single Mode:

A. The Header Account must be Cash, Bank / Bank OCC Account

B. The Header Account cannot be Cash, Bank / Bank OCC Account

C. One of the Line Accounts must be Cash, Bank / Bank OCC Account

D. The Header Account gets Credited

STQ 12.4: In Single Mode Receipt Voucher

A. The header account is credited

B. The line account is debited

C. The header account is debited

STQ 12.5: In Single Mode Payment Voucher

A. The header account is Debited

B. The line account is debited

C. The line account is credited

STQ 12.6: In Single Mode Receipt Voucher

A. The Line account with negative value is Debited

B. The Line account with negative value is Credited

C. The Header account is Credited

STQ 12.7: What is the difference between Single & Double mode voucher entry. Which type of Vouchers can be entered in Single Mode and what are the advantage / disadvantage of Single Mode. Which mode you will like to use?

STQ 12.8: Explain, the ledger Accounts that you will enter in Header and in Line area (with sign) in Single Mode:

A. Rs.1000 Withdrawn from HDFC Cash Credit A/c (under Bank OCC)

B. Rs 3000 Cash deposited into Syndicate Bank Current A/c

C. A Cheque for Rs 1000 drawn on HDFC Cash Credit A/c deposited into Syndicate Bank Current A/c

D. Sales made to a Customer for Rs 120 in cash) Sales made to a Customer for Rs 120 through Credit Card

F. Salary Paid in Cash as follows:

Gross Salary	3500
Less PF (deduction)	350
Net Amount Paid	3150

Accounts Voucher Printing 13

After Voucher entry, you may also print the voucher.

13.1 Voucher printing Modes

You may print voucher at 2 stages:

- **On line Voucher Printing during voucher entry**: Just after you have completed the voucher data entry, you may print the voucher before saving it. This way, you print only the current voucher instantly upon entry.
- **Off line Voucher Printing of saved Voucher**: You may print all vouchers of a day at one go (through Multi Voucher Printing option), after the vouchers have been saved

13.2 Tally Configuration for Voucher Printing

At Voucher printing screen (Fig 13.6), click *F12: Configure* to get the Voucher printing Configuration Screen for the respective voucher types (Fig 13-1, 13-2, 13-4). Set the configuration options as desired.

The standard values in the configuration screen are pre set to fit voucher in A4 size stationery. However, you may change them to adjust according to the size of stationery you use.

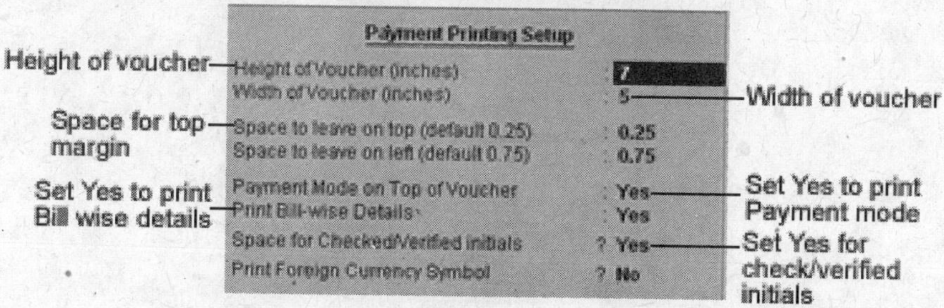

Fig 13-1: Payment Voucher Configuration

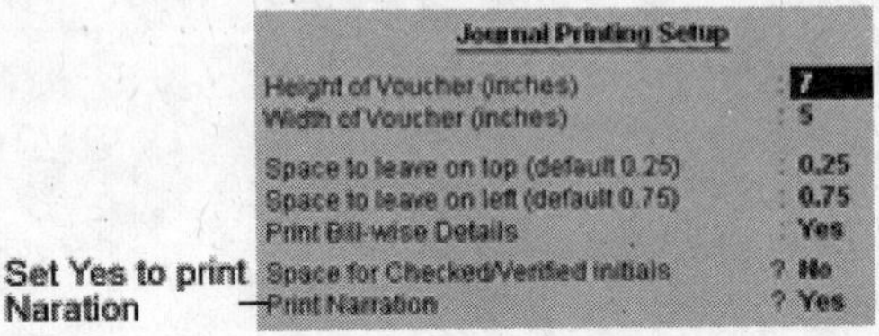

Fig 13-2: Contra & Journal Voucher Configuration

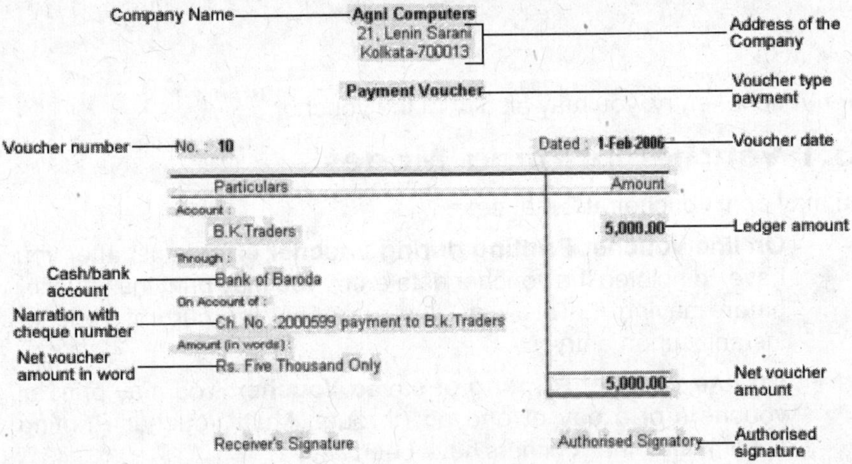

Fig 13-3 : Payment Voucher

The Height, Width & Top Margin may be specified. The spaces of each column / field are proportionately adjusted by voucher dimension set in the configuration (Height, Width) by Tally (Fig 13-5)

To leave space for voucher signatories, set *Yes* at Space for *Checked / Verified.*

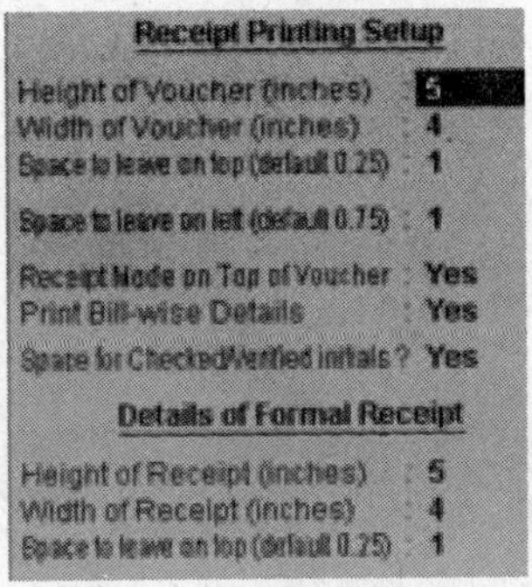

Fig 13-4: Receipt Voucher & Formal Receipt Configuration

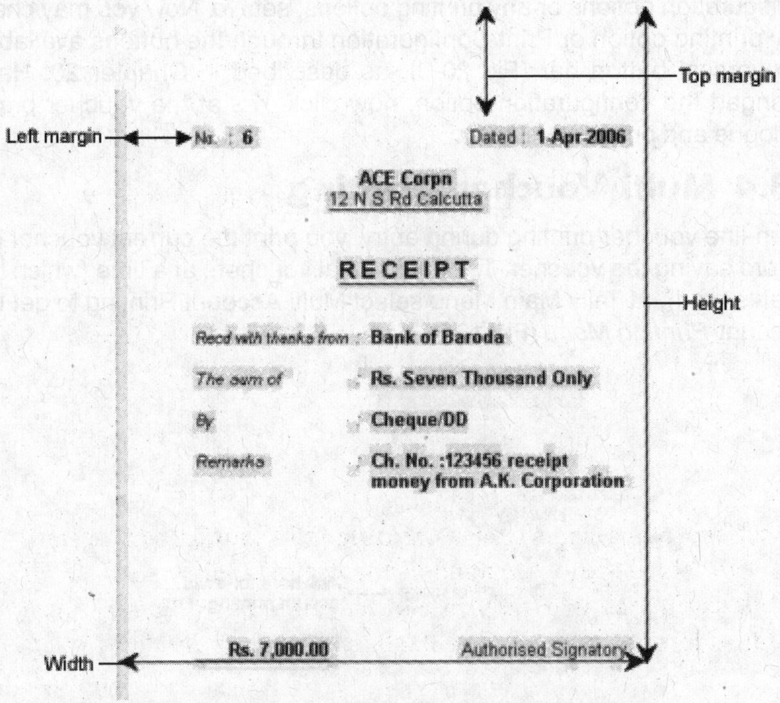

Fig 13-5 : Money Receipt (Formal Receipt)

13.3 On Line Voucher Printing

To print the Voucher before saving, press Alt+P (or click *Print* button) at voucher entry screen. You will get the Voucher Printing dialogue (Fig 13-6).

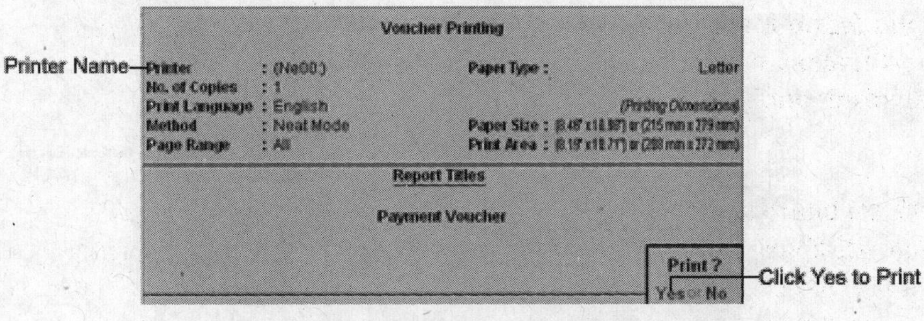

Fig 13-6: Voucher Printing dialogue

Click *Yes* at *Print? Yes or No.* (Fig 13-6) to print the Voucher as per existing *Voucher Printing Configuration* (Fig 13-1, 13-2, 13-4). To change any configuration options or any printing options, set *No*. Now you may change any printing option or Print Configuration through the buttons available at the vertical button bar (Fig 20-3), as described in Chapter 20. Having changed the configuration option, now click *Yes* at the voucher printing dialogue and print the voucher.

13.4 Multi Voucher printing

In on-line voucher printing during entry, you print the current voucher only, before saving the voucher. To print several vouchers at a time (which have been saved), at Tally Main Menu select Multi Account Printing to get Multi Account *Printing Menu* (Fig 13-7).

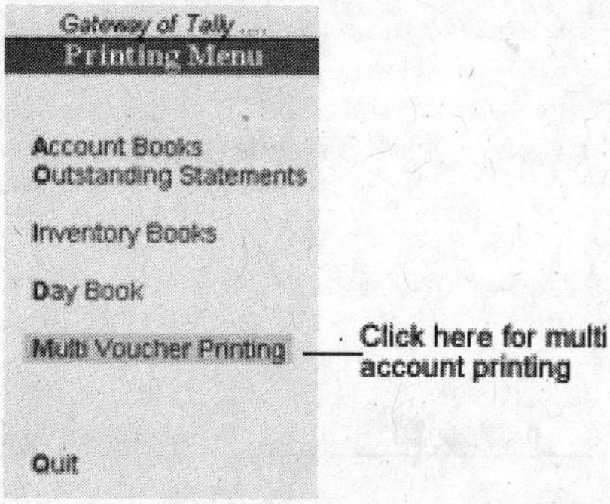

Fig 13-7: Multi Account Printing Menu

At Multi Account Printing Menu (Fig 13-7), select *Multi Voucher Printing* to get Multi Voucher Printing Dialogue (Fig 13-8).

Select the Voucher Type (Fig 13-8) and Date Range (*From* & *To* Date). All the vouchers of the selected voucher type within the specified date range will be printed.

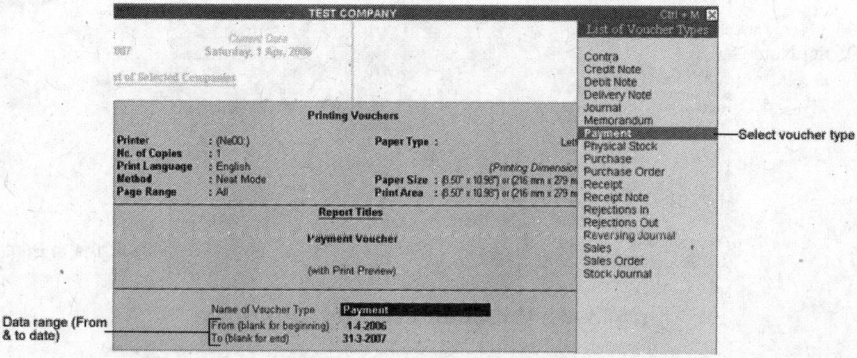

Fig 13-8: Multi Voucher Printing Dialogue

13.5 Voucher Title

At Printing Dialogue screen (Fig 13-8), at vertical button bar (Fig 20-2), click *Title* button to set the Voucher Title, option for Company Name, Address printing etc (Fig 13-9).

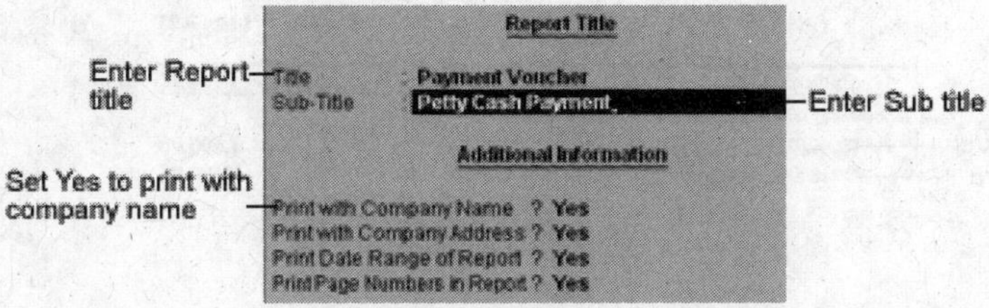

Fig 13-9: Voucher Title Configuration

Using the buttons at bar (Fig 20-2), you may set other printing options also as described in chapter 20 : Reports Printing.

13.6 Specimen of Printed Vouchers

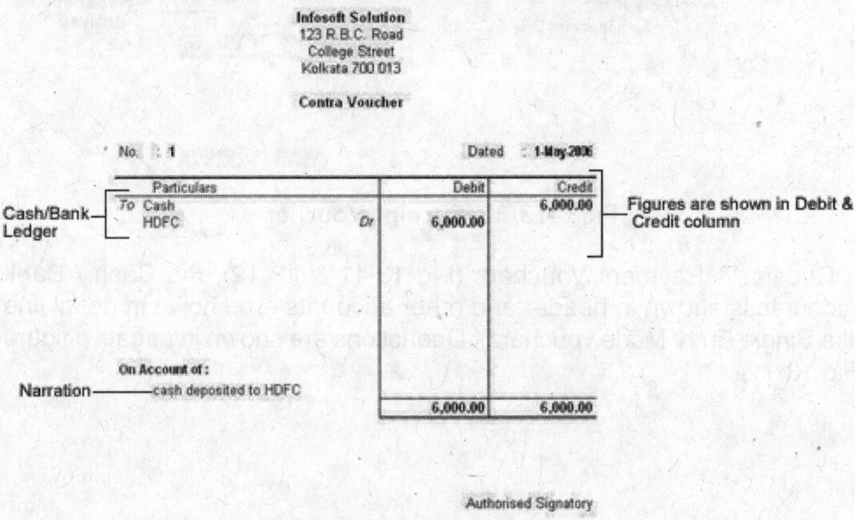

Fig 13-10: Contra Voucher

In Contra & Journal Vouchers (Fig 13-10 & 13-13), the Ledger Amounts (including Cash / Bank Accounts) are shown under Debit & Credit Columns (like Double Entry mode voucher)

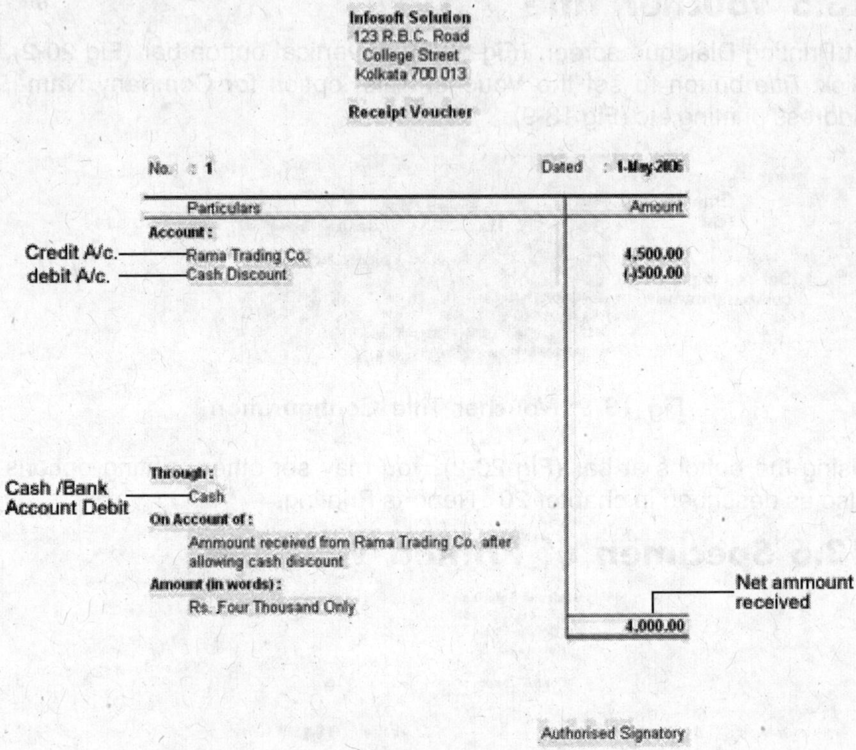

Infosoft Solution
123 R.B.C. Road
College Street
Kolkata 700 013

Receipt Voucher

No. : 1 Dated : 1-May-2006

Particulars	Amount
Account :	
Rama Trading Co.	4,500.00
Cash Discount	(-)500.00
Through :	
Cash	
On Account of :	
Ammount received from Rama Trading Co. after allowing cash discount	
Amount (in words) :	
Rs. Four Thousand Only	4,000.00

Authorised Signatory

Fig : 13-11 Receipt Voucher

In Receipt & Payment Vouchers (Fig 13-11 & 13-12), the Cash / Bank Accounts is shown in header and other accounts are shown in detail line (like Single Entry Mode vouchers). Deductions are shown in negative figure (Fig 13-11).

Infosoft Solution
123 R.B.C. Road
College Street
Kolkata 700 013

Payment Voucher

No. : 1 Dated : 1-Apr-2006

Particulars	Amount
Account :	
Suresh Kumar	5,000.00
Interest	60.00
Through : Cash	
On Account of : Payment to Suresh Kumar with Interest	
Amount (in words) : Rs. Five Thousand Sixty Only	5,060.00

Receiver's Signature: Authorised Signatory

Fig : 13-12 Payment Voucher

Agni Computers
21, Lenin Sarani
Kolkata-700013

Journal Voucher

No. : 4 Dated : 1-Feb-2006

Particulars		Debit	Credit
A.K. Traders	Dr	5,000.00	
To Software Contracts			5,000.00
On Account of : For software contracts.		5,000.00	5,000.00

Figures are shown in Debit & Credit column

Fig : 13-13 Journal Voucher

Self Test Questions

STQ 13.1: To print Money Receipt (Formal Receipt)

A. You must have set *Yes* at *Print Money Receipt* Option at Receipt Voucher Printing Configuration

B. You must have set *Yes* at *Print Formal Receipt* at *Receipt Voucher* Type

C. You must enter *Payees Name* at the Print Dialogue of *Receipt Voucher* Printing

STQ 13.2: To print Cheques

A. You must have set *Yes* at *Print Cheques* Option at Payment Voucher Printing Configuration

B. You must have set *Yes* at *Print Cheque* at *Payment Voucher* Type

C. You must have set *Yes* at *Enable Cheque Printing* at Advanced Company Operations set up

D. You must enter *Payees Name* at the Print Dialogue of *Payment Voucher* Printing

STQ 13.3: To print Cheques

A. You must have selected the respective Bank Account at *Company Cheque Details* at *Advanced Company Operations* set up

B. You must have set *Yes* at *Print Cheque* at the respective Bank Account

C. You must have set *Yes* at *Cheque Printing* at Print Dialogue of *Receipt Voucher* Printing

D. You must enter *Payees Name* at the Print Dialogue of *Payment Voucher* Printing

STQ 13.4: How you can print :

A. Money Receipt only immediately on completion of Receipt Voucher Entry

B. Both Money Receipt & Receipt Voucher immedialely on completion of Receipt Voucher Entry

C. All Money Receipts for the day at the day end at a time

D. Both Money Receipt & Receipt Voucher for the day at day end at a time Accounts Voucher Printing

14 Accounts Master Lists

In this chapter we show how to print List of Masters, i.e. List of Account Groups & Account Ledgers.

14.1 List of Accounts

Select *Display > List of Accounts* to see the list of all Accounts Masters. Normally, you get the List of Ledgers (Fig 14-1) showing the complete Chart of Accounts of all Accounts Groups & Ledgers.

At the Button Bar, you get the buttons for each Master type activated. Select the button to get respective List of Accounts.

Fig 14-1: Buttons to select the List of Masters

14.1.1 List of Groups

Click *G:Groups* button to get the list of Account Groups in alphabetical order of Primary Groups with subordinate Groups placed in hierarchical order, with *Alias* Names of some Reserved Groups displayed in parenthesis (Fig 14-2).

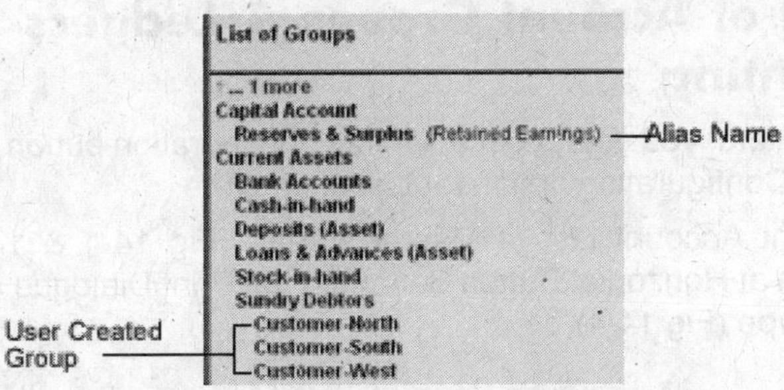

Fig 14-2: List of Account Groups

14.1.2 List of Ledgers

At List of Accounts screen (Fig 14-2), click *L: Ledgers* button at Button Bar (Fig 14-1) to show the List of Account Groups & Ledgers (the complete chart of accounts) in hierarchical structure (Fig 14-3).

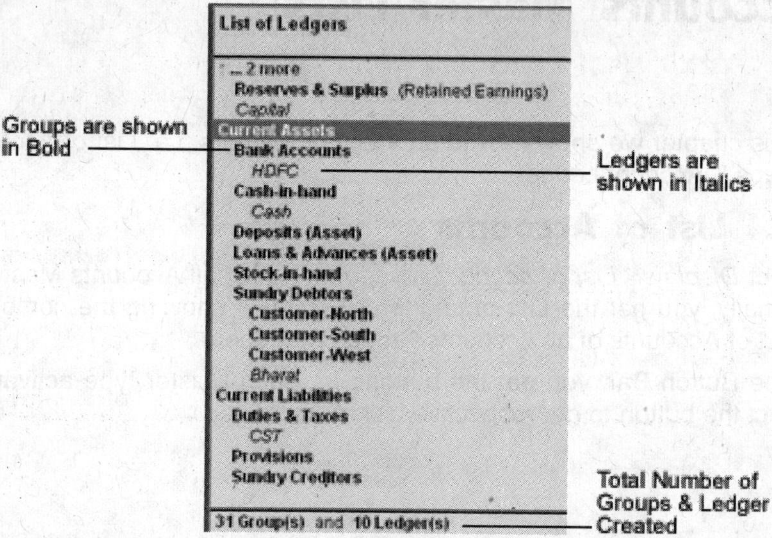

Fig 14-3: List of Ledger Accounts

14.2 Modification / Deletion through List of Masters

In the List of Master, place the cursor on the master record and press ↵ to get the Alteration screen for the Master record (Fig 10-12 & 10-14). You may carry out alteration & deletion in the master record as explained in Chapter 10 (Ref 10.5).

14.3 List of Account Groups & Ledgers Printing

At List of Masters, you do not get any F12: Configuration button. So, there is no Report Configuration option for List of Masters.

At the current Account List of Master screen (Fig 14-1 & 14-2), click *P:Print* button at Horizontal Button Bar to get the Print Dialogue and select the Master Type (Fig 14-4).

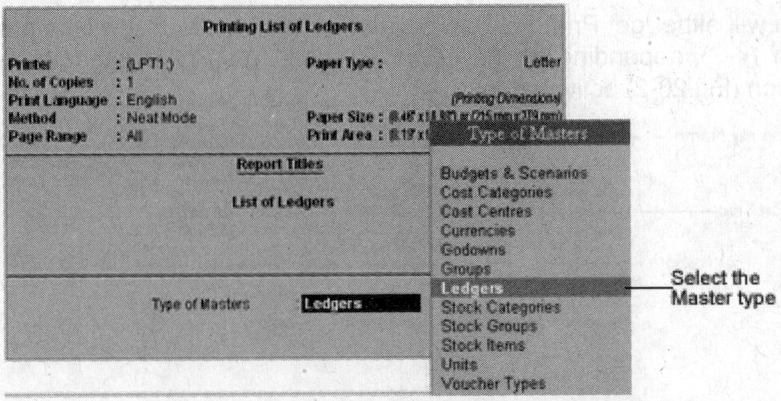

Fig 14-4: Account Master List Printing

At Account Master List Printing (Fig 14-4), click *Titling* button at Vertical Button Bar (Ref 20.3) and set the Report Title / Sub-Title (Fig 14-5). In the same way, you may change the other print options through various button available at Vertical button bar (Fig 20-2), as described in Chapter 20.

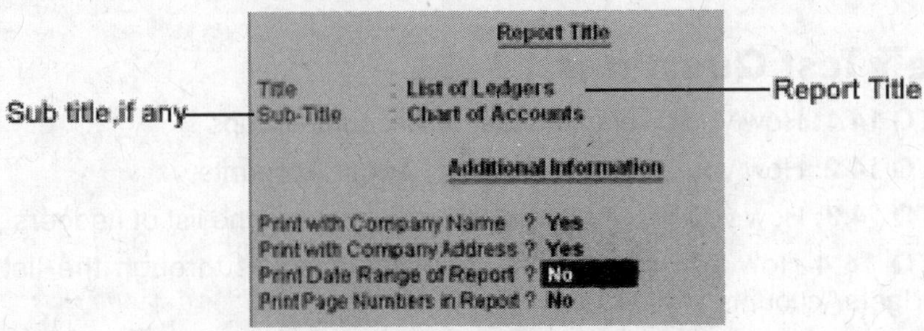

Fig 14-5: Account Master List Title set up

After setting up the respective print options, press *Y* at Print dialogue box (Fig 14-6).

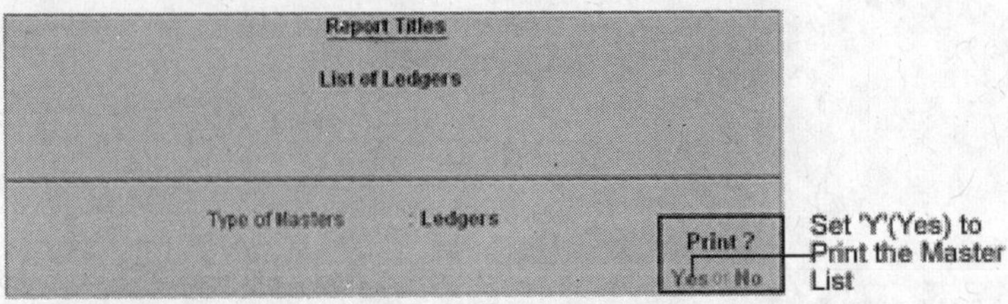

Fig 14-6: Master List Print Dialogue

You will either get Print Preview screen, or the Master List will be printed (Fig 14-7), depending on the *I:Print Preview / No Preview* toggle button option (Fig 20-2) activated.

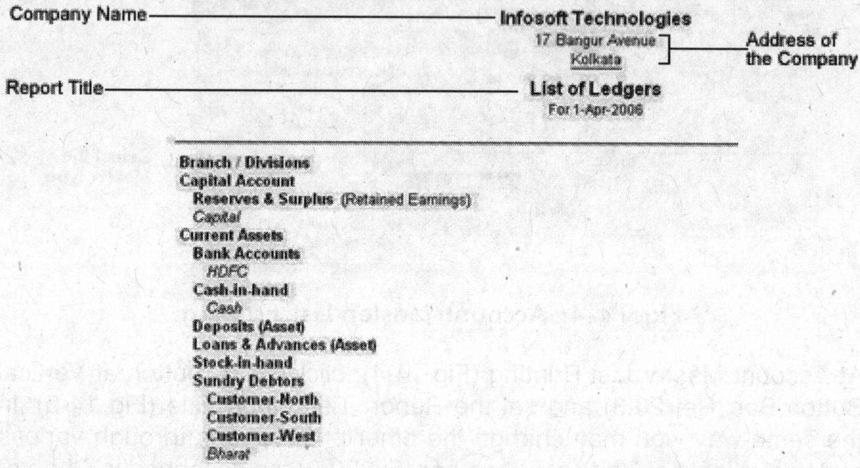

Fig 14-7: List of Ledgers

Self Test Questions

STQ 14.1: How you display the List of Account Groups

STQ 14.2: How you display the List of Ledger Accounts

STQ 14.3: How you Modify Account Group through the list of Ledgers

STQ 14.4 How you can Delete a ledger Account through the list of LedgersAccounts Master Lists

Accounts Voucher Lists

15

As soon as you enter voucher, its effect is reflected everywhere and you may view any report on screen or print on paper at any point of time to get the updated figures.

Apart from conventional printed reports, Tally provides powerful display facility to view Reports at various levels of details and contents, on screen.

15.1 Voucher Lists

In this Chapter, we discuss about various types of Voucher Lists. This is the lowest level report, which contains a list of Vouchers. When you drill down through any Voucher in Voucher list, you get the Voucher in Alteration mode (Ref 11.8)

The following reports constitute a Voucher list:

- Voucher Register
- Day Book
- Group Voucher
- Ledger

15.1.1 Voucher Register

Select *Display > Account Books > Journal Register* and then select a month to get the Journal Voucher Register for the month (Fig 15-1).

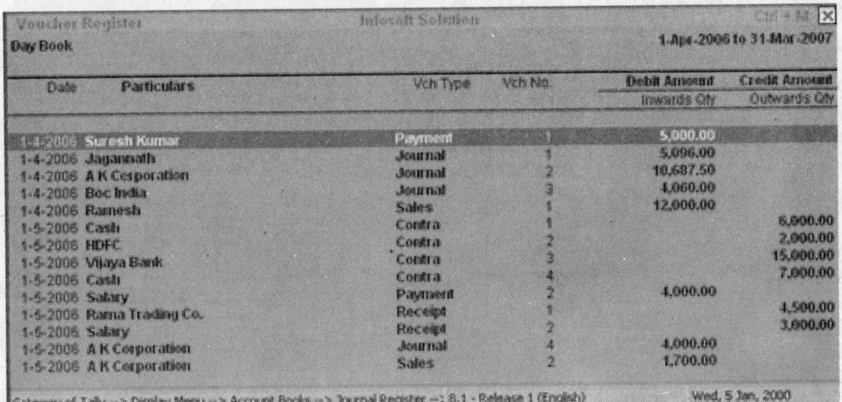
Voucher Register — Infosoft Solution — Ctrl + M

Day Book — 1-Apr-2006 to 31-Mar-2007

Date	Particulars	Vch Type	Vch No.	Debit Amount Inwards Qty	Credit Amount Outwards Qty
1-4-2006	Suresh Kumar	Payment	1	5,000.00	
1-4-2006	Jagannath	Journal	1	5,096.00	
1-4-2006	A K Cerporation	Journal	2	10,687.50	
1-4-2006	Boc India	Journal	3	4,060.00	
1-4-2006	Ramesh	Sales	1	12,000.00	
1-5-2006	Cash	Contra	1		6,000.00
1-5-2006	HDFC	Contra	2		2,000.00
1-5-2006	Vijaya Bank	Contra	3		15,000.00
1-5-2006	Cash	Contra	4		7,000.00
1-5-2006	Salary	Payment	2	4,000.00	
1-5-2006	Rama Trading Co.	Receipt	1		4,500.00
1-5-2006	Salary	Receipt	2		3,000.00
1-5-2006	A K Corporation	Journal	4	4,000.00	
1-5-2006	A K Corporation	Sales	2	1,700.00	

Gateway of Tally --> Display Menu --> Account Books --> Journal Register --: 8.1 - Release 1 (English) — Wed, 5 Jan, 2000

Fig 15-1: Voucher Register (Condensed)

At Voucher Register, you may define columns for Columnar Report for Ledgers & Account Groups (Ref 17.1).

15.1.1.1 Default Voucher Register

The default report lists vouchers of all types. The particulars column shows the first ledger account transacted and the amount column shows the corresponding ledger amount.

15.1.1.2 Voucher Register Configuration

Click F12: Configuration and set the various configuration options as shown in Fig 15-3.

Fig 15-2 : Buttons at Voucher Register

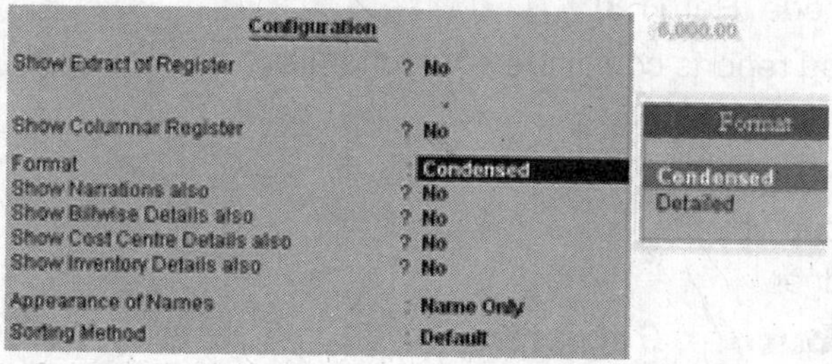

Fig 15-3: Voucher Register Report Configuration

15.1.1.3 Detailed Voucher Register

At Voucher Register (Fig 15-1), click *F1: Detailed* toggle button to get Detailed Voucher Register (Fig 15-4) (Click *F1: Condensed* to get back to Voucher register). You may also select *Detailed* at *Format* field in Voucher Register Configuration screen (Fig 15-3) to get Detailed Voucher Register.

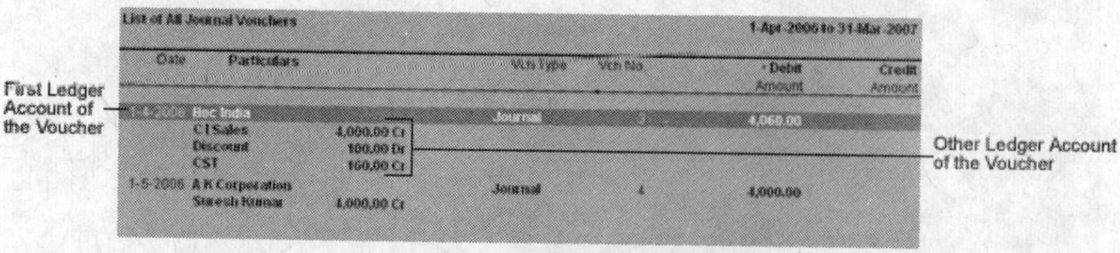

Fig 15-4: Detailed Voucher Register

15.1.1.4 Voucher Register Extract

Voucher Register Extract shows net figures of Groups & Ledger in hierarchical order. The Groups are shown in bold and ledgers are shown in normal font.

At Voucher Register (Fig 15-3), click *F6: Extract* button (Fig 15-2) to get Voucher Register Extract (Fig 15-6) for the selected period (click *F6: Voucher* toggle button to get back Voucher Register).

You may also select *Yes* at *Show Voucher Register Extract* at Voucher Register Configuration options (Fig 15-3) to get Voucher Register Extract.

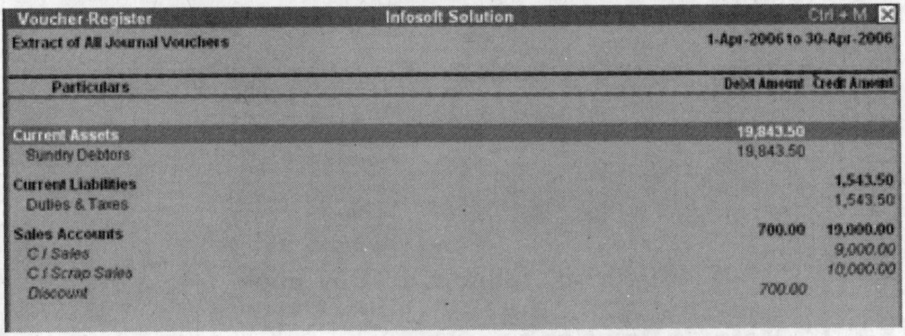

Fig 15-5: Voucher Register Extract

15.1.1.5 Voucher Register for Specified Voucher Types

At Voucher Register (Fig 15-1), Click *F4:Vch Type* button and select the Voucher Type to get Voucher Register for the selected Voucher Type (Fig 15-6) only (useful to get a separate list for a selected Voucher type) or select *All Vouchers* to get Voucher Register of all Vouchers (Fig 15-1). The heading shows the name of selected Voucher Types (in case of All voucher Types selected, the heading shows *Day Book* (Fig 15-1).

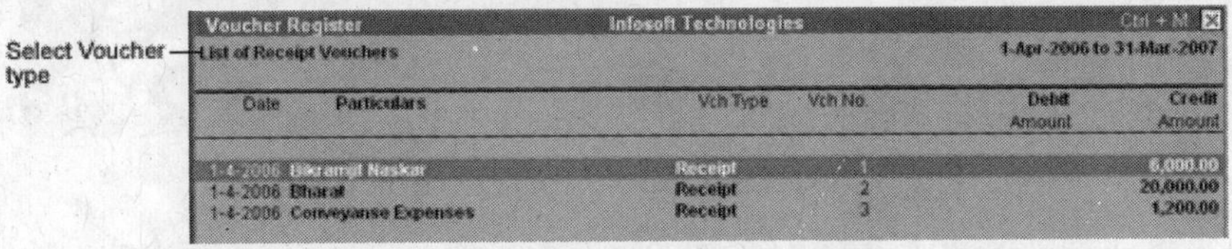

Fig 15-6: Voucher Register (selected Voucher Type)

15.1.2 Day Book

Like Voucher Register, Day Book also shows list of Vouchers (Fig 15-9) and the contents are similar to Voucher list of all Voucher Types (Fig 15-1).

Select Display > Day Book.

15.1.2.1 Day Book Configuration Options

At Day Book screen (Fig 15-1), click *F12: Configuration* and set the options as desired (Fig 15-7).

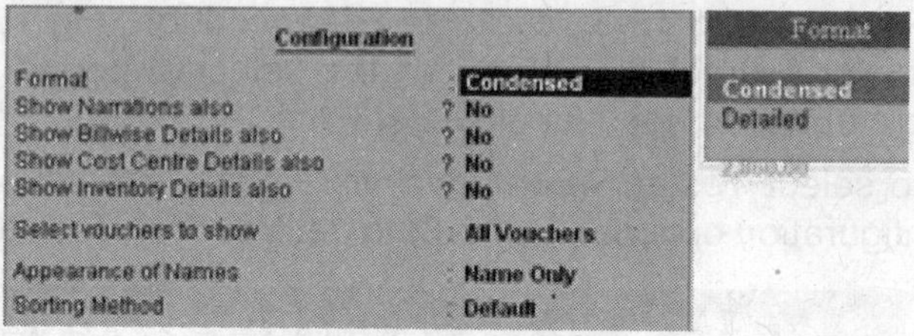

Fig 15-7: Day Book Configuration options

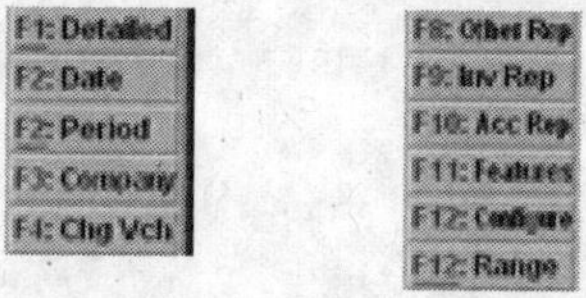

Fig 15-8 : Buttons at Day Book

15.1.2.2 Default Day Book

The default report lists vouchers of all types. The particulars column shows the first ledger account transacted and the amount column shows the corresponding ledger amount.

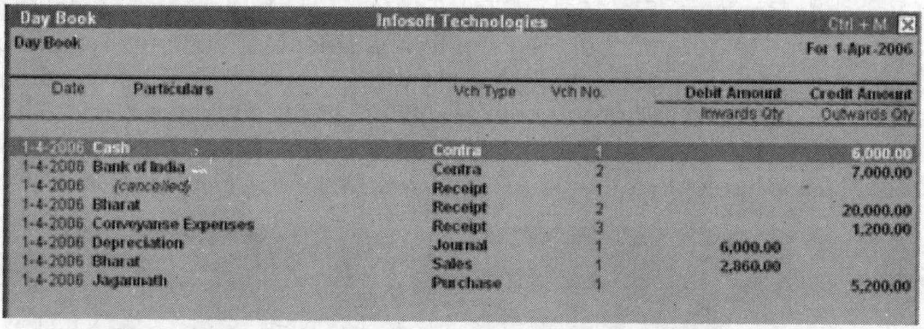

Fig 15-9: Day Book for current date

Initially, you get list of all Vouchers for the Current Date (one day) only (the report period is shown at the header, for reference). Cancelled vouchers are also listed showing zero amount (Fig 15.2)

- To get the report for any other Date (for one day only), Click *F2: Date* Button and change the current Date (Fig 8-6). Press - (minus sign) to get List of Vouchers for previous day, + (plus sign) to display for next date.

- To get List of Vouchers for a period, click *F2: Period* button and enter Date Range (Fig 8-5). Now the report period will show the Vouchers for the selected period.

15.1.2.3 Day Book for specified Voucher Type

At Day Book (Fig 15-9), Click *F4:Vch Type* button (Fig 15-8) and select the Voucher Type to get Day Book for the selected Voucher Type only (useful to get a separate list for a selected Voucher type) or select *All Vouchers* to get Day Book of all Vouchers (Fig 15-9).

15.1.2.4 Detailed Day Book

At Day Book (Fig 15-1), click *F1: Detailed* button to get Detailed Day Book (click *F1: Condensed* toggle button to get back Condensed Day Book) showing all ledger accounts of each voucher (Fig 15-15). You may also select *Detailed* at Day Book Configuration screen (Fig 15-7) to get Detailed Day Book.

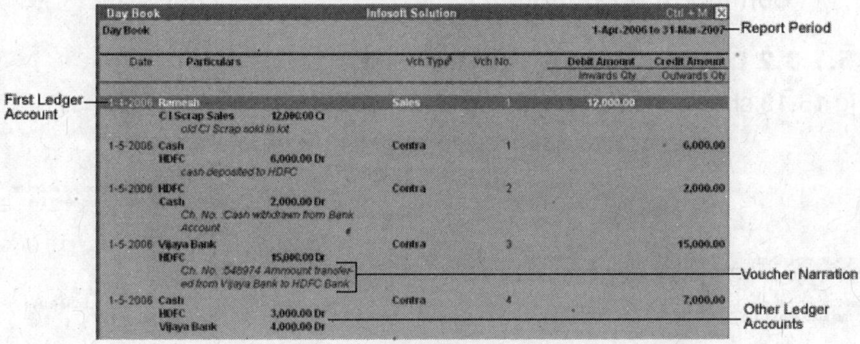

Fig 15-10 : Day Book in Detail Format

15.1.2.5 Day Book with Voucher Narration

At Day Book Configuration screen (Fig 15-7), set *Yes* at *Show Narration also*, to get the Day Book showing Voucher Narration (Fig 15-15)

15.1.3 Group Vouchers List

Group Vouchers List (Fig 15-13) shows the list of Vouchers for a selected Account Group (i.e all vouchers having transaction with any child ledger of the selected Account Group).

To get this report:

- Select *Display > Account Books > Group Vouchers* and select the Account Group to get the default list of all Vouchers (for the current period) relating to the selected Account Group.

Click *F7: Voucher* button at Group Summary to get the details of selected ledger accounts [Display > *Account Books* > *Group Summary*].

15.1.3.1 Configuration Options of Group Voucher List

At Group Voucher list (Fig 15.13), click *F12: Configuration* to get Group Voucher Configuration screen (Fig 15-11) and set the options.

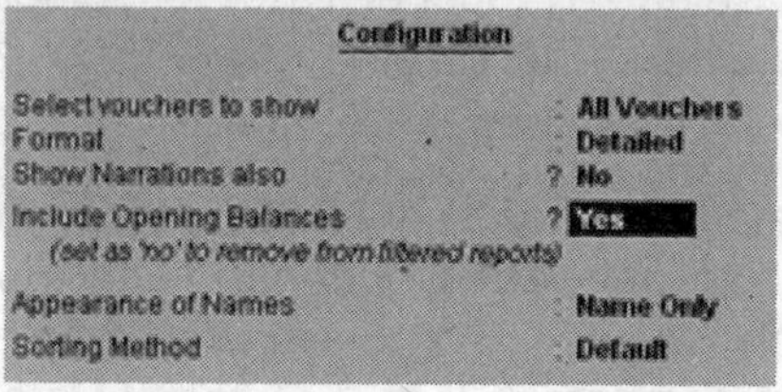

Fig 15-11: Group Vouchers List Configuration options

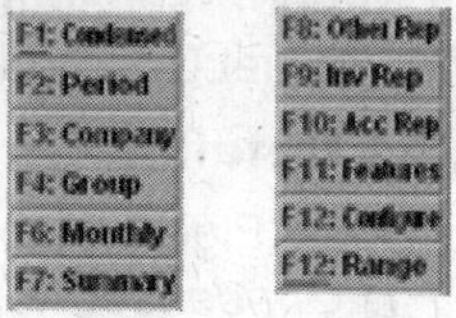

Fig: 15-12 Buttons at Group Vouchers List

15.1.3.2 Default Group Voucher List

Fig 15-13 shows the default Group Voucher List

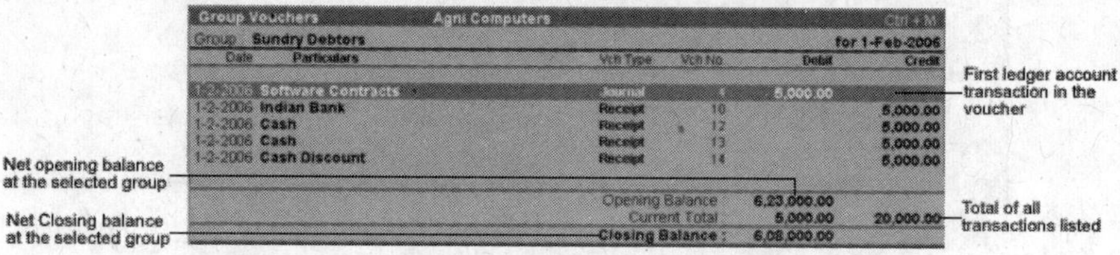

Fig 15-13: Group Voucher list

Particulars column shows the first complementary ledger account in the voucher and the amount shows the amount in respect of the child Ledger account of the selected Group.

Example :

Sales	8,99,700.00 Cr
Discount	500.00 Dr
Packing Charges	800.00 Cr
Customer a/c (under Sundry Debtors)	9,00,000.00 Dr

Now if you see the Group Vouchers for Sundry Debtors Group, the above Voucher will show *Sales* at Particulars Column and 9,00,000.00 at amount column (though the amount for Sales Ledger Account is 8,99,700.00). The amount represents the amount related to the ledger under the selected

Group (Sundry Debtor). The ledger shown in the Particular columns is the first Ledger other than the child Ledger of the selected Group, transacted in the voucher.

15.1.3.3 Debit / Credit Group Voucher List

At Group Voucher Fig 15-14 shows the Group Voucher list of Vouchers having Debit Entry only (select *Debit Entry only* at *Select Voucher to show* at Configuration - Fig 15-11) for the transacted Ledger under the selected Group.

Group Vouchers — Agni Computers — Ctrl + M

Group : Sundry Debtors — for 1-Apr-2005

Date	Particulars	Vch Type	Vch No.	Debit	Credit
1-4-2005	Sales	Sales	1	9,00,000.00	
1-4-2005	Software Contracts	Journal	1	80,000.00	
		Opening Balance :		34,500.00	
		Current Total :		9,80,000.00	
		Closing Balance :		10,14,500.00	

Fig 15-14: Group voucher (Debit entries only) including opening balance

Group Vouchers — Agni Computers — Ctrl + M

Group : Sundry Debtors — for 1-Apr-2005

Date	Particulars	Vch Type	Vch No.	Debit	Credit
1-4-2005	Cash	Receipt	1		50,000.00
1-4-2005	Indian Bank	Receipt	2		1,35,000.00
1-4-2005	Sales	Sales	1	9,00,000.00	
1-4-2005	Cash	Receipt	3		25,000.00
1-4-2005	Indian Bank	Receipt	4		50,000.00
1-4-2005	Indian Bank	Receipt	5		60,000.00
1-4-2005	Indian Bank	Receipt	6		30,000.00
1-4-2005	Indian Bank	Receipt	7		50,000.00
1-4-2005	Software Contracts	Journal	1	80,000.00	
		Opening Balance :			
		Current Total :		9,80,000.00	4,00,000.00
		Closing Balance :		5,80,000.00	

Fig 15-15: Group voucher List without opening balance

Fig 15-15 shows the Group Voucher List without Opening Balance (Set *No* at *Include Opening Balance* at Configuration – Fig 15-11). The closing balance shows the net amount of the listed voucher only. This is helpful to get the one way transactions (like *Sales* or *Payments* of Sundry Debtors) relating to all ledgers of a selected Account Group.

Like Voucher Register & Day Book, toggle through *F1: Detailed / Condensed* button to get Detailed & Condensed list of Group Voucher.

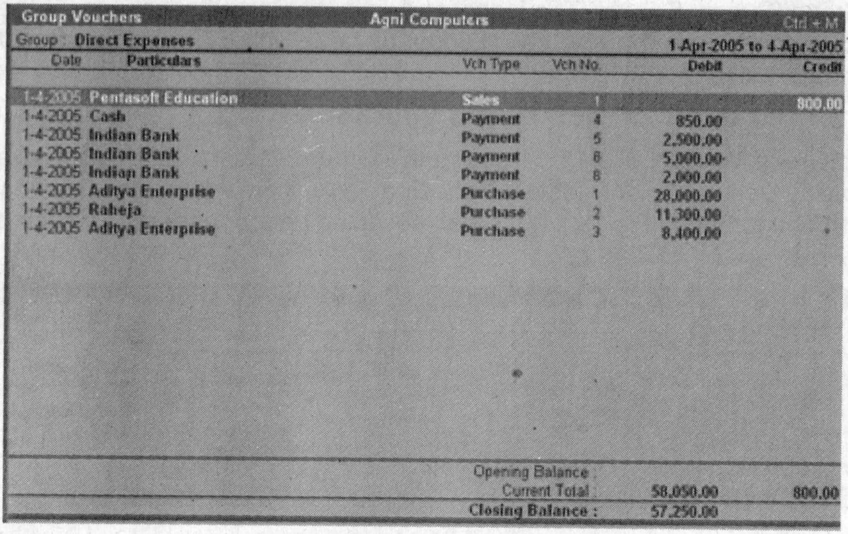

Fig 15-16: Detailed Group Voucher list

At Group Vouchers list (Fig 15-13/ 15-15), click *F2: Period* and enter the period to get Group Voucher for any specified Period.

To view Group Voucher of another Group, click F4: Group button at Group Vouchers list (Fig 15-13/ 15-15) and select the Group.

15.1.4 Ledger

This Report shows the list of Vouchers (Fig 15-18) in which the selected Ledger Account has been transacted.

You get this report (Fig 15-19) from:

- Ledger [*Display > Account Books > Ledger > Ledger Account*].
- Select a month from the Ledger Monthly Summary
  - *Display > Account Books > Group Summary > Account Group > Ledger Account > Month.*
  - *Display > Account Books > Cash / Bank Book -> Account Group -> Ledger Account - > Month.*

15.1.4.1 Ledger Configuration

At Ledger (Fig 15.19), click *F12: Configuration* to get Ledger Configuration screen (Fig 15-17) and set the options.

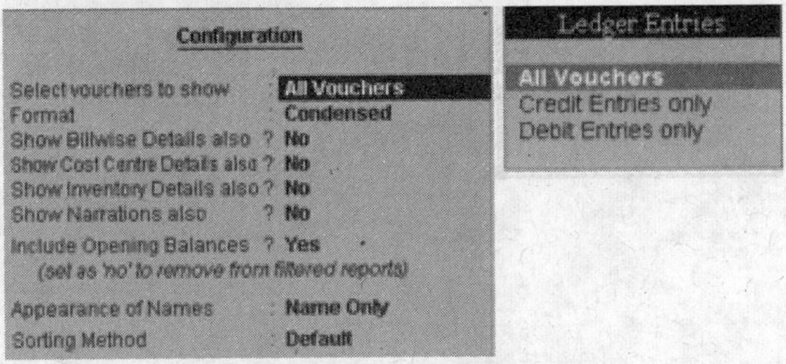

Fig 15-17: Ledger Configuration Options

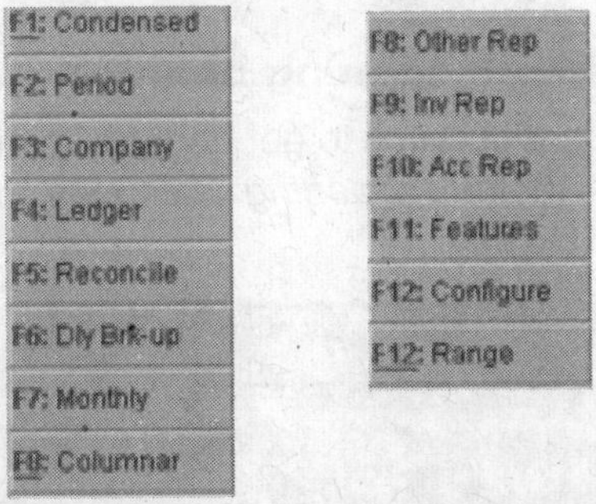

Fig 15-18: Buttons at Ledger

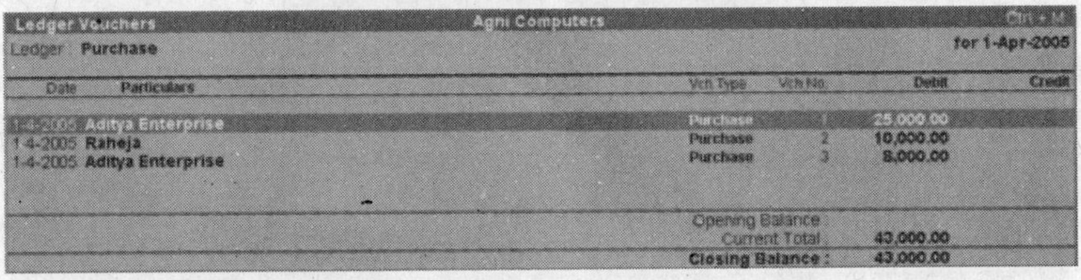

Fig 15-19: Ledger

15.1.4.2 Detailed Ledger

At Ledger (Fig 15-19), click *F1: Detailed button* to get Detailed Ledger (Fig 15-18).

You may also select *Detailed* at *Format* field at Ledger Configuration screen (Fig 15-17), to get Detailed Ledger (Fig 15-20). In case of voucher with only 2 ledgers transacted, the particulars column shows the complementary ledger account. In case of voucher with more ledgers transacted, the first line in particulars column shows (as per details) followed by all complementary ledger accounts (Fig 15-20)

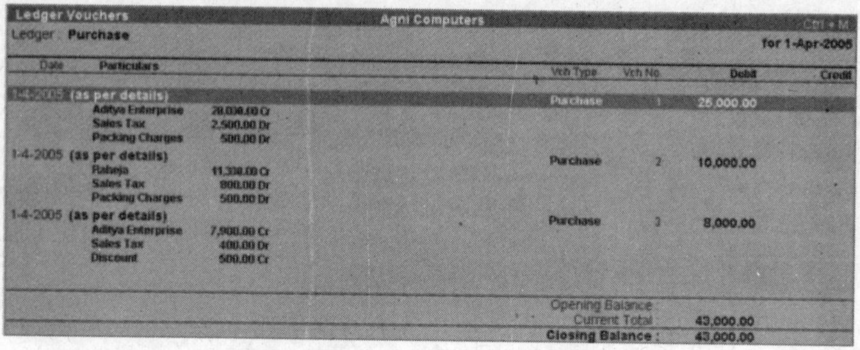

Fig 15-20: Ledger Details

15.1.4.3 Ledger without opening balance

At Ledger, click *F12: Configuration* to get Ledger Configuration screen (Fig 15-17) and set *No* at *Include Opening Balances* to get ledger without opening balance (Fig 15-21).

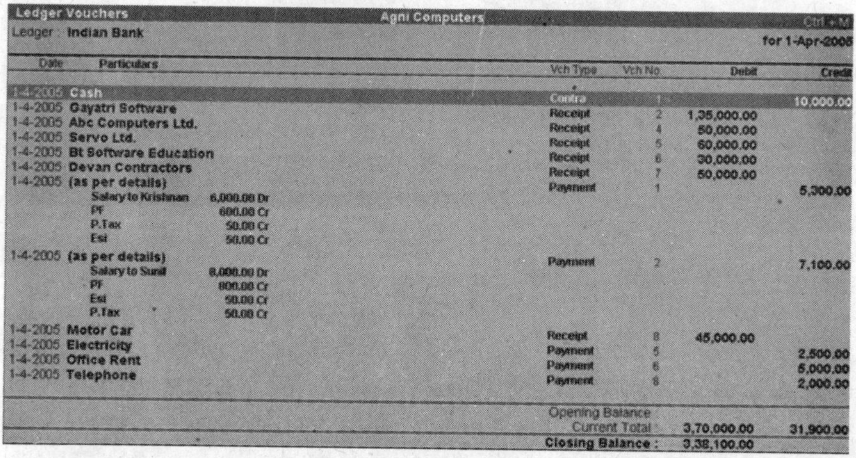

Fig 15-21: Ledger (Detailed) without opening balance

15.1.4.4 Debit / Credit Ledger

At Ledger Configuration screen (Fig 15-17), at *Select Vouchers to Show*, set *Debit Entries Only* to get only Debit entries (Fig 15-12). Similarly, you may set the option to get Ledger with Credit Entries only. This is useful to get one side transaction figures (e.g to get Sales Figures only of a Customer).

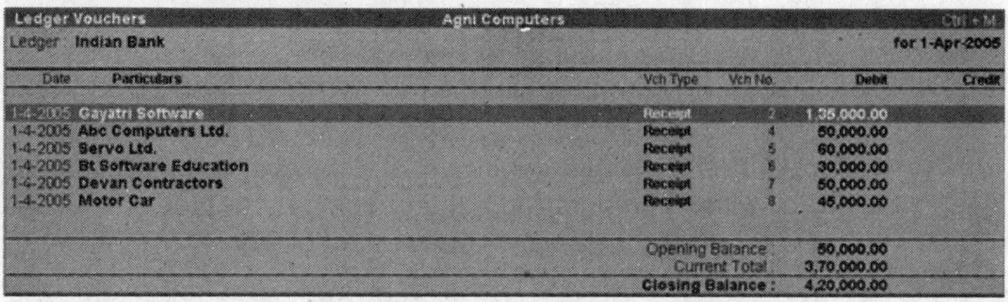

Fig 15-22:Ledger (with Debit Entries Only)

15.2 Operations at Voucher lists

At any of the voucher lists, you may perform the following operations :

- **Voucher Insertion**: Press Alt+I to *Insert* a Voucher. The Voucher Creation Screen appears to create new Voucher. The new voucher will be inserted immediately before the selected voucher. For example, in Fig 15-22, you place cursor at Receipt Voucher # 5 and press Alt+I and enter a Receipt Voucher dt 1-4-2005.. A new Receipt Voucher # 5 will be created and all subsequent Receipt Voucher(including existing Voucher No. 5) number will get increased by 1.
- **Adding a Voucher**: Press Alt+A to *Add* a Voucher. Voucher creation screen appears to create new Voucher. The new voucher will be appended after the last voucher. For example, in Fig 15-22, press Alt+A and enter a Receipt Voucher dt 1-4-2005.. A new Receipt Voucher # 9 will be created and all subsequent Receipt Voucher number will get increased by 1.
- **Duplicating a Voucher**: Select a Voucher from the list and press Alt+2 to *Duplicate* the Voucher. Tally will create another Voucher carrying data from the selected voucher, which you may modify and save. Helpful to create Voucher similar to the selected voucher (e.g creating a Payment voucher for conveyance expenses carrying data from a similar voucher).
- **Voucher Deletion**: Press Alt+D to *Delete* the voucher. A confirmation will be sought, press *Y* to Delete the Voucher. For example, in Fig 15-22, place the cursor at Voucher # 5 and press Alt+D. Press Y to confirm deletion. The original voucher # 5 will get deleted and Voucher # 6 will get re-numbered as Voucher # 5. All subsequent Receipt Voucher number will also get decreased by 1.
- **Voucher Cancellation**: Press Alt+X to *Cancel* the Voucher. Press **Y** to confirm cancellation at Cancel? Yes or No prompt (in the

Voucher listing, cancelled vouchers are also listed, with zero value). Tally will reserve the voucher number and will not allot it to next voucher created. For example, in Fig 15-22, place the cursor at Voucher # 5 and press Alt+X. Press Y to confirm Cancellation. The voucher # 5 will get cancelled (the number will be shown in Day Book with no amount figures). All subsequent Receipt Voucher number will remain unchanged even after deletion.

- **Voucher Modification** : Press ↵ at any Voucher to get the Voucher in Alteration mode to carry out any modification.

15.3 Operations at Display Screen

You may perform the following operations in display screens, as applicable.

15.3.1 Exploding / Collapsing Details in Display screen

In condensed reports, you may press Shift + ↵ key on the summary figure line (Fig 15-23) to get the exploded report showing next level details (Fig 15-24). Press Shift + ↵ key again to collapse the details to show the summary line only (Fig 15-23)

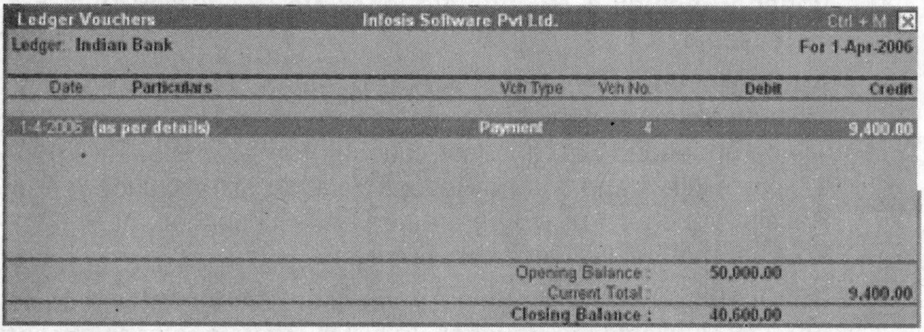

Fig 15-23: Collapsed Report

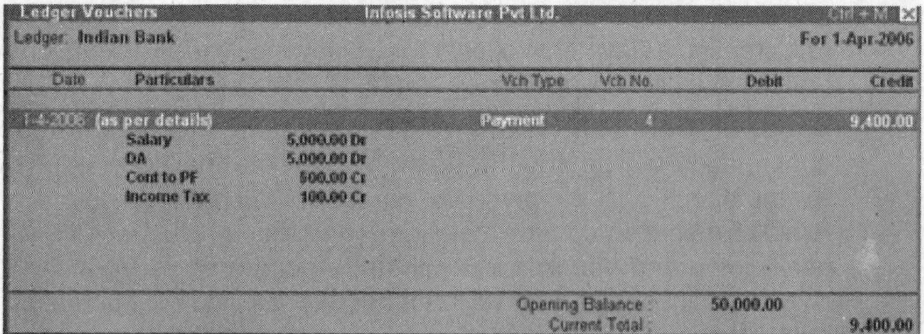

Fig 15-24: Exploded Report

15.3.2 Master Alteration through Reports Display

While displaying a report, press Ctrl + ↵ on the Group / Ledger. to get the Group / Ledger in alteration mode (Ref 10.5), to carry out Alteration of the Master record.

15.3.3 Hiding Report Lines in Display

To remove a line in the display screen (to hide the line), place the cursor on the record (Fig 15-25) and press Alt+R. The record is removed from the Report (but no data gets deleted) as shown in Fig 15-26. Thus you may get an edited report on screen, deleting some lines.

15.3.4 Restoration of Hidden Lines in Reports Display

To Restore (bring back) all the hidden lines (Fig 15-25), press Alt+S. To restore only last hidden line, press Alt+U

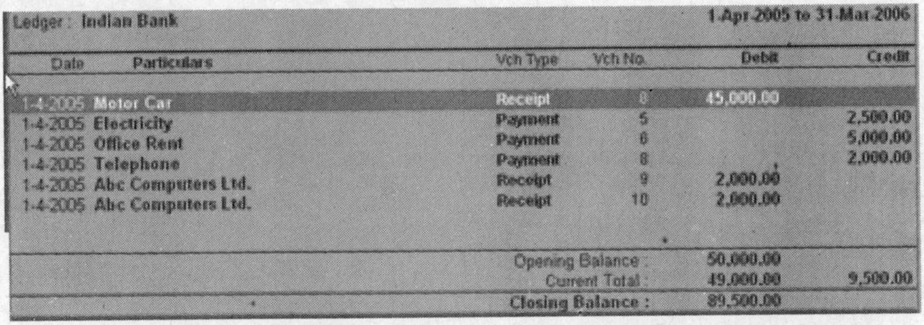

Ledger : Indian Bank — 1-Apr-2005 to 31-Mar-2006

Date	Particulars	Vch Type	Vch No.	Debit	Credit
1-4-2005	Motor Car	Receipt	8	45,000.00	
1-4-2005	Electricity	Payment	5		2,500.00
1-4-2005	Office Rent	Payment	6		5,000.00
1-4-2005	Telephone	Payment	8		2,000.00
1-4-2005	Abc Computers Ltd.	Receipt	9	2,000.00	
1-4-2005	Abc Computers Ltd.	Receipt	10	2,000.00	
		Opening Balance :		50,000.00	
		Current Total :		49,000.00	9,500.00
		Closing Balance :		89,500.00	

Fig 15-25: Original (and Restored with Alt+S) report

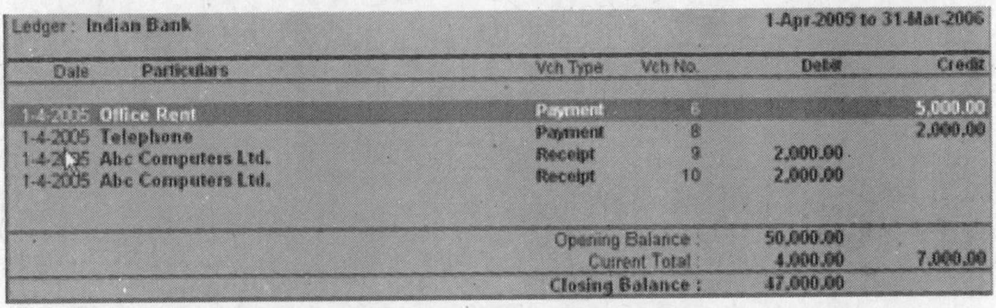

Ledger : Indian Bank — 1-Apr-2005 to 31-Mar-2006

Date	Particulars	Vch Type	Vch No.	Debit	Credit
1-4-2005	Office Rent	Payment	6		5,000.00
1-4-2005	Telephone	Payment	8		2,000.00
1-4-2005	Abc Computers Ltd.	Receipt	9	2,000.00	
1-4-2005	Abc Computers Ltd.	Receipt	10	2,000.00	
		Opening Balance :		50,000.00	
		Current Total :		4,000.00	7,000.00
		Closing Balance :		47,000.00	

Fig 15-26: Report after removing a line (with Alt+R)

Self Test Questions

STQ 15.1: In voucher list, how you can explode a voucher to show details and how to collapse to hide the details

STQ 15.2: How you hide a record in the voucher list and restore it back?

STQ 15.3: Explain the report options to get Group / Ledgerwise summary of all transactions for a specified period.

STQ 15.4: Explain the report options to display only list of Receipt Vouchers

STQ 15.5: How to get a list of all the vouchers related to Sundry Debtors

STQ 15.6: What do you mean by Voucher Duplication and how to do it. Do you get 2 vouchers of same number through Voucher Duplication?

Day Book Summaries

16

In this chapter, we discuss about next level reports to voucher listing, showing compiled figures of several vouchers. You reach any of the voucher list by drilling down through these reports :

- Account Group Summary
- Ledger Summary
- Monthly Summaries
- Cash Bank Summary

16.1 Account Group Summary

This report shows the summary of Account Groups.

Select *Display > Account Books > Group Summary.*

Select an Account Group to get Group Summary for the Group (else select *Primary* to get Primary Group Summary).

16.1.1 Group Summary Configuration

Click *F12: Configure* at Group Summary (Fig 16-3/16-4) or Ledger Summary (Fig 16-9). You get the Account Group Summary configuration screen (Fig 16-1) to set the report options.

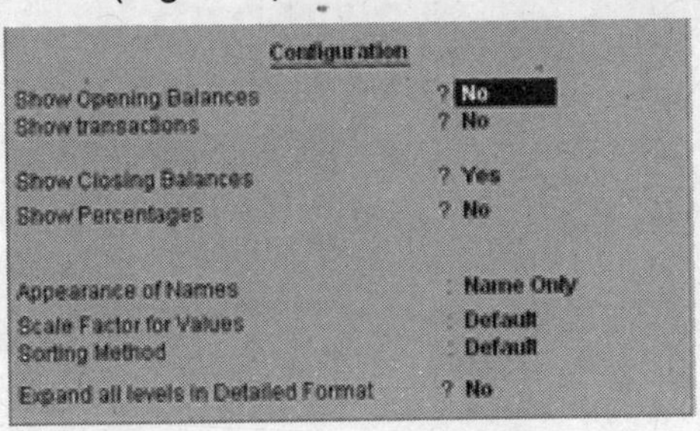

Fig 16-1: Configuration Options at Group & Ledger Summary

Fig: 16-2 Buttons for Group & Ledger Summary

16.2 Primary Group Summary

The default Group Summary shows the figures of all Primary Groups (Fig 16-3).

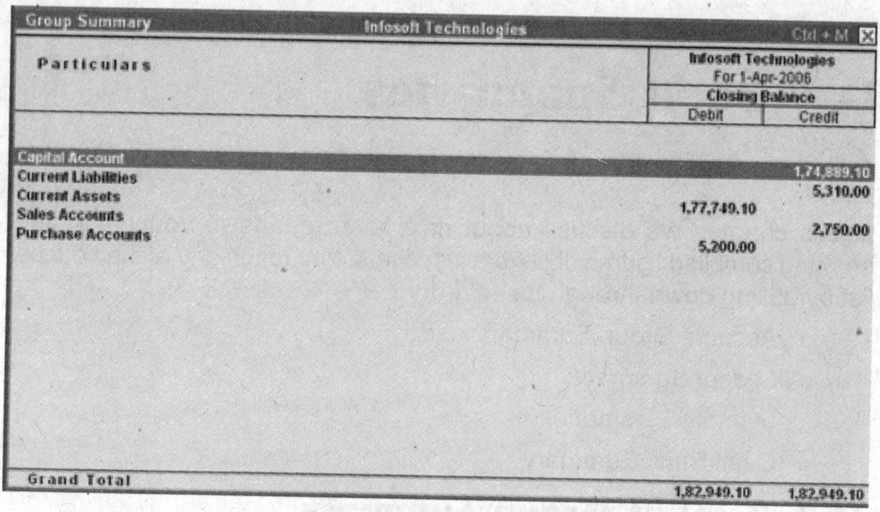

Fig 16-3: Primary Group Summary

16.2.1 Group Summary of a selected Group

At Primary Group Summary (Fig 16-3), drill down through any Account Group to get figures of next level Groups and Ledgers (Fig 16-4).

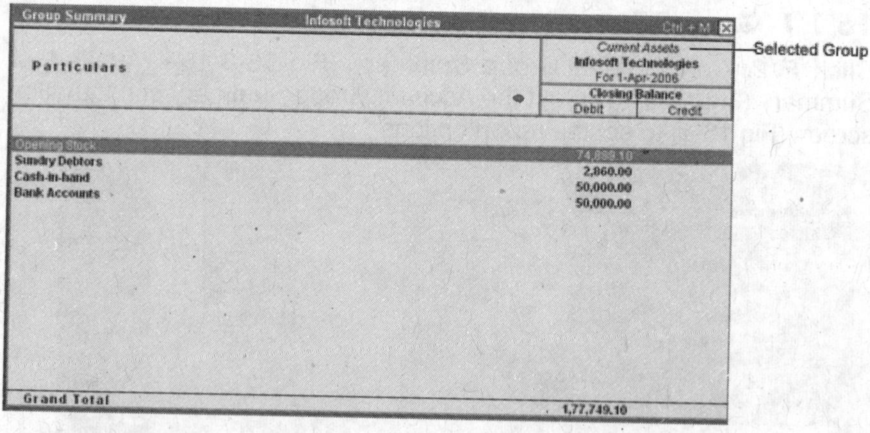

Fig 16-4: Group Summary of a selected Group

16.2.2 Drill Down from Group Summary

When you drill down through Group summary, you get the reports as follows :

Item through which Drilled	*Next Level Report*
Account Group	Group Summary (Fig 16-4)
Ledger Account	Ledger Monthly Summary (Fig 16-13)

16.2.3. Ledgerwise Group Summary

At Group Summary, Click F5:Ledgwise button (Fig 16-2) to get list of Ledgers for the selected Group in alphabetical order (Fig 16-5).

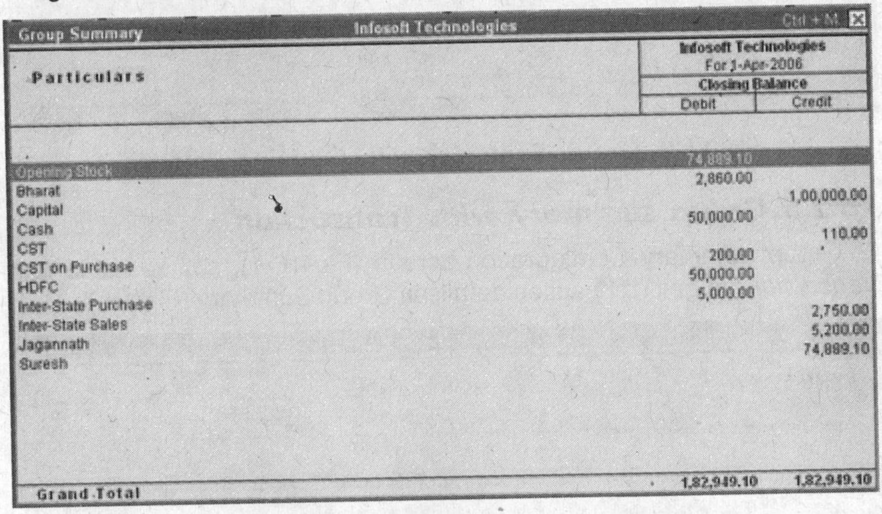

Fig: 16-5 Led-wise Group summary

16.2.4 Group summary with opening balance

At Account Group Summary configuration screen (Fig 16-1), set *Yes* at *Show Opening Balances* to get Group Summary with Opening Balance (Fig 16-6). The Opening Balance figure shows the sum of Opening Balance of all Child Ledgers of the respective Group.

The Transaction figure shows the sum of Debit & Credit transactions of all Child Ledgers of the respective Group.

Group Summary — Infosoft Technologies — Ctrl + M

Particulars	Infosoft Technologies For 1-Apr-2006			
	Opening Balance		Closing Balance	
	Debit	Credit	Debit	Credit
Opening Stock	74,889.10		74,889.10	
Bharat			2,860.00	
Capital		1,00,000.00		1,00,000.00
Cash	50,000.00		50,000.00	
CST				110.00
CST on Purchase			200.00	
HDFC	50,000.00		50,000.00	
Inter-State Purchase			5,000.00	
Inter-State Sales				2,750.00
Jagannath				5,200.00
Suresh		74,889.10		74,889.10
Grand Total	1,74,889.10	1,74,889.10	1,82,949.10	1,82,949.10

Fig 16-6 Group Summary with Opening Balance

16.2.5 Group summary with Transaction

At Group Summary Configuration screen (Fig 16-1), set *Yes* at *Show transactions* to get Transaction details in Group Summary (Fig 16-7)

Group Summary — Infosoft Technologies — Ctrl + M

Particulars	Infosoft Technologies For 1-Apr-2006		
	Transactions		Closing Balance
	Debit	Credit	
Opening Stock			74,889.10 Dr
Bharat	*2,860.00*		2,860.00 Dr
Capital			1,00,000.00 Cr
Cash			50,000.00 Dr
CST		*110.00*	110.00 Cr
CST on Purchase	*200.00*		200.00 Dr
HDFC			50,000.00 Dr
Inter-State Purchase	*5,000.00*		5,000.00 Dr
Inter-State Sales		*2,750.00*	2,750.00 Cr
Jagannath		*5,200.00*	5,200.00 Cr
Suresh			74,889.10 Cr
Grand Total	*8,060.00*	*8,060.00*	

Fig 16-7 Group Summary with Transaction

16.2.6 Percentage wise Group Summary

At Group Summary Configuration screen (Fig 16-1), set Yes at *Show Percentage* to get Group Summary with percentage figures (Fig 16-8)

Group Summary — Infosoft Technologies — Ctrl + M

Particulars	Infosoft Technologies For 1-Apr-2006 Closing Balance			
	Debit		Credit	
Opening Stock	74,889.10	40.93%		
Bharat	2,860.00	1.56%		
Capital			1,00,000.00	54.66%
Cash	50,000.00	27.33%		
CST			110.00	0.06%
CST on Purchase	200.00	0.11%		
HDFC	50,000.00	27.33%		
Inter-State Purchase	5,000.00	2.73%		
Inter-State Sales			2,750.00	1.50%
Jagannath			5,200.00	2.84%
Suresh			74,889.10	40.93%
Grand Total	1,82,949.10	100.00%	1,82,949.10	100.00%

Fig 16-8 Group Summary with percentage details

16.3 Ledger Summary

It shows the Summary of each Ledger for the current period.

At Group Summary (Fig 16-3 /16-4), click *F5: Ledwise* button (Fig 16-2) to show the Ledger Summary of all child Ledgers of the Groups (Fig 16-9).

Group Summary — Infosoft Technologies — Ctrl + M

Particulars	Current Assets Infosoft Technologies For 1-Apr-2006 Closing Balance	
	Debit	Credit
Opening Stock	74,889.10	
Bharat	2,860.00	
Cash	50,000.00	
HDFC	50,000.00	
Grand Total	1,77,749.10	

Fig 16-9: Ledger Summary

16.4 Monthly Summaries

Now we explain Account Group & Ledger Account Monthly Summary showing the monthly / quarterly break up of Selected Account Group / Account Ledger.

16.4.1 Group Monthly Summary

This report shows the Monthly break up of selected Account Group (Fig 16-10).

At Group Summary:

- [*Display > Account Books > Group Voucher* - > select a Group – Fig 15-13/ 15-15]
- [*Display > Account Books > Group Summary* -> select a Group - Fig 16-3/ 16-4]

Click *F6: Monthly* to get Monthly Summary for the selected Group.

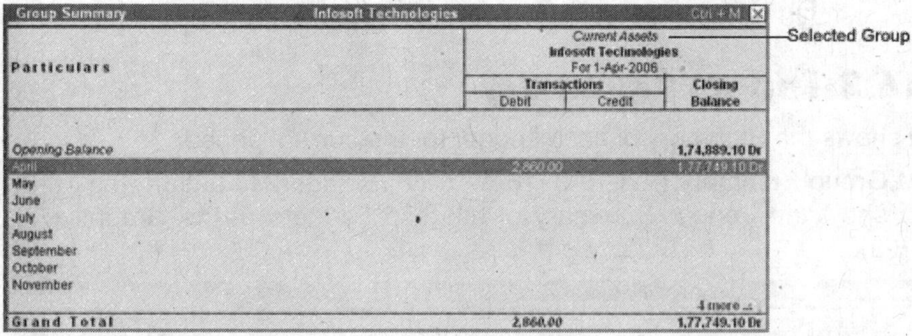

Fig 16-10: Group Monthly Summary for a Group

16.4.2 Ledger Monthly Summary

This report shows the monthly break up of a Ledger (Fig 16-13).

To get this report:

- At Group Summary (Fig 16-4), drill down through a Ledger
- At Ledger Summary (Fig 16-9), drill down through a Ledger
- Click *F7: Monthly* at Ledger Vouchers *[Display > Account Books > Ledger - > select a Ledger* - Fig 15-19*]*.
- Drill down through a Cash/Bank Ledger from Cash / Bank Book *[Display > Account Books > Cash Bank Book* - Fig 16-15*]*.

16.4.3 Monthly Summary Configuration

At Account Group or Ledger Account Monthly/ Quarterly summary (Fig 16-13) & Ledger Daily Break up (Fig 16-14), click *F12: Configure* button to get Monthly Summary Configuration screen (Fig 16-11), to set the options as desired.

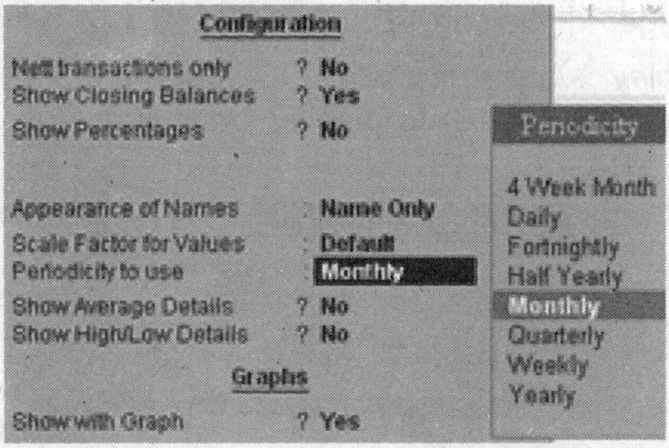

Fig 16-11: Account Group & Ledger Monthly Summary Configuration

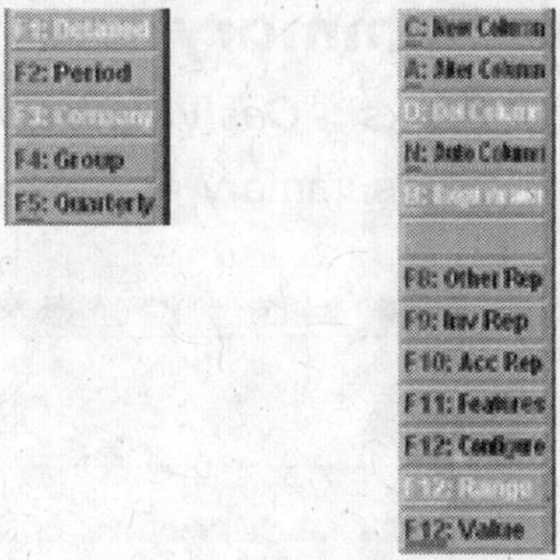

Fig16-12:Buttons at Ledger Monthly Summary

Toggle between Monthly & Quarterly summary figures through *F5: Quarterly / Monthly* button.

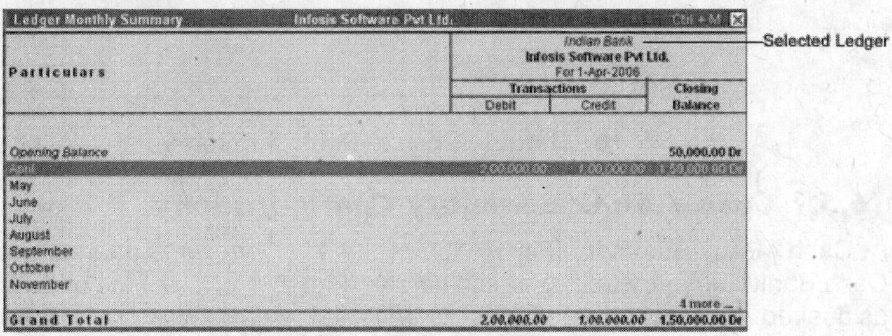

Fig 16-13: Ledger Monthly Summary

16.4.4 Ledger Daily Break Up

Like Ledger Monthly summary, this report shows the Daily summary of the selected Ledger for the current period (Fig 16-14).

At Ledger (*Display > Account Books > Ledger* – Fig 15-19), Click F6: Dly Brk-up button (Fig 15-18) to display *Daily Break-up* of transactions for the Ledger.

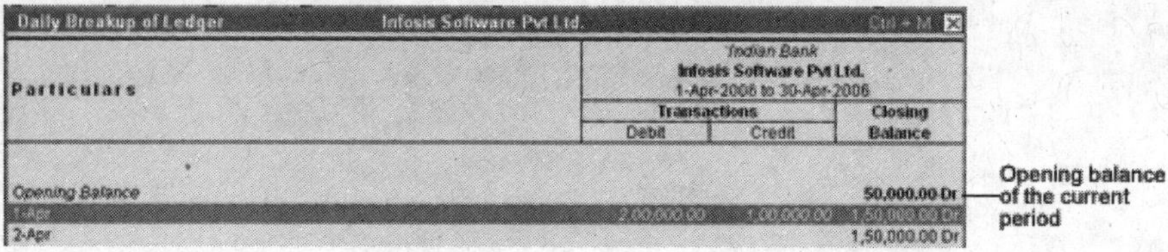

Fig 16-14: Daily Break Up

16.5 Cash/Bank Summary

Select Display > Account Books > Cash/Bank Books.

This report shows Groupwise summary of Cash, Bank and Bank OCC Accounts (Fig 16-15).

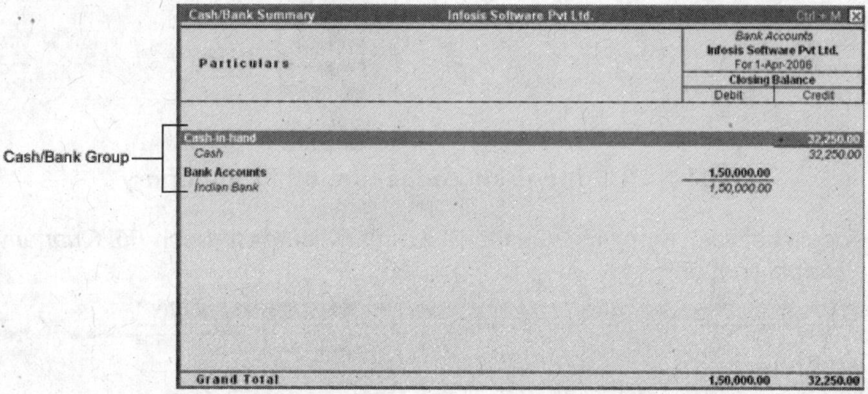

Fig 16-15: Default Cash / Bank Summary

16.5.1 Cash / Bank Summary Configuration

At Cash / Bank Summary (Fig 16-15), click *F12: Configure* button to get Cash Bank Summary Configuration screen (Fig 16-16), to set the options as desired.

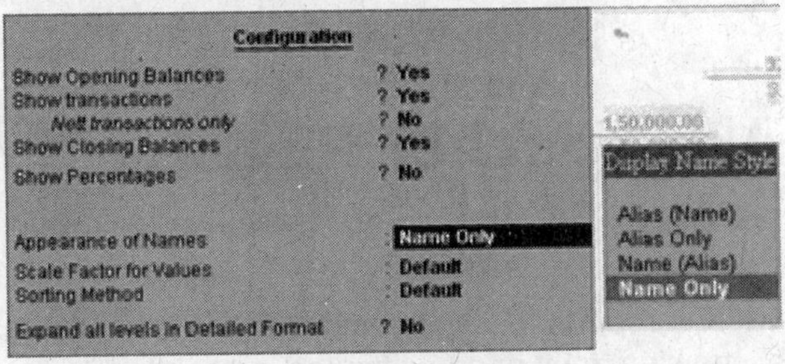

Fig 16-16: Cash Bank Summary Configuration

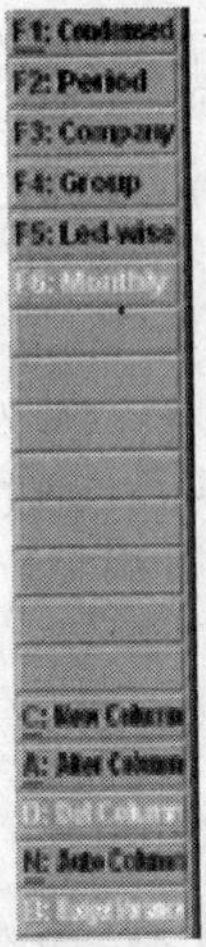

Fig 16-17: Button Bar at Cash Bank Summary

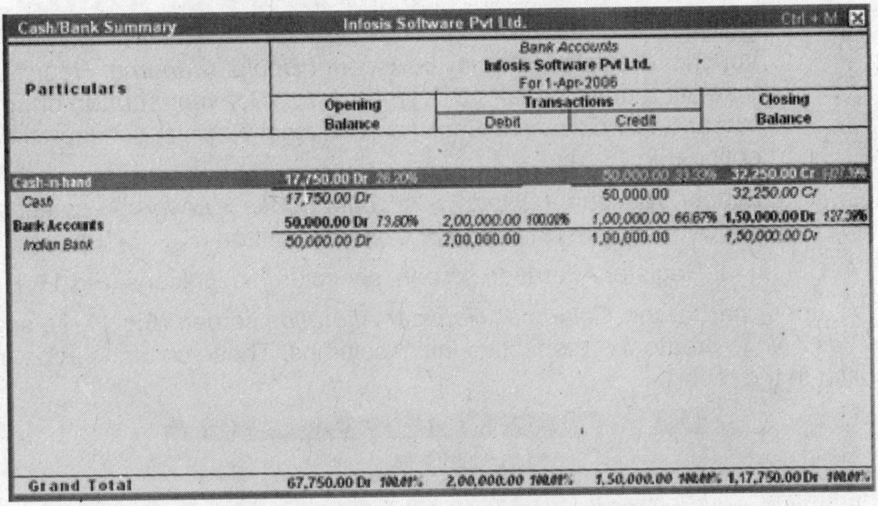

Fig 16-18: Cash Bank Summary (in detailed format) with all columns & percentage figures.

Self Test Questions

STQ 16.1: How you get Account Group Monthly Summary for a selected Group

STQ 16.2: How you get Account Ledger Monthly Summary for a selected Ledger.

Columnar A/c Voucher Register 17

So far we have seen various reports in which each ledger transaction is printed in separate line, showing debit or credit figures, as applicable.

However, businessmen often prefer columnar reports in very compact form (see Fig 17-2). These reports give detailed (each voucher detail) as well as summary figures (column totals for each ledger / group), provide more information at a glance, are compact in format and simpler to apprehend.

17.1 Voucher Register Column Definitions

Tally provides useful facilities to define report columns by the user to print various types of columnar reports (Fig 17-1).

You get Column Definition screen (Fig 17-1) at:

- Voucher Register (*Display > Account Books > Journal Register* > select a month - Ref 15.1.1), Click *F5: Columnar* button or set *Yes* at *Show Columnar Register* at Voucher Register configuration option (Fig 15-3).
- Ledger Vouchers (*Display > Account Books > Ledger* -> select a Ledger – Fig 15-19. Click *F8: Columnar* button (Fig 15-18).

At Columnar Register Alteration screen, set column definitions (Fig 17.1).

At upper part of the *Columnar Register Alteration* screen (Fig 17-1), set *Yes / No* to create the respective initial columns. These columns appear first in the report.

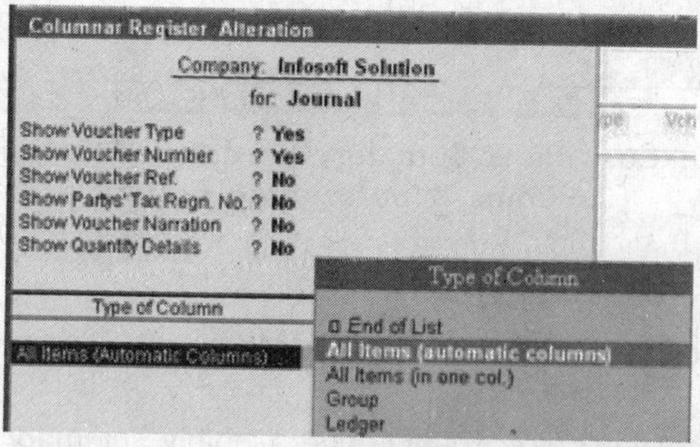

Fig 17-1: Columnar Register column definition

At the lower part of the *Columnar Register Alteration* screen (Fig 17-1), set the Amount columns

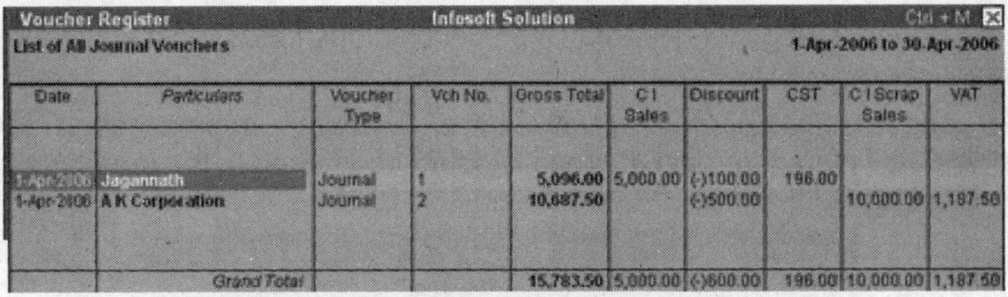

Fig 17-2: All Items(automatic columns)

Fig 17-2 shows the report as per columns set up in Feb 17-1.

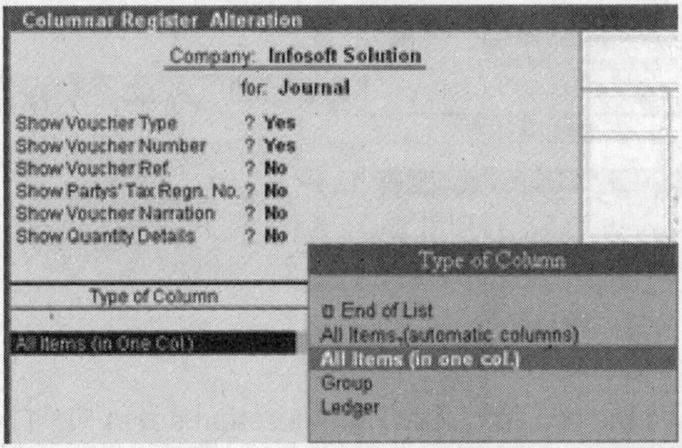

Fig 17-3: Column Register for column definition for all items in one column

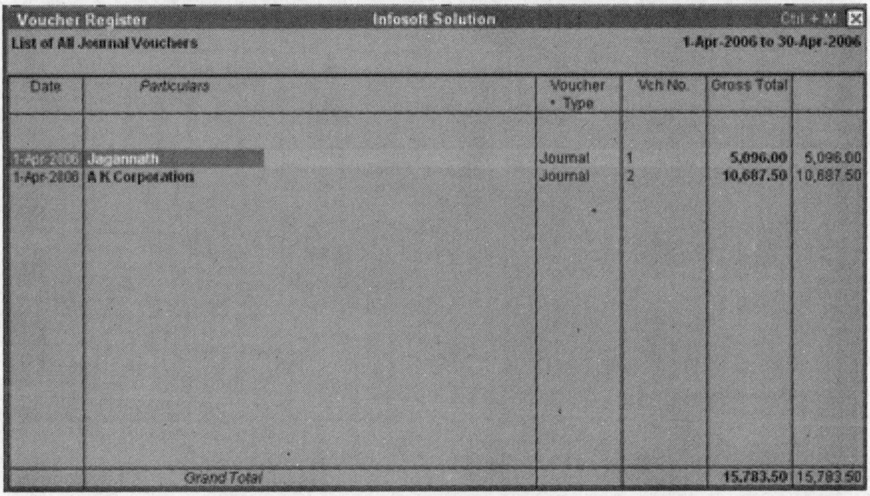

Fig 17-4: All Items in one column

Fig 17-4 shows the report as per columns set up in Feb 17-3.

17.1.1 All Ledger Columns Voucher Register

Like Voucher Register, you may also set columns for associated Ledgers in vouchers.

At Ledger, select *All Items (Automatic Columns)* to automatically create individual column for each Ledger Account transacted in the Vouchers for the period.

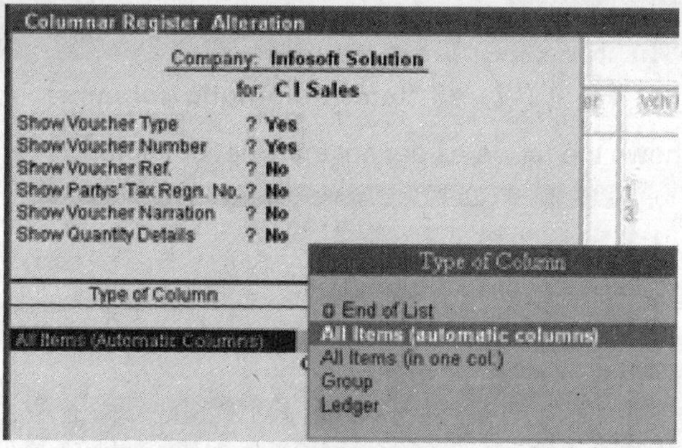

Fig 17-5: Column definition for Voucher Register

Fig 17-6 shows the report as per configuration set in Fig 17-5

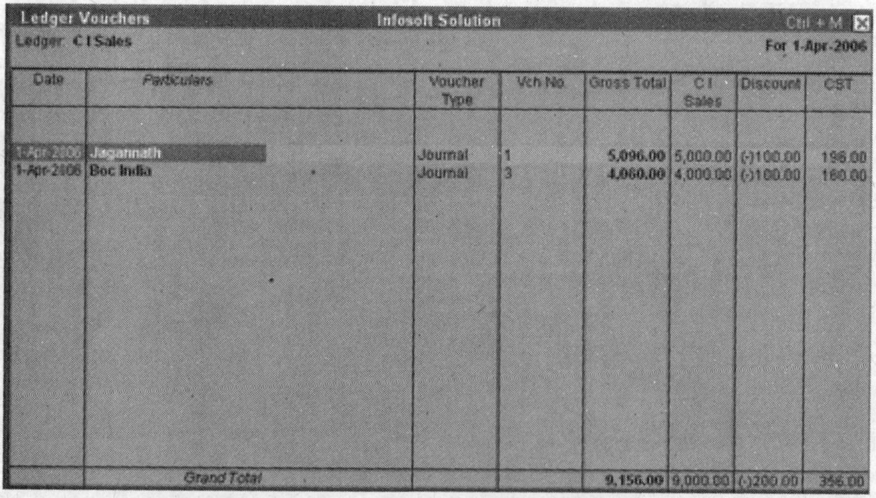

Fig 17-6: Columnar Voucher Register

17.1.2 Column Set Up for Accounts Voucher Register

To create column for Account Group / Account Ledger:

- Select Group to create column for the summed up figures of all ledgers of an Account Group
- Select Ledger to create column for Ledger Accounts
- Select All Items (in One column) to combine the remaining Ledgers (Items which are not selected individually) in one Column only.

Now specify the column definition for Group / Ledger columns.

Select Related Items (Automatic Columns)

- When you select Ledger, a column will be auto created for each ledger account transacted in the Vouchers.
- When you select Group, a column will be created for each Account Group in which the figures of all ledgers accounts transacted in the voucher, falling under the Account Group will be placed.
- When you select Related Items (in One Column, figures of related, Ledgers will be clubbed together into one column named others).

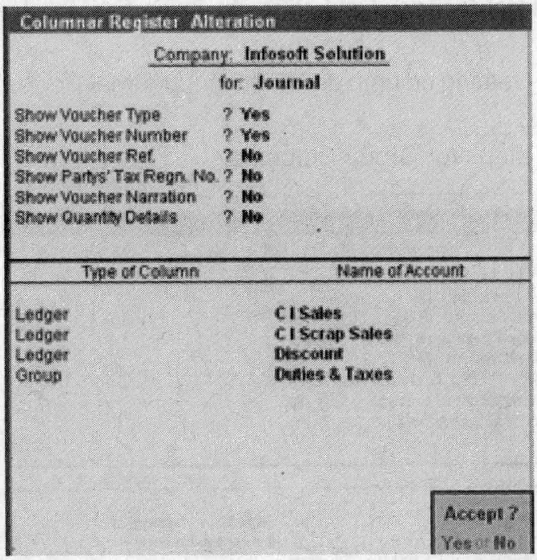

Fig 17-7: Voucher Register column set up for specified Groups/ Ledgers

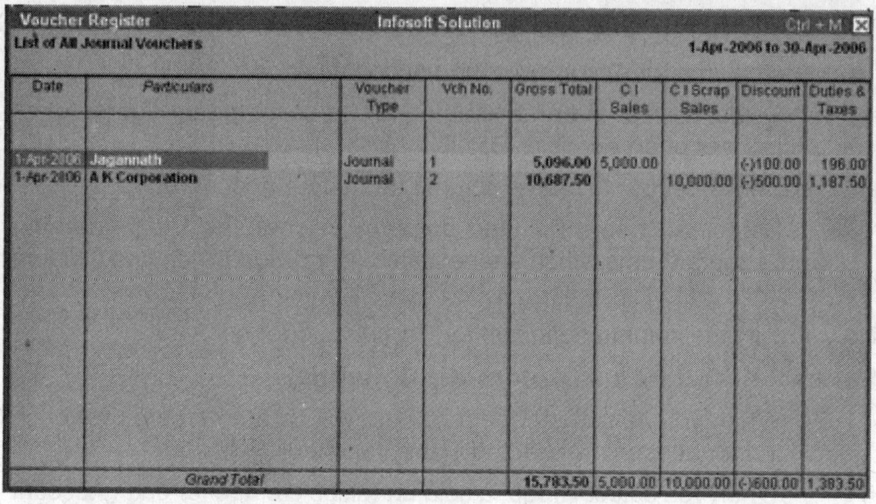

Fig 17-8: Voucher Register with Ledger & group

17.1.3 Columnar Multi Ledger Register

At Ledger (Fig 15.19), Click *F8: Columnar* to get Column Alteration screen and specify Ledgers for each Column to get Columnar Multi Ledger Register (Fig 17-10).

The process of creating column definitions for Journal Register and Ledger is similar.

We explain the steps for Group Columns.

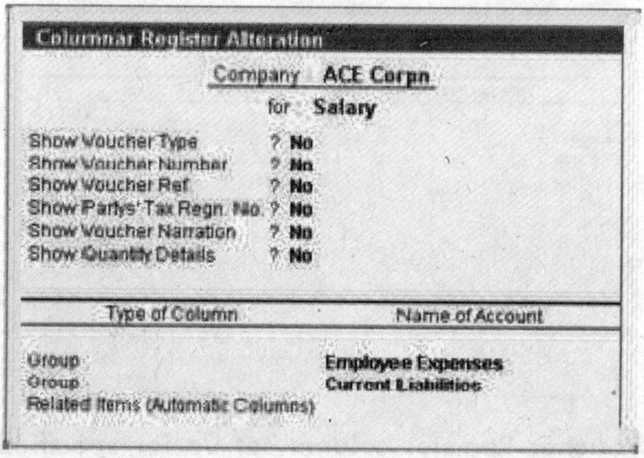

Fig 17-9: Column Definition for Account Group (clubbed ledger columns)

Fig 17-10 shows the Report as per column definition shown in Fig 17-9. The columns show the net figure of all the transacted child ledgers under the specified Group. So, the column (Employee Expenses) shows the total of all Pay heads placed under the Group Salary (or its child Group) and the column (Current Liabilities) shows the total of all Deduction heads placed under the Group Current (or its child Group)

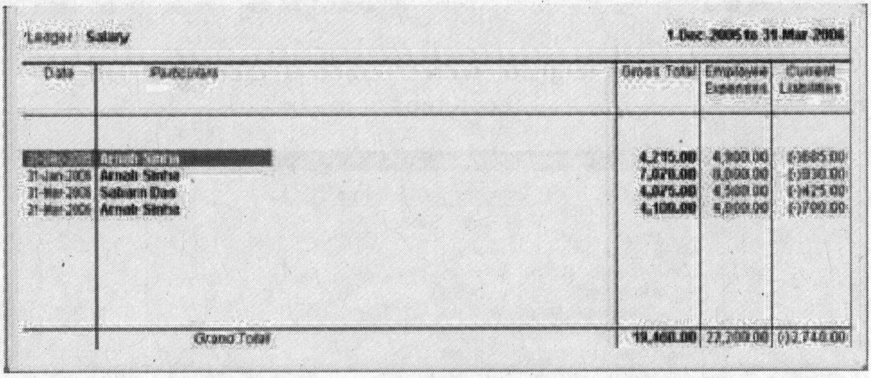

Fig 17-10: Salary Register with Account Group columns (clubbed ledger columns)

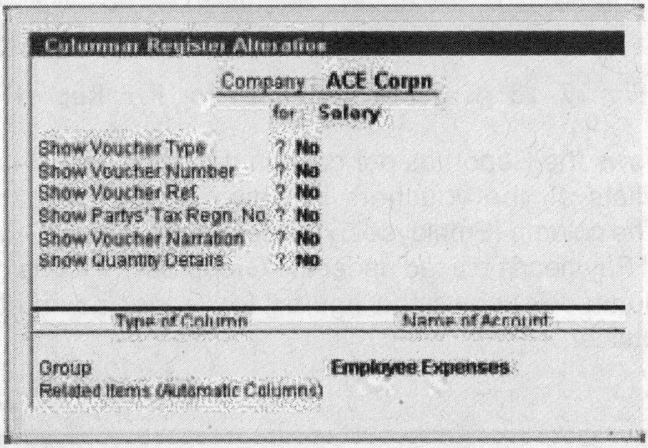

Fig 17-11: Salary Register column definition for clubbed & individual ledger columns

Fig 17-12 shows the Report as per column definition shown in Fig 17-11. In this report, the column (Employee Expenses) represents a Group showing the total of all Pay heads placed under the Group Salary (or its child Group) and the Columns PF, ESI & P Tax represent individual ledger columns. These are the complementary ledger accounts transacted (Ledger Accounts other than the selected Group).

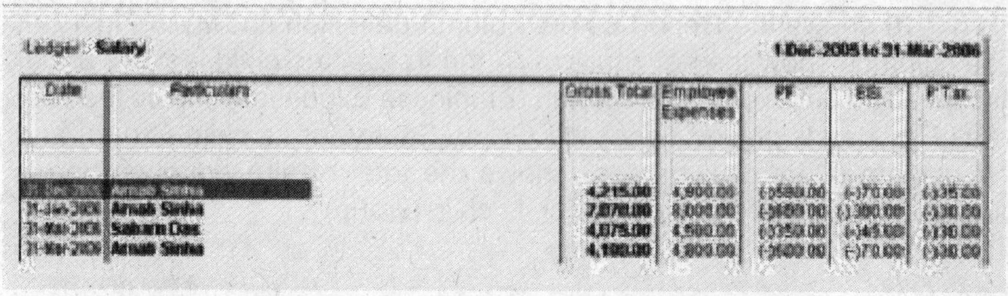

Fig 17-12: Salary Register with clubbed & individual ledger columns

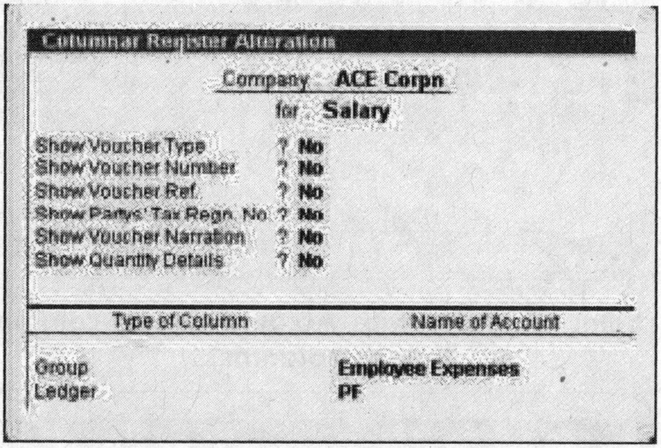

Fig 17-13: Column definition for P F Report

Fig 17-14 shows the Report as per column definition shown in Fig 17-13. This report lists all the vouchers in which Salary Ledger has been transacted. The column (Employee Expenses) represents a Group showing the total of all Pay heads placed under the Group Salary (or its child Group) and the Column PF shows the figures for ledger account PF in the respective voucher.

Fig 17-14: P F Report

17.1.4 Petty Cash Book

Using the columnar feature of Ledger, you may print Petty cash Book in columnar format. To maintain Petty Cash:

- Create a Petty Cash Ledger Account and Main Cash Account (under Cash – in –Hand).
- To transfer money from Main cash to Petty Cash, create a Contra voucher as usual.
- In all payments from Petty Cash, create payment voucher. Select Petty Cash Account.

To print Columnar Petty Cash Book, select *Display > Account Book > Ledger*, select Petty cash Account. Click *columnar* button and set the columns (Fig 17-15).

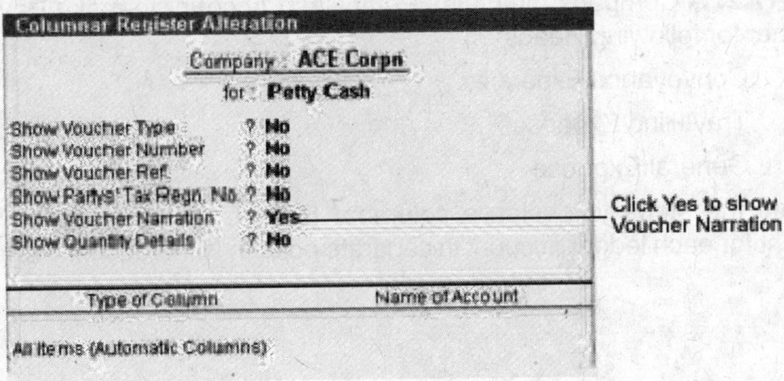

Fig 17-15: Column definition for Petty Cash Book

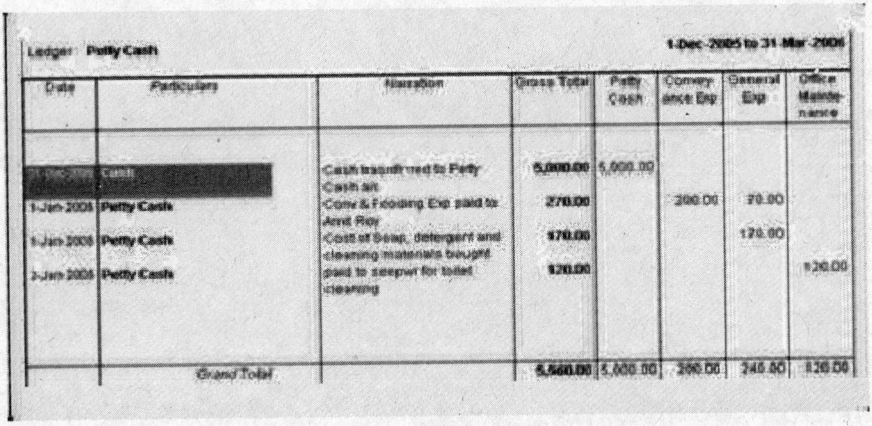

Ledger : Petty Cash — 1-Dec-2005 to 31-Mar-2006

Date	Particulars	Narration	Gross Total	Petty Cash	Conveyance Exp	General Exp	Office Maintenance
[illegible]	Cash	Cash transferred to Petty Cash a/c	5,000.00	5,000.00			
1-Jan-2006	Petty Cash	Conv & Fooding Exp paid to Amit Roy	270.00		200.00	70.00	
1-Jan-2006	Petty Cash	Cost of Soap, detergent and cleaning materials bought	170.00			170.00	
3-Jan-2006	Petty Cash	paid to seepwr for toilet cleaning	120.00				120.00
	Grand Total		5,560.00	5,000.00	200.00	240.00	120.00

Fig 17-16: Petty Cash Book

So, all the vouchers having a transaction with Petty Cash Ledger account are listed.

Fig 17-16 shows the Report as per column definition shown in Fig 17-15-

Columnar Registers are very handy and helpful to print the assorted voucher lists to form a special type of Day Books in a compact form. With a bit of planning and innovation, you can get useful reports very quickly.

Self Test Questions

STQ 17.1: Show how to print the voucher list with showing Employee Name & Net Pay like:

V Date	Employee Name	Net Pay
31-7-2006	Arnab Sinha	4400

STQ 17.2: A Company maintains Petty Cash Account to make Payment Voucher for following Heads

- Conveyance Expenses
- Travelling Expenses
- General Expense

Explain the steps to design a columnar Petty Cash Register showing amount for each ledger account in separate column with Voucher Narration.

Trial Balance

18

Trial Balance is a list of all Account Groups / Ledger showing the net Closing Balance (Fig 18-1 & 18-2). This is the immediate higher level report of Ledger.

18.1 Trial Balance

The default Trial Balance shows the Primary Groups (Fig 18-1) with balance for each Group. The total of debits & credits must Tally. The opening balance difference, if any, is shown as the last Item balancing the Debit & Credit totals.

Select Display > Trial Balance.

18.1.1 Trial Balance Configuration

At Trial Balance (Fig 18-3 / 18-4), click *F12: Configure* to get Trial Balance Configuration options (Fig 18-1).

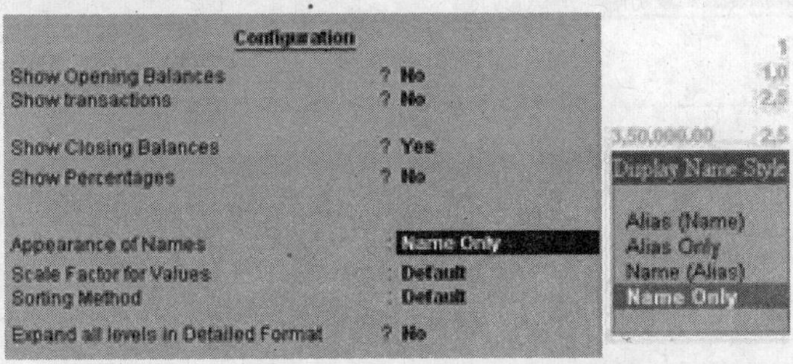

Fig 18-1: Trial Balance Configuration options

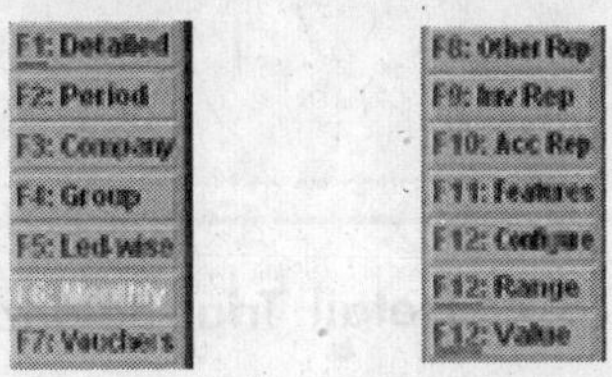

Fig: 18-2: Buttons at Trial Balance

Trial Balance — Infosis Software Pvt Ltd. — Ctrl + M

Particulars	Infosis Software Pvt Ltd. For 1-Apr-2006 Closing Balance	
	Debit	Credit
Capital Account		17,400.00
Loans (Liability)		1,00,000.00
Current Liabilities		2,50,250.00
Fixed Assets	3,50,000.00	2,50,000.00
Current Assets	4,99,900.00	32,250.00
Sales Accounts		2,00,000.00
Grand Total	8,49,900.00	8,49,900.00

Fig 18-3: Primary Group Trial Balance

18.1.2 Detail Trial Balance

At Primary Group Trial Balance (Fig 18-3), click *F1: Detailed* button (Fig 18-2) to get *Detail Trial Balance* showing next level Groups/ Ledgers (Fig 18-4). Click *F1: Condensed* toggle button to get back to Primary Group Trial Balance (Fig 18-3).

Trial Balance — Infosis Software Pvt Ltd. — Ctrl + M

Particulars	Infosis Software Pvt Ltd. For 1-Apr-2006 Closing Balance	
	Debit	Credit
Capital Account		17,400.00
Ajay Kr.Ghosh(Propriter)		*17,400.00*
Loans (Liability)		1,00,000.00
Rajesh Kumar(Loan)		*1,00,000.00*
Current Liabilities		2,50,250.00
Provisions		14,550.00
Sundry Creditors		2,35,700.00
Fixed Assets	3,50,000.00	2,50,000.00
Furniture	1,00,000.00	50,000.00
Motor Car	2,50,000.00	2,00,000.00
Current Assets	4,99,900.00	32,250.00
Opening Stock	2,35,550.00	
Sundry Debtors	34,500.00	
Cash-in-hand		
		32,250.00
		5 more ...
Grand Total	8,49,900.00	8,49,900.00

Fig 18-4: Detail Trial Balance

18.1.3 Exploded Trial Balance

In Detailed Trial Balance you get only top 2 level Group/ Ledgers (Fig 18-4). To get full hierarchical details upto the lowest level ledger (Fig 18-5), set *Yes* at *Expand all levels in Detailed Format* at the Configuration screen (18-1).

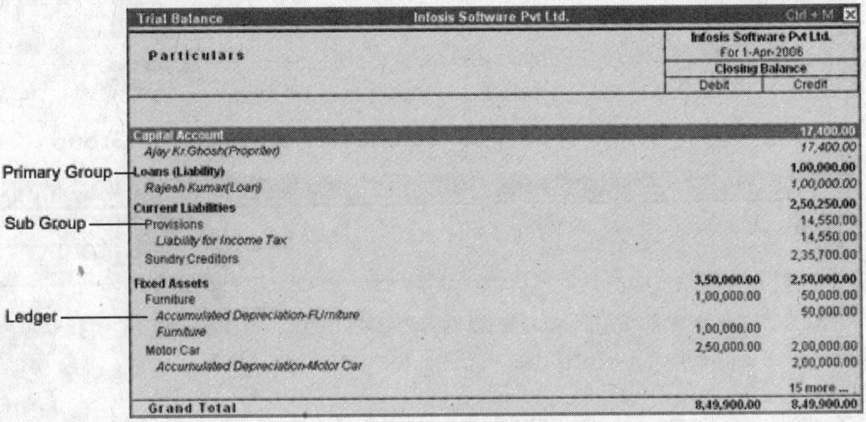

Particulars	Infosis Software Pvt Ltd. For 1-Apr-2006 Closing Balance	
	Debit	Credit
Capital Account		17,400.00
Ajay Kr.Ghosh(Propriter)		*17,400.00*
Loans (Liability)		**1,00,000.00**
Rajesh Kumar(Loan)		*1,00,000.00*
Current Liabilities		**2,50,250.00**
Provisions		14,550.00
Liability for Income Tax		14,550.00
Sundry Creditors		2,35,700.00
Fixed Assets	**3,50,000.00**	**2,50,000.00**
Furniture	1,00,000.00	50,000.00
Accumulated Depreciation-FUrniture		50,000.00
Furniture	1,00,000.00	
Motor Car	2,50,000.00	2,00,000.00
Accumulated Depreciation-Motor Car		2,00,000.00
		15 more ...
Grand Total	8,49,900.00	8,49,900.00

Fig 18-5: Exploded Trial Balance

18.1.4 Drill Down from Trial Balance

When you drill down through any Item of default Trial Balance, you get the reports as follows :

Item through which Drilled	*Next Level Report*
Account Group	Group Summary of the selected Group (Fig 16-4)
Ledger Account	Ledger Monthly Summary of the selected ledger (Fig 16-13)

18.2 Ledgerwise Trial Balance

At Primary Group Trial Balance (Fig 18-3) or at Group Trial Balance (Fig 18-6/18-7), click *F5: Led-wise toggle button (Fig 18-2) to get Ledgerwise* Trial Balance of all subordinate ledgers of the selected Group (Fig 18-6). So at Primary Trial Balance, you get All Ledgers in alphabetical order (Fig 18-7).

Trial Balance	Infosis Software Pvt Ltd.	Ctrl + M
Particulars	*Current Assets* **Infosis Software Pvt Ltd.** For 1-Apr-2006 **Closing Balance**	
	Debit	Credit
Opening Stock	2,35,550.00	
Advance to Staff	12,350.00	
A.K.Shina	34,500.00	
Cash		32,250.00
Indian Bank	1,50,000.00	
Tds	67,500.00	

Fig 18-6: Ledgerwise Trial Balance of an Account Group

Trial Balance	Infosis Software Pvt Ltd.	Ctrl + M
Particulars	**Infosis Software Pvt Ltd.** For 1-Apr-2006 **Closing Balance**	
	Debit	Credit
Opening Stock	2,35,550.00	
Accumulated Depreciation-FUrniture		50,000.00
Accumulated Depreciation-Motor Car		2,00,000.00
Advance to Staff	12,350.00	
Ajay Kr.Ghosh(Propriter)		17,400.00
A.K.Shina	34,500.00	
Cash		32,250.00
Furniture	1,00,000.00	
Indian Bank	1,50,000.00	
Liability for Income Tax		14,550.00
Metrics Computers		2,35,700.00
Motor Car	2,50,000.00	
Rajesh Kumar(Loan)		1,00,000.00
Software Devlopment		2,00,000.00
Tds	67,500.00	
Grand Total	**8,49,900.00**	**8,49,900.00**

Fig 18-7: Ledgerwise Trial Balance (All Ledgers)

18.3 Trial Balance with Percentage figures

At Trial Balance Configuration (Fig 18-1), set Yes at *Show Percentage* to to get Trial Balance with Percentage figures (Fig 18-8).

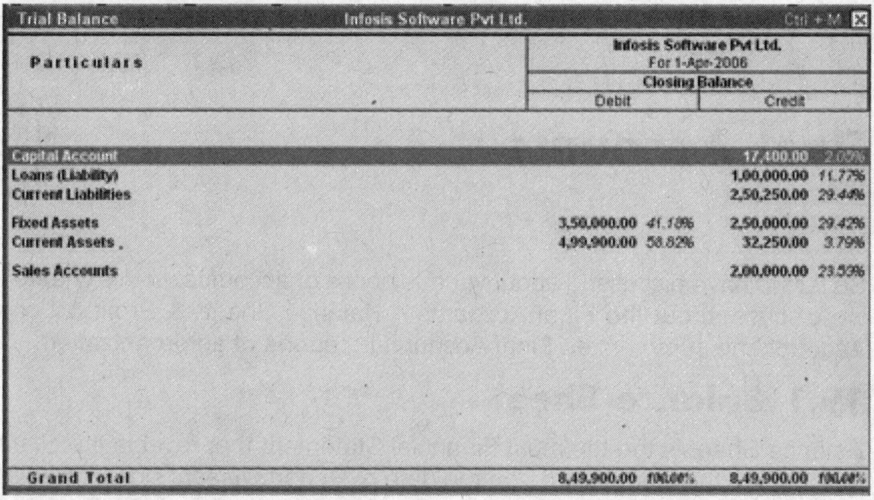

Trial Balance — Infosis Software Pvt Ltd. — Ctrl + M

Particulars	Infosis Software Pvt Ltd. For 1-Apr-2006 Closing Balance			
	Debit		Credit	
Capital Account			17,400.00	2.05%
Loans (Liability)			1,00,000.00	11.77%
Current Liabilities			2,50,250.00	29.44%
Fixed Assets	3,50,000.00	41.18%	2,50,000.00	29.42%
Current Assets	4,99,900.00	58.82%	32,250.00	3.79%
Sales Accounts			2,00,000.00	23.53%
Grand Total	8,49,900.00	100.00%	8,49,900.00	100.00%

Fig 18-8: Trial Balance with percentage figure

Self Test Questions

STQ 18.1: Specify the options to get Extended Trial Balance with lowest level details with Opening Balance, Transactions and Closing balance for a specified period.

STQ 18.2: Specify the options to get Trial Balance with all ledgers in alphabetical order, showing Closing Balance as on 31-Dec-2005 (FY is 1-4-2005 to 31-3-2006).

Final Accounts

19

So far we have discussed about various books of accounts. In this chapter, we discuss about the Final Accounts – Balance Sheet & Profit & Loss Account, the summarized Final Accounting reports of an organization.

19.1 Balance Sheet

Balance Sheet is the top most Financial Statement that reveals the *State of Affairs* of the Company as on the date of Report. *Assets* side lists what the Company *Owns* and *Liabilities* side lists what it *Owes*. All *Real* and *Personal* accounts appear in Balance Sheet.

19.1.1 Primary Balance Sheet

The default Balance Sheet shows Closing Balance for Primary Groups of *Liabilities* in one side, *Assets* on the other in horizontal (T) format (Fig 19-1). You may move the cursor around the two sides with the help of Left & Right arrow keys.

Select *Balance Sheet* at Gateway to get Primary Balance Sheet (Fig 19-1).

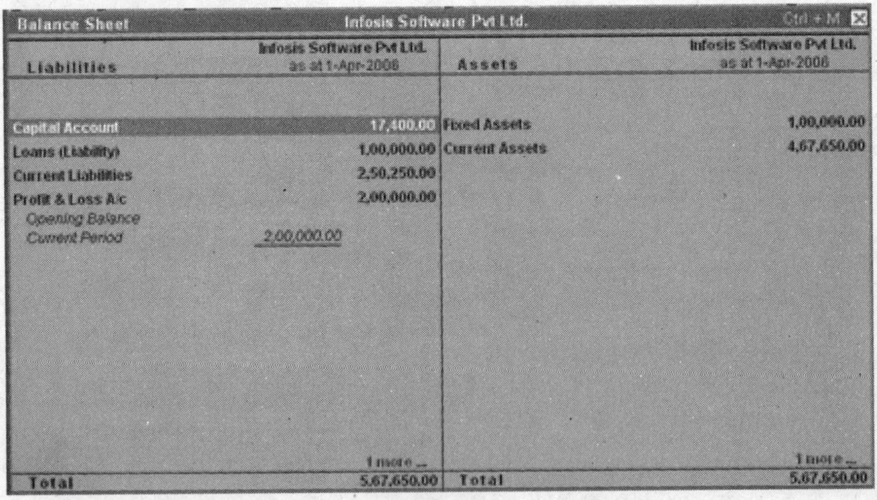

Fig 19-1: Primary Balance Sheet

19.1.2 Detailed Balance Sheet

At Primary Balance Sheet (Fig 19-1), click the *F1: Detailed* toggle button (Fig 19-4) to get Detailed Balance Sheet showing next level Group/ Ledger details (Fig 19-2). Click *F1: Condensed* to get back Primary Balance Sheet (Fig 19-1).

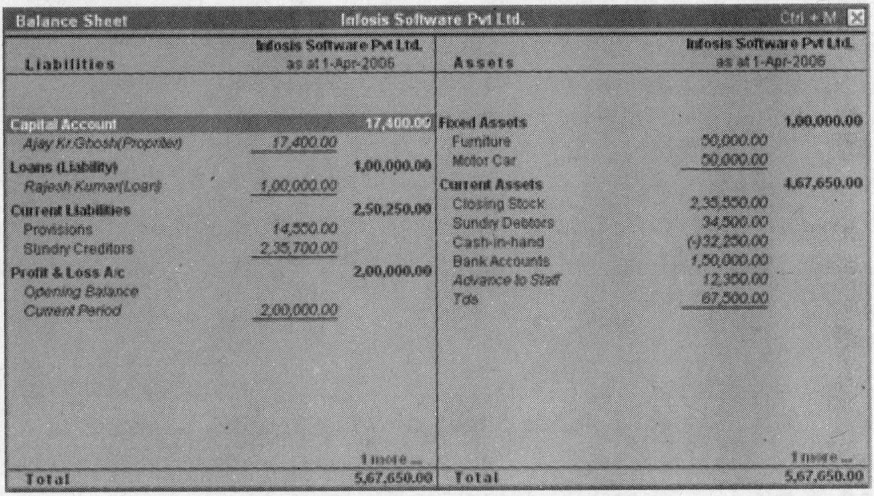

Fig 19-2: Balance Sheet - Detailed

19.1.3 Balance Sheet Configuration

At Balance Sheet (Fig 19-1 / Fig 19-2) click *F12: Configure* to get Balance Sheet Configuration options (Fig 19-3).

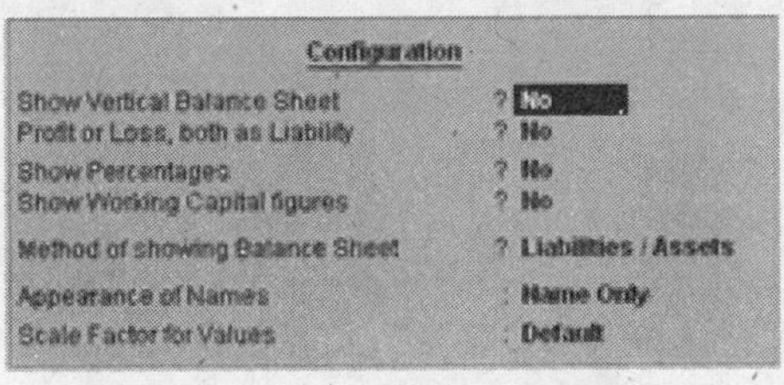

Fig 19-3: Balance Sheet Configuration

Fig 19-4 Buttons at Balance Sheet

19.1.4 Sources & Application of Funds

To get the Balance Sheet showing Sources & Application of Funds (Fig 19-5), set *Yes* at *Show Vertical Balance Sheet* at Configuration options (Fig 19-3).

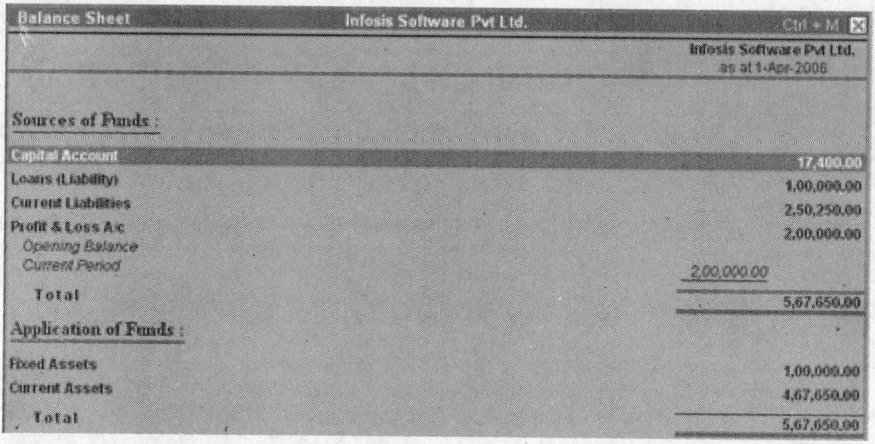

Fig 19-5: Vertical Balance Sheet showing Sources & Application of funds

19.1.5 Loss as Negative Profit in Balance Sheet

To show Profit/ Loss in Liability side only (Loss as negative profit) in Balance Sheet (in T Format only - Fig 19-6), set *Yes* at *Profit or Loss both at Liability* at Balance Sheet Configuration screen (Fig 19-3).

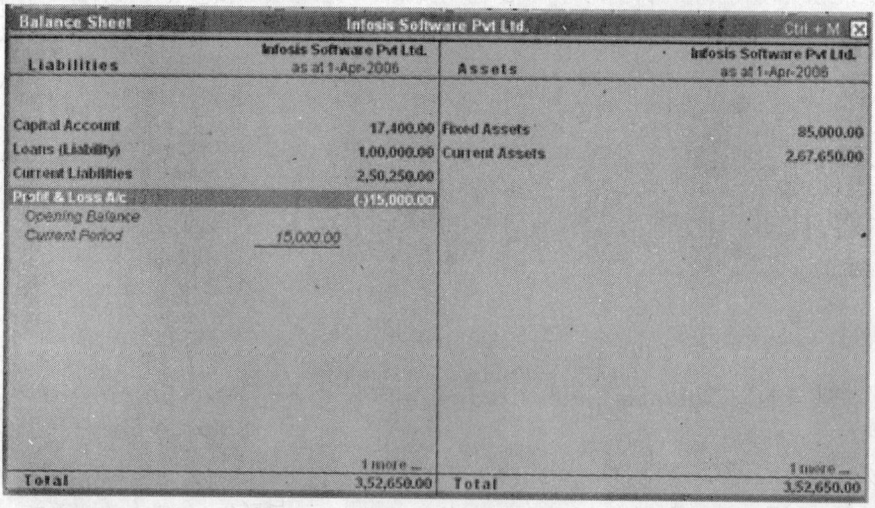

Fig 19-6: Balance Sheet showing Profit / Loss in Liabilities side

To show Loss in Asset side in Balance Sheet (in T Format only - Fig 19-7), set *No* at *Profit or Loss both at Liability* at Balance Sheet Configuration (Fig 19-3).

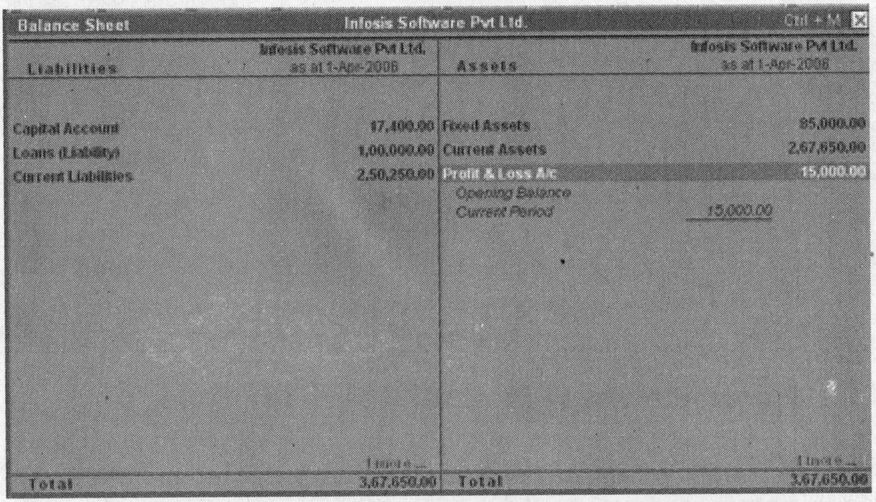

Fig 19-7: Balance Sheet showing Loss in Asset side

19.1.6 Balance Sheet with Percentage Figures

To show Percentage figures of Primary Groups in Balance Sheet (Fig 19-8), set *Yes* at *Show Percentages* at Configuration (Fig 19-3).

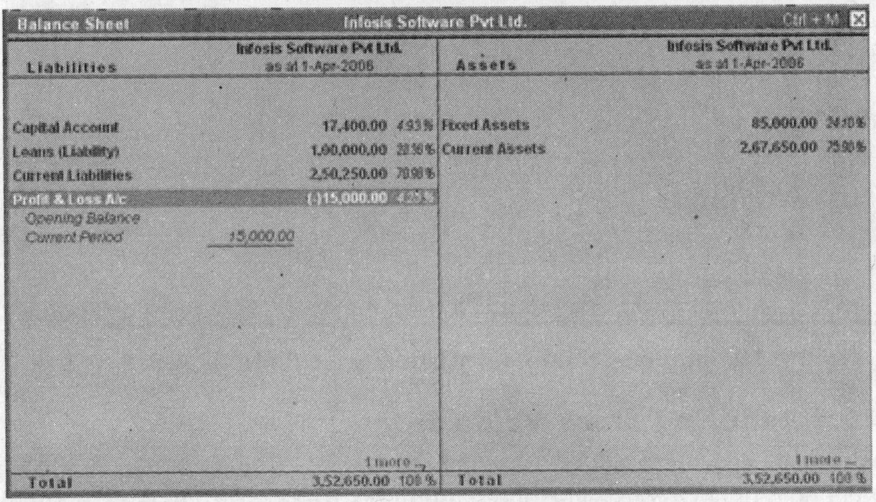

Fig 19-8: Balance Sheet with percentage figure

19.1.7 Balance Sheet showing Working Capital

To get the Balance Sheet showing working capital (Fig19-9), set *Yes* at *Show working Capital figures* at Balance Sheet Configuration (Fig 19-3).

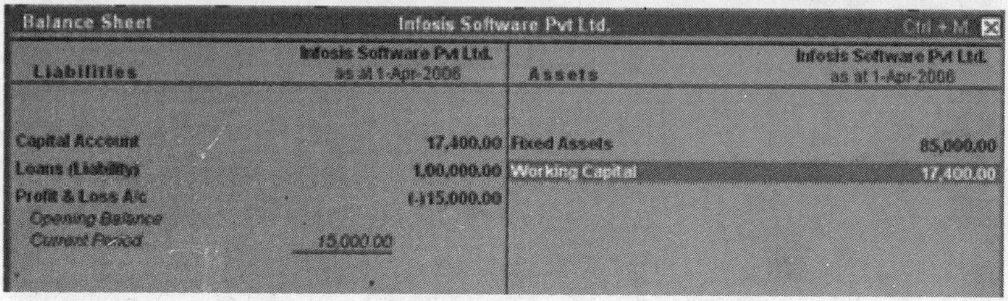

Fig 19-9 : Balance Sheet with Working Capital figures (in T Format)

19.1.8 Balance Sheet in Asset / Liability Style

At Balance Sheet Configuration (Fig 19-3), select *Assets / Liabilities* at *Method of Showing Balance Sheet*, to show Balance Sheet in reverse way (used in some countries) as shown in Fig 19-10.

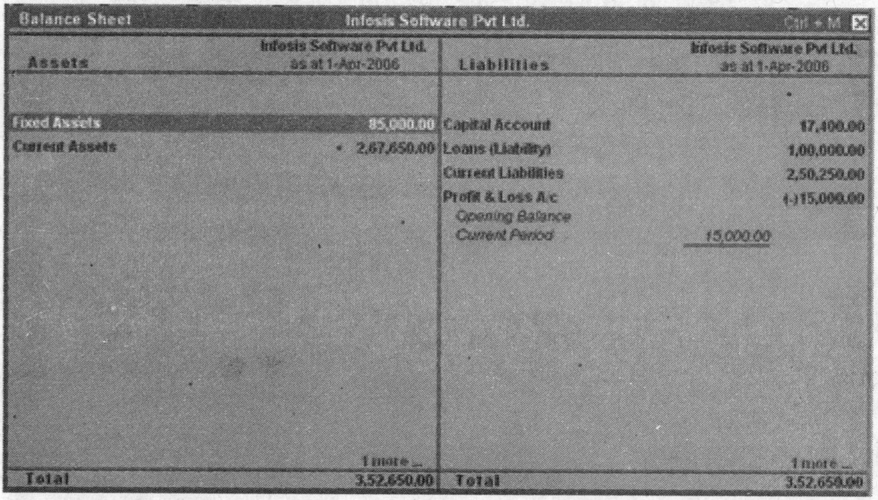

Fig 19-10: Balance Sheet with Liability at Right & Asset at Left

19.1.9 Closing Stock Value Entry

We have explained how you may enter closing stock value through Ledger Accounts under Stock –in-Hand Group (Fig 10-21). You may also enter Closing Stock value from Balance Sheet. Drill down through Current Assets

> Closing Stock > Stock Ledger. Press ↵ at desired Ledger under the Stock-in-hand Group to get it in Alteration mode (10-21). Now enter value of Stock for any date (Ref 10.7).

Value of Stock as entered would be carried to Balance Sheet (Fig 19-11) & Profit & Loss Account at Closing Stock (Fig 19-12).

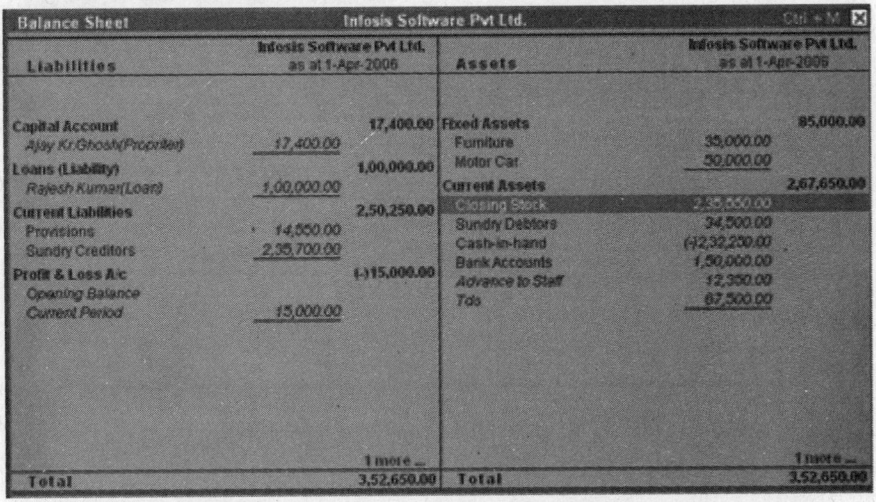

Fig 19-11: Closing Stock value carried in Balance Sheet

19.1.10 Drill Down from Balance Sheet

When you drill down through any Item of default Balance Sheet, you get the reports as follows :

Item through which Drilled	*Next Level Report*
Account Group (other than Closing Stock)	Group Summary (Fig 16-3)
Ledger Account	Ledger Monthly Summary (Fig 16-13)
Profit & Loss Account	P L Statement (Fig 19-12)

19.2 Profit & Loss Statement

The Profit & Loss Statement (popularly known as Profit & Loss Account) displays the figures of all Nominal Accounts and the Net Profit/ Loss (Fig 19-12). Sales, Closing Stock, Direct and Indirect Income heads appear in the Income side; Opening Stock, Purchase, Direct and Indirect Expenses appear in the Expenditure side. *Excess* of Income over Expenditure is shown as *Nett Profit*, *Deficit* is shown as *Nett Loss*.

Select *Profit & Loss Account at Gateway* to get Primary Profit & Loss Statement (Fig 19-12).

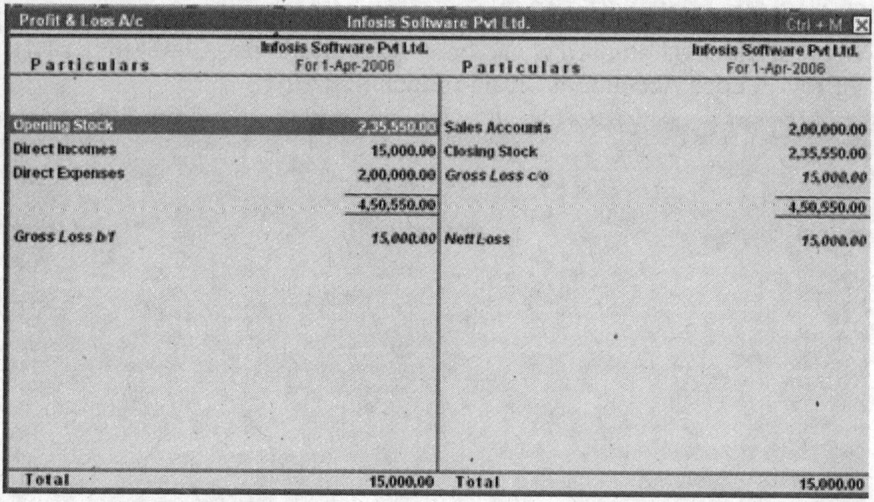

Profit & Loss A/c — Infosis Software Pvt Ltd. — Ctrl + M

Particulars	Infosis Software Pvt Ltd. For 1-Apr-2006	Particulars	Infosis Software Pvt Ltd. For 1-Apr-2006
Opening Stock	2,35,550.00	Sales Accounts	2,00,000.00
Direct Incomes	15,000.00	Closing Stock	2,35,550.00
Direct Expenses	2,00,000.00	*Gross Loss c/o*	*15,000.00*
	4,50,550.00		4,50,550.00
Gross Loss b/f	*15,000.00*	*Nett Loss*	*15,000.00*
Total	15,000.00	Total	15,000.00

Fig 19-12: Profit & Loss Statement

19.2.1 Detailed P L Statement

At Profit & Loss Statement (Fig 19-12), click the *F1: Detailed* toggle button to show next level details (Click *F1: Condensed* to get back Condensed Format – Fig 19-12) as shown in Fig 19-13.

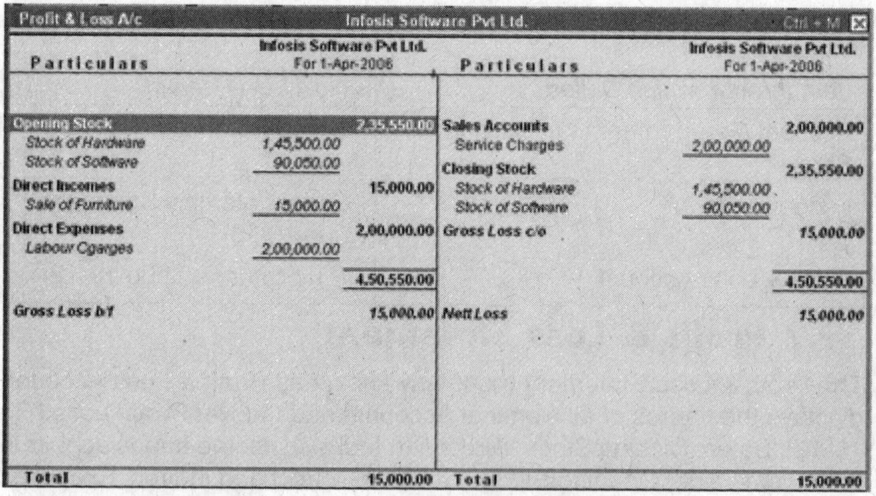

Profit & Loss A/c — Infosis Software Pvt Ltd. — Ctrl + M

Particulars		Infosis Software Pvt Ltd. For 1-Apr-2006	Particulars		Infosis Software Pvt Ltd. For 1-Apr-2006
Opening Stock		2,35,550.00	Sales Accounts		2,00,000.00
Stock of Hardware	*1,45,500.00*		*Service Charges*	*2,00,000.00*	
Stock of Software	*90,050.00*		Closing Stock		2,35,550.00
Direct Incomes		15,000.00	*Stock of Hardware*	*1,45,500.00*	
Sale of Furniture	*15,000.00*		*Stock of Software*	*90,050.00*	
Direct Expenses		2,00,000.00	*Gross Loss c/o*		*15,000.00*
Labour Cgarges	*2,00,000.00*				
		4,50,550.00			4,50,550.00
Gross Loss b/f		*15,000.00*	*Nett Loss*		*15,000.00*
Total		15,000.00	Total		15,000.00

Fig 19-13: Profit & Loss Statement - Detailed

19.2.2 Profit & Loss Statement Configuration options

At Profit & Loss Statement (Fig 19-12 / 19-13), click *F12: Configure* to get Profit & Loss Statement Configuration screen (Fig 19-14).

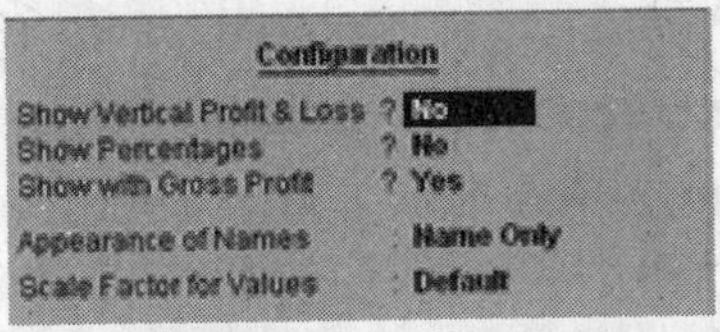

Fig 19-14: Profit & Loss Statement Configuration

Fig 19-15 : Buttons at P L Statement

19.2.3 Profit & Loss Statement – Vertical form

To show P L Statement in Vertical format (Income Heads first followed by the Expenses heads - Fig 19-16), set *Yes* at *Show Vertical Profit & Loss* at Configuration options (Fig 19-14).

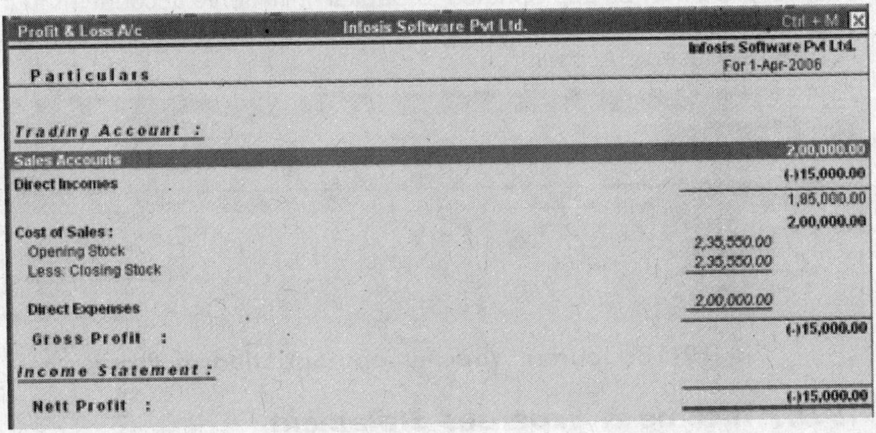

Fig 19-16: Profit & Loss Account – Vertical Format

19.2.4 Trading and Profit & Loss Account

To get the figures of Gross & Net Profit (popularly known as Trading & Profit Loss A/c), set *Yes* at *Show with Gross Profit* (Fig 19-14) at Configuration options.

Trading Account excludes *Indirect Income* and *Indirect Expenses* and computes *Gross Profit/Loss* reflecting the operational *Profit/Loss* of the organisation. In Profit & Loss Account (second part of the Report), *Gross Profit/Loss* is carried and *Indirect Income* and *Indirect Expenses* are taken into account to compute *Nett Profit/Loss* of the organization (Fig 19-13).

19.2.5 Profit & Loss Account with percentage figures

To get Profit & Loss Account with percentage figures (Fig 19-17), set *Yes* at *Show Percentage* at Profit & Loss Configuration options (Fig 19-14).

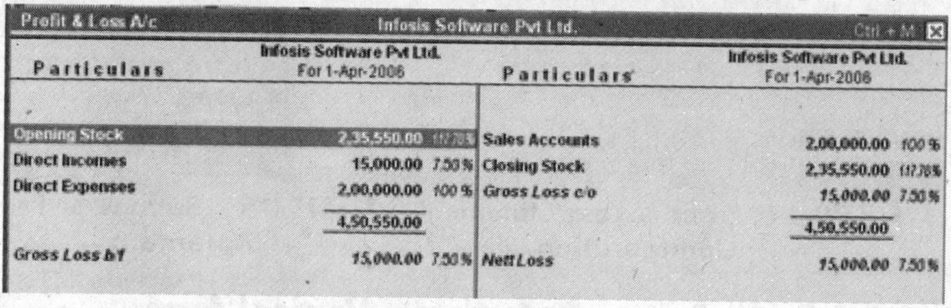

Fig 19-17: P L statement with percentage figure

19.2.6 Profit & Loss Appropriation

The Net profit may be appropriated to Capital or Reserve account through Journal Voucher. Fig 19-18 shows a typical JV to transfer from P L Account to Reserve Account.

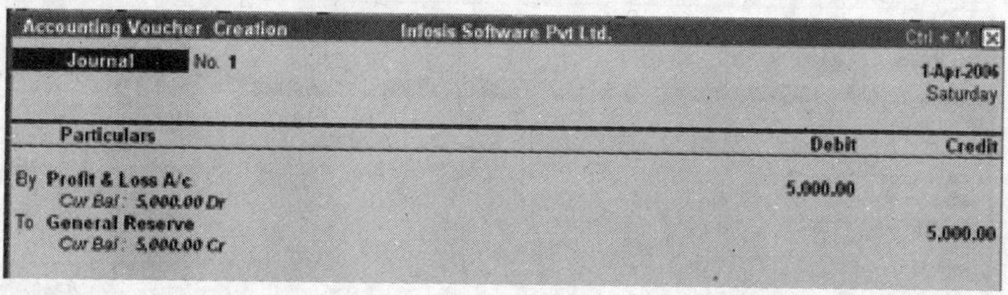

Fig 19-18: Journal Voucher appropriation of Profit

19.2.7 Income & Expenses Statement

To get Income & Expenditure Account (Fig 19-21) for Non-Profit Organisation (instead of Profit & Loss Account), click *F11: Features* button and set *Yes* at *Use Income/Expense Statement instead of P & L* (Fig 19-19)

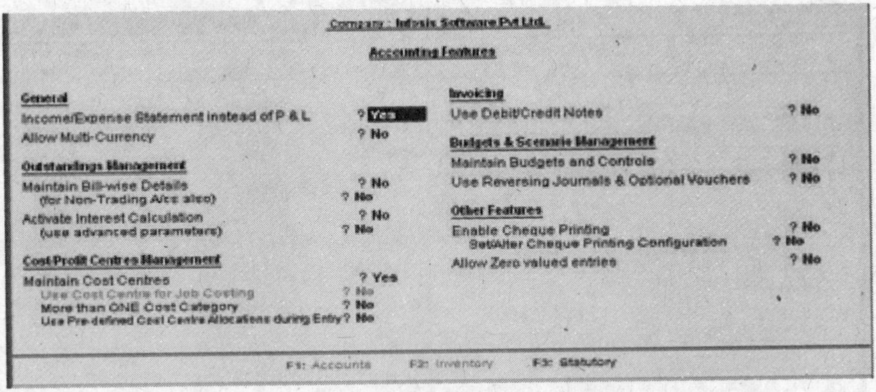

Fig 19-19: Income & Expenses Account set up option

Consequently, the menu option *Profit & Loss Accounts* changes to *Income & Expenses* Account (Fig 19-20).

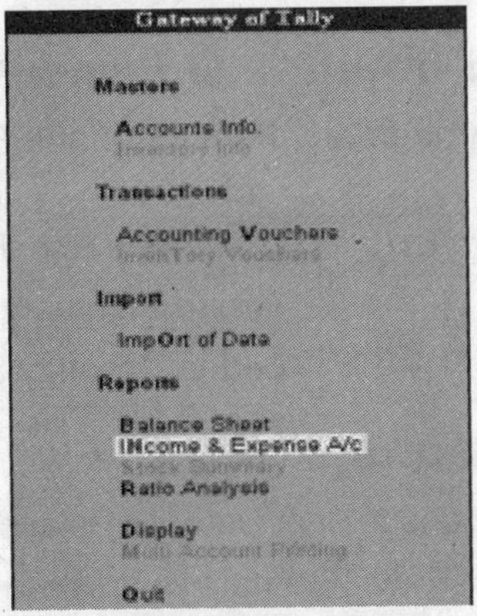

Fig 19-20: Income & Expenses Statement in Main Menu

The Name of the Report changes to *Income & Expenditure Statement* (Fig 19-21).The Profit is shown as Excess of Income over Expenditure & Loss is shown as Excess of Expenditure over Income (Fig 19-21).

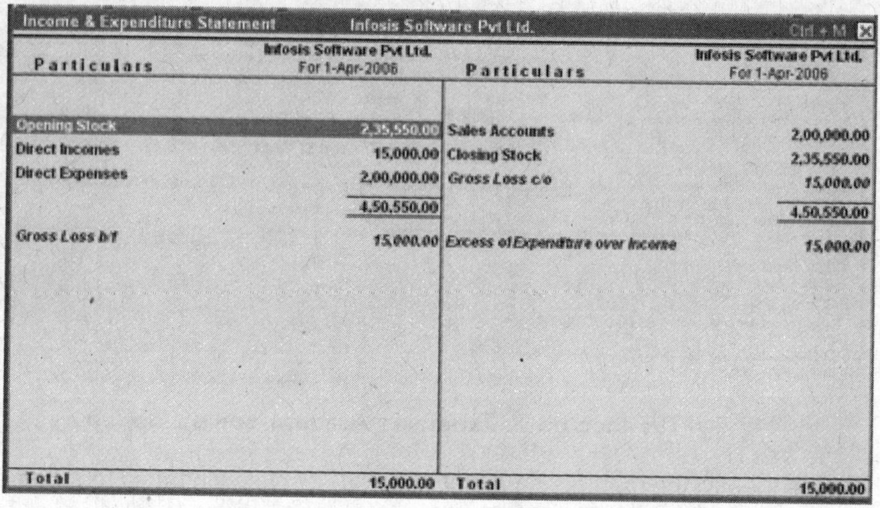

Fig 19-21 : Income & Expenditure Statement

19.2.8 Drill Down from P L Statement

When you drill down through any Item of default P L Statement, you get the reports as follows :

Item through which Drilled	*Next Level Report*
Account Group	Group Summary (Fig16-3)
Ledger Account	Ledger Monthly Summary (Fig 16-13)

Self Test Questions

STQ 19.1: Show the options to print Detailed Balance Sheet with % figures.

STQ 19.2: How to enter Raw Materials & Finished Stock Value as on 31-08-2006 through Balance Sheet.

Reports Printing

20

So far we have seen various accounting reports on screen and traversed reports at various levels. In this chapter, we explain how you may print these reports also on the Printer.

We also discuss Multi Account Reports printing. These are static reports and you cannot drill down through them. However, you may view the report on screen (to see how the printed report looks like) through *Print Preview* (Ref 20.4)

You may print Vouchers and various reports like Day Book, Registers, Final Accounts and Summary Reports in Dot Matrix, Inkjet or Laser Printers.

20.1 Printing from Display mode

In Display mode, you can print the current voucher / report you are viewing. Click the Print button (or press Alt+P) to get *Print Configuration* Screen (Fig 20-1).

20.2 Print Configuration Screen

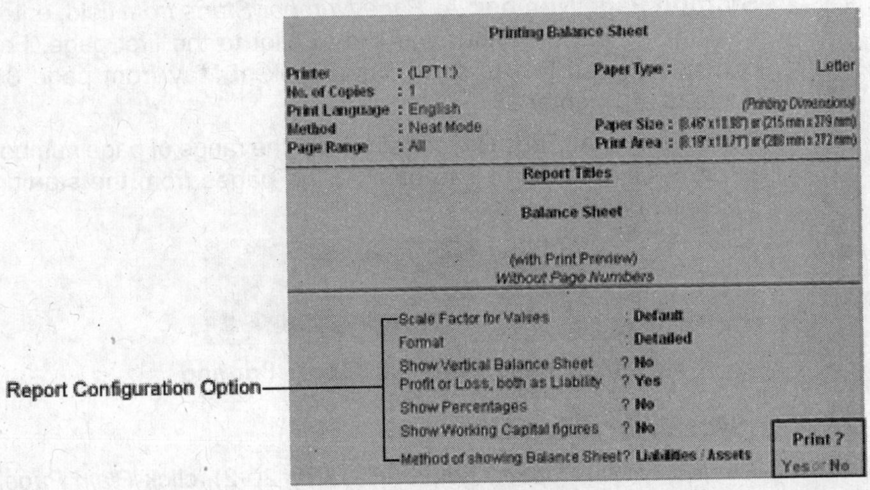

Fig 20-1: Printing Configuration screen

The Print configuration screen may be broadly split in 3 parts as shown in Fig 20-1.

- The Top part displays *Common Printing Information* about selected Printer, Paper Type, No. of Copies, Printing method, Printing Range, Paper Size and Print Area etc.
- The Middle part displays *Report Title* & related information
- The third part may display the Report specific configuration options.

20.3 Buttons at Printing screen

Fig 20-2 shows the buttons at Print Configuration screen (Fig 20-1) through which you may alter configuration settings of the current report, as explained next.

Fig 20-2: Buttons for Print Configuration screen

20.3.1 Page Filter

To print only specified pages of the report, click *Page No* button (Fig 20-2) and set the page filter to print specified pages of the report (Fig 20-3).

- **Starting Page Number**: At *Page Number Starts from* field, enter the starting page number you like to allot to the first page. For example, if you like to start Cash Book of May from page 35 (instead of 1), enter 35.
- **Page Range**: At *Page Range* field, enter the range of page number to print (else select ALL to print all the pages from the starting page number specified).

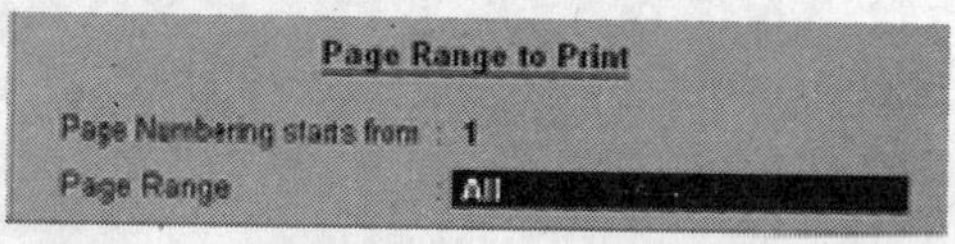

Fig 20-3: Page Filter at Report Printing

20.3.2 Stationery Type

At *Pre –Printed / Plain Paper* toggle button (Fig 20-2), click *Plain Paper* (to print with heading), else select *Pre-printed* to print on pre-printed stationery (headings not printed)

20.3.3 Print Format

Click *Print Format* button (Fig 20-2) and set as follows:

Print Mode

At *Print Mode* field (Fig 20-4/ 20-5), select from the following options.

- **Non Impact Printer**: Select *Neat Mode* (the report looks better but printing is slow in Dot Matrix Printer) for Non Impact printer (like Ink Jet / Laser printer) as shown in Fig 20-5.
- **Dot Matrix Printer**: Select *Dot Matrix Format* to print in Dot Matrix Printer. Further select the Printer Driver (Epson FX 80 / Epson LQ 850 compatible) as shown in Fig 20-4.
- **Saving On Media**: Select Quick / Draft (Fig 20-8) Format to save report data in any media (Ref 20.3.6)

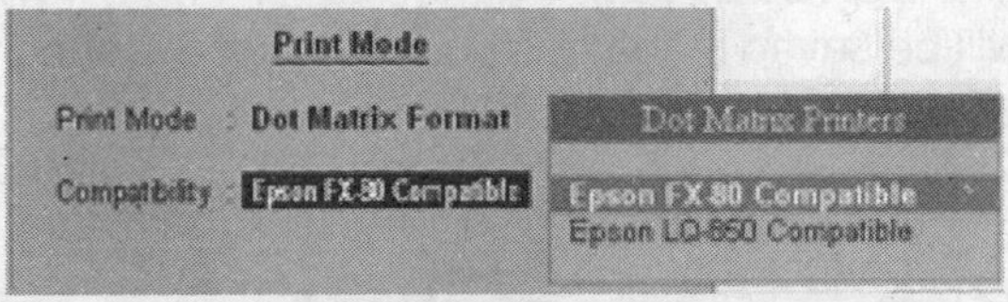

Fig 20-4: Dot Matrix Printer Driver selection

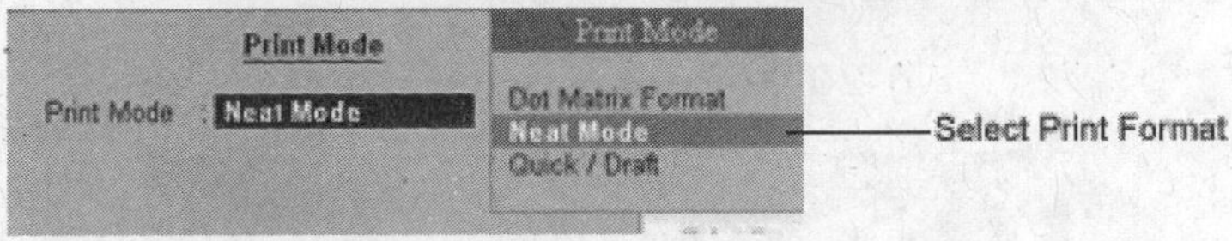

Fig 20-5: Selection of Print Format

20.3.4 Multiple Copies

To print multiple copies, click *Copies* button (Fig 20-2) and enter the number of copies (Fig 20-6).

Fig 20-6: Number of Copies option

20.3.5 Printer Selection

If more than one printer is installed in your system, click *Select Printer* (Fig 20-7) button to switch to another printer (or to save data in disk) and specify the following:

- **Print to a file**: At *Print to a File* prompt, set N (for No) to print the report on paper (this appears when you have selected *Quick / Draft Mode* in Print Format – Ref Fig 20-8)
- **Printer Name**: At *Printer Name* prompt, select the Printer from the list of installed printer (Fig 20-7).

20.3.6 Saving Report on Media

To save the report on any Media (if you have selected *Quick/ Draft* at Print Format – Ref 20.3.3), click *Select Printer* button (Fig 20-2) and then specify as follows :

- **Print to a file**: Set *Y* (for Yes) to save the Report on media (Fig 20-7)
- **File Name**: Tally proposes a filename depending on the selected report (like BSHEET.PRN). Change the filename if you like to. The report will be saved in the designated file at the specified directory (Fig 20-7)

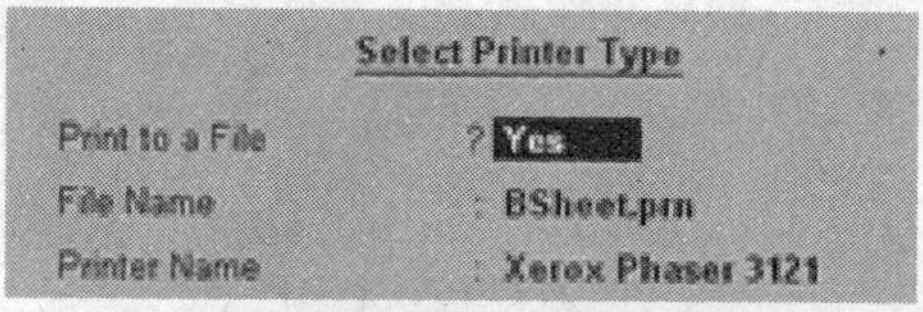

Fig 20-7: Printer Selection

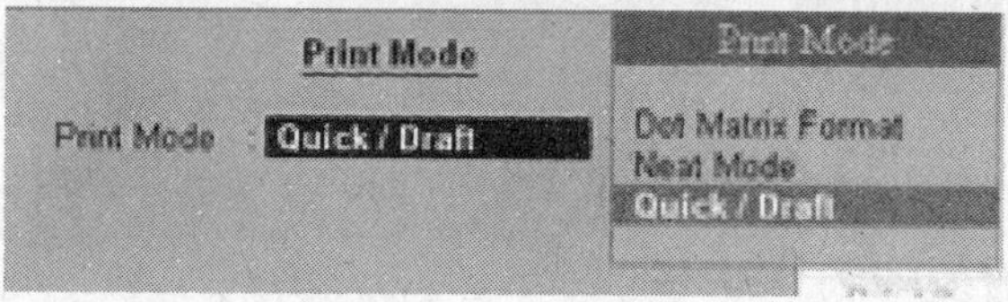

Fig 20-8: Saving Report in a file

20.3.7 Report Title

The Middle part displays *Report Title* and related Information.

To change report title or any option in Report Title, click *Titling* button (Fig 20-2) to specify Title, Sub-title and set other report printing options as follows (Fig 20-9).

- **Title**: Tally proposes a Report Title. Change it if you like.
- **Sub-Title**: You may enter a Sub-Title for the report (to print under the Title in first page only).
- **Additional Information**: Set *Yes / No* at the respective options (Fig 20-9), as required.

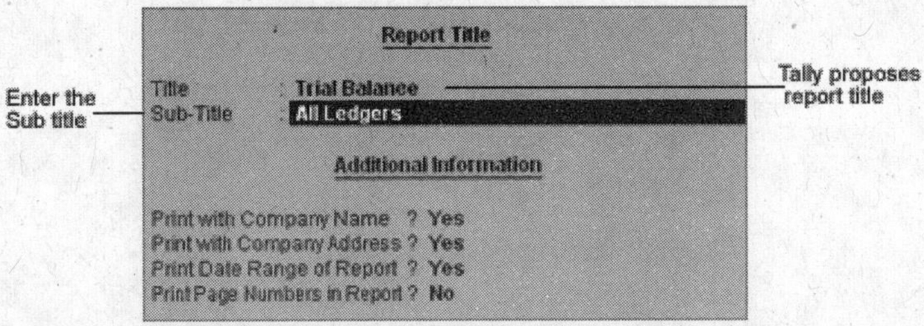

Fig 20-9: Report Title & other Report options set up

Fig 20-10 shows the first page of the Report Title and Fig 20-11 shows the Report Title of subsequent pages. The Company Address and Report Sub Title in printed only on the first page of the Report (Fig 20-10).

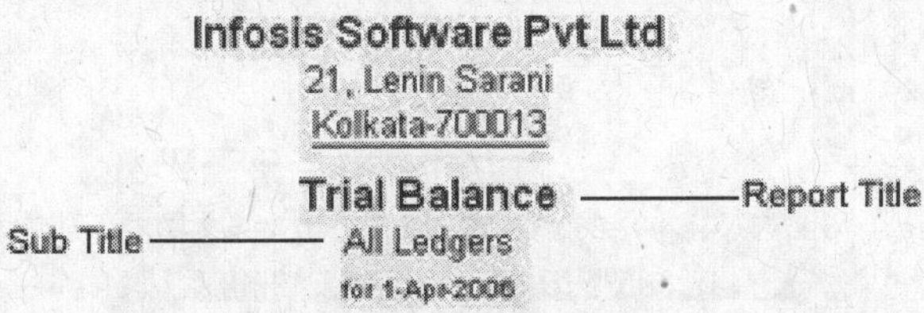

Fig 20-10: Report Title in first page

Fig 20-11: Report Title in subsequent pages

20.4 Report Preview on screen

In *Neat* Mode (Ref 20.3.3), you may click *Print Preview* button (Fig 20-2) to see how the report (Fig 20-12) will look like when printed.

At Print Preview screen (Fig 20-12), click *Zoom* button to expand the report in full size (Fig 20-13).

Use **PgUp, PgDn**, *(also PgRight, PgLeft)* **Home** and **End** buttons (Fig 20-12) to pan through long / wide or multi-page report.

Click *In Inches / In MMs* toggle button (Fig 20-12) to toggle the top and left ruler into Inches / mm scale. This helps you to estimate the page length and width of the actual report area.

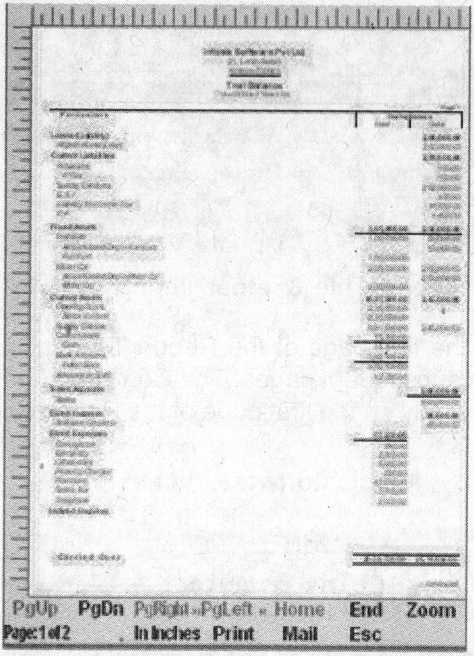

Fig 20-12: Print Preview (reduced size)

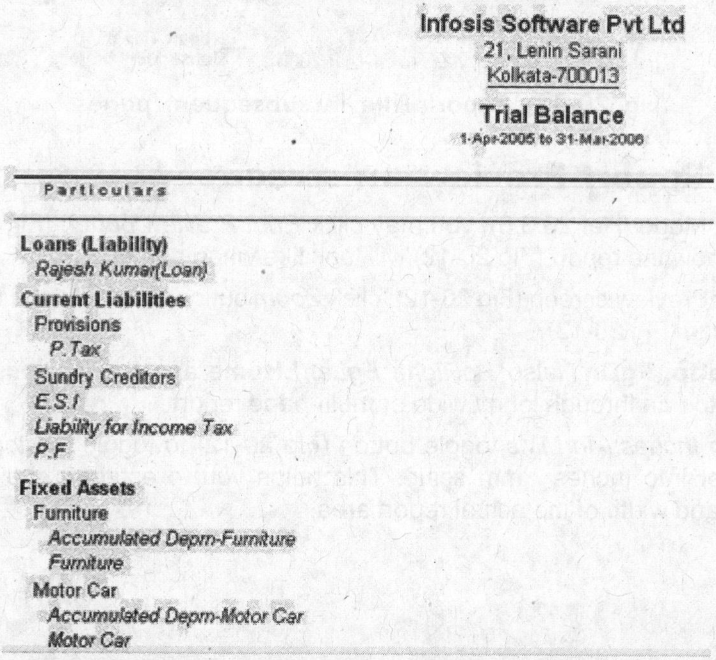

Infosis Software Pvt Ltd
21, Lenin Sarani
Kolkata-700013

Trial Balance
1-Apr-2005 to 31-Mar-2006

Particulars

Loans (Liability)
Rajesh Kumar(Loan)
Current Liabilities
Provisions
P.Tax
Sundry Creditors
E.S.I
Liability for Income Tax
P.F
Fixed Assets
Furniture
Accumulated Deprn-Furniture
Furniture
Motor Car
Accumulated Deprn-Motor Car
Motor Car

Fig 20-13: Expanded view of Print Preview through Zoom button

Self Test Questions

General Questions

STQ 20.1: You have printed the Cash Book for April 2006, the last page number being 21. Now you want to print the May 2006 Cash Book and start the page number as 22. Explain the options.

STQ 20.2: After printing unto page 45, the printer stopped. Now you like to print the rest of the cash book for the month, starting from page # 46. Explain the options

STQ 20.3: Explain the options to save a report on disk file.

Multi Account Reports Printing 21

Apart from Display, you may print few types of Static Reports (no drill down possible) through Multi Account Print option, useful to print multiple Items at a time.

In this chapter we discuss about the general features and printing options of Multi Account printing.

21.1 Multi Account Printing Menu

Select *Multi Account Printing* from Tally Main Menu (Fig 2.7) to get Multi Account Printing Menu (Fig 21-1).

Select the appropriate menu option and finally select the desired report to be printed from the menu.

Fig 21-1: Multi Account Printing Menu

21.2 Multi Account Print Configuration

Having selected the report, the Print Configuration screen appears showing the prompt *Print? Yes or No* (Fig 21-2).

- **Printing with currently set Configuration**: Type *Y* to print the report as per currently set configuration options.
- **Changing the Configuration options**: To change the configuration option, type *No*. Now change the desired option as discussed in Chapter 20, press Ctrl+A to save the changed option and then type Y to print the report.

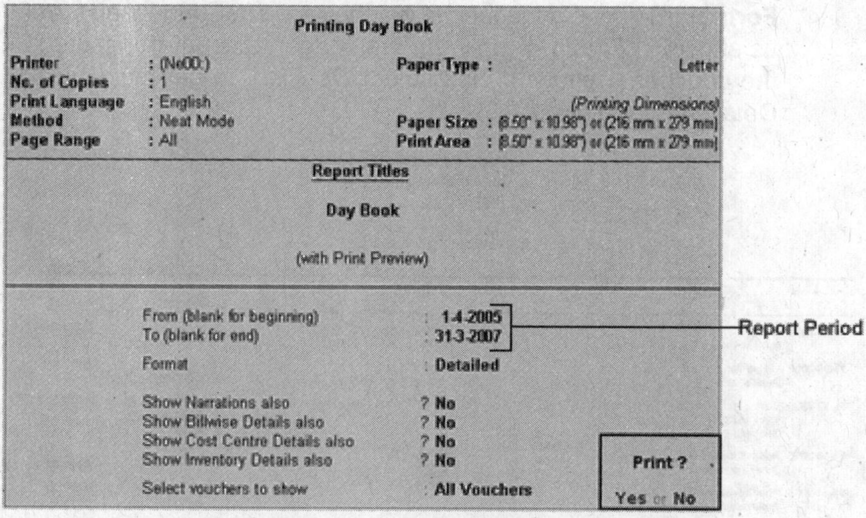

Fig 21-2: Multi Account Day Book Print Dialogue

All report buttons work in the same way as discussed in Chapter 20 (Ref 20.4).

21.3 Multi Account Day Book

Select Multi Account Printing > Day Book to print Day Book showing list of Vouchers.

Set the respective options (Fig 21-3) to print the Day Book (21-4).

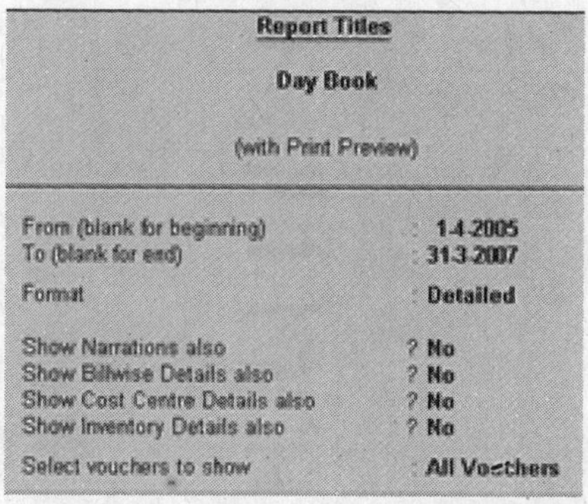

Fig 21-3: Multi Account Day Book printing Options

- **Report Period**: Enter the period at *From* & *To* fields for which you like to print the report. Leave blank to print from beginning to the end of Current Period set.

- **Format :** Select *Condensed* to get the report in Condensed format as shown in Fig 21-4 (only the first ledger account transacted in the voucher is shown), else select *Detailed* to get the report in Detailed format (Fig 21-5).

Agni Computers
21, Lenin Sarani
Kolkata-700013

Day Book
1-Apr-2006 to 31-Mar-2007

Page 1

Date	Particulars	Vch Type	Vch No.	Debit Amount	Credit Amount
31-10-2006	Cash	Contra	1		7,000.00
	Bank of India			7,000.00	
31-10-2006	Vijaya Bank	Contra	2		15,000.00
	Bank of India			15,000.00	
31-10-2006	Cash	Contra	3		7,000.00
	Bank of India			3,000.00	
	Bank of Baroda			4,000.00	
31-10-2006	Aditya Enterprise	Sales	1	8,000.00	
	Sales Account				8,000.00
31-10-2006	Abc Computers Ltd.	Purchase	1		9,000.00
	Purchase Account			9,000.00	

Fig: 21-4 Multi Account Day Book (Condensed Format)

Agni Computers
21, Lenin Sarani
Kolkata-700013

Day Book
1-Apr-2005 to 31-Mar-2007

Page 1

Date	Particulars	Vch Type	Vch No.	Debit Amount Inwards Qty	Credit Amount Outwards Qty
1-4-2005	Salary to Krishnan	Payment	1	6,000.00	
	Indian Bank				5,300.00
	PF				600.00
	P.Tax				50.00
	Esi				50.00
1-4-2005	Salary to Sunil	Payment	2	8,000.00	
	Indian Bank				7,100.00
	PF				800.00
	Esi				50.00
	P.Tax				50.00
1-4-2005	*(cancelled)*	Payment	3		
1-4-2005	Conveyance	Payment	4	850.00	
	Cash				850.00
1-4-2005	Electricity	Payment	5	2,500.00	
	Indian Bank				2,500.00
1-4-2005	Office Rent	Payment	6	5,000.00	
	Indian Bank				5,000.00
1-4-2005	Salary to Sweeper	Payment	7	300.00	
	Cash				300.00
1-4-2005	Telephone	Payment	8	2,000.00	
	Indian Bank				2,000.00
1-4-2005	M/s Raj Enterprise	Receipt	1		50,000.00
	Cash			50,000.00	

Fig 21-5: Multi Account Day Book (Detailed Format)

At Multi Account Day Book Print Dialogue (Fig 21-3), set Yes at *Show Narrations also* to print Voucher Narrations also in Day Book.

Agni Computers
21, Lenin Sarani
Kolkata-700013

Day Book
1-Apr-2005 to 31-Mar-2007

Page 1

Date	Particulars	Vch Type	Vch No.	Debit Amount Inwards Qty	Credit Amount Outwards Qty
1-4-2005	**Salary to Krishnan**	Payment	1	6,000.00	
	Indian Bank				5,300.00
	PF				600.00
	P.Tax				50.00
	Esi				50.00
	Ch. No. :999994 salary paid to Krishnan.				
1-4-2005	**Salary to Sunil**	Payment	2	8,000.00	
	Indian Bank				7,100.00
	PF				800.00
	Esi				50.00
	P.Tax				50.00
	Ch. No. : 999993 salary paid to sunil.				
1-4-2005	(cancelled)	Payment	3		
	Ch. No. : 999994 salary paid to Shikanth.				
1-4-2005	**Conveyance**	Payment	4	850.00	
	Cash				850.00
	conveyance expenses for client visits and go the income tax office for some tax related matters.				
1-4-2005	**Electricity**	Payment	5	2,500.00	
	Indian Bank				2,500.00
	Ch. No. :999995 paid for electricity for the month of March.				

Fig 21-6:Multi Account Day Book (with Narration)

21.4 Multi Account Books

At Multi Account Printing menu (Fig 21-1), select Account Books to get Multi Account Books printing menu (Fig 21-7) for printing of Multi Accounts Books like Cash Book, Bank Book, Ledger, Sales, Purchase, Journal as discussed next.

Fig 21-7: Multi Account Printing menu for Account Books

21.4.1 Multi Account Journal Register

At Account Books Printing menu (Fig 21-7), select *Journal Register* to get Journal printing dialogue (Fig 21-8) for printing of Journal Register (Fig 21-9).

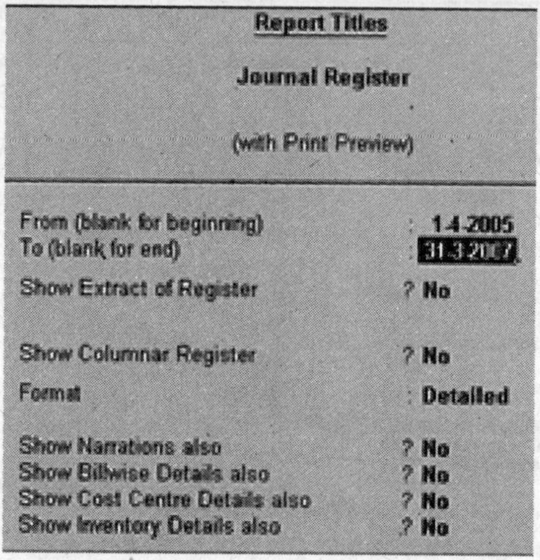

Fig 21-8: Multi Account Journal Register Configuration

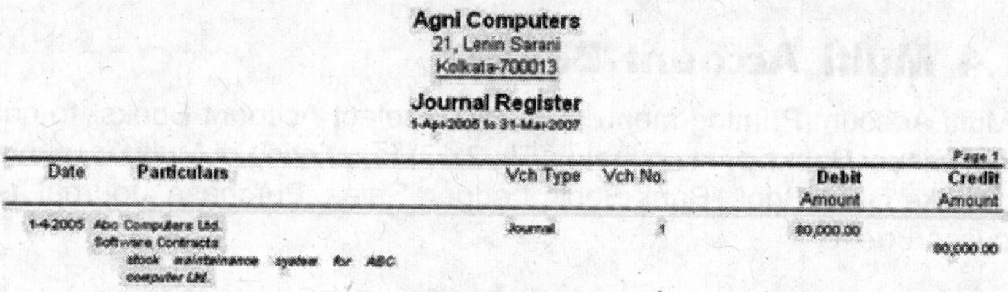

Agni Computers
21, Lenin Sarani
Kolkata-700013

Journal Register
1-Apr-2005 to 31-Mar-2007

Page 1

Date	Particulars	Vch Type	Vch No.	Debit Amount	Credit Amount
1-4-2005	Abc Computers Ltd.	Journal	1	80,000.00	
	Software Contracts				80,000.00
	stock maintainance system for ABC computer Ltd.				

Fig 21-9: Multi Account Journal Register (Detailed Format – with Narration)

21.4.2 Multi Account Cash Books

At Multi Account Books Printing menu (Fig 21-7), select Cash Book(s) to get Cash Book printing options (Fig 21-10). Select the Cash Account to print the Cash Book (like Fig 21-11).

Report Titles

Cash Book

(with Print Preview)

From (blank for beginning)	: **1-4-2005**
To (blank for end)	: **31-3-2007**
Style of Report	: **Normal Ledger**
Select vouchers to show	: **All Vouchers**
Format	: **Detailed**
Show Billwise Details also	? **No**
Show Cost Centre Details also	? **No**
Show Inventory Details also	? **No**
Show Narrations also	? **No**
Include Opening Balances *(set as 'no' to remove from filtered reports)*	? **Yes**
Method of Balancing	: **Monthly**
Start fresh page for each Account	? **Yes**

Fig 21-10: Cash / Bank Book printing options

21.4.3 Multi Bank Book(s)

At *Account Books Printing* menu (Fig 21-7), select the Bank Account to get Bank Book printing options (similar to Cash Book printing options - Fig 21-10). Fig 21-11 shows a sample Cash / Bank Book.

Agni Computers
21, Lenin Sarani
Kolkata-700013

Cash Book
1-Apr-2005 to 31-Mar-2007

Page 1

Date	Particulars	Vch Type	Vch No.	Debit	Credit
1-4-2005	To **Opening Balance**			**17,850.00**	
1-4-2005	To **M/s Raj Enterprise**	Receipt	1	50,000.00	
	To **Bt Software Education**	Receipt	3	25,000.00	
	By **Conveyance**	Payment	4		850.00
	By **Salary to Sweeper**	Payment	7		300.00
2-4-2005	By **A.K Shina**	Payment	9		10,000.00
	By **Abc Computers Ltd.**	Payment	10		5,000.00
4-4-2005	By **Bt Software Education**	Payment	11		5,000.00
	By **A.K Shina**	Payment	12		6,000.00
				92,850.00	27,150.00
	By **Closing Balance**				65,700.00
				92,850.00	**92,850.00**
1-4-2006	To **Opening Balance**			**65,700.00**	
1-4-2006	To **Indian Bank**	Contra	1	10,000.00	
				75,700.00	
	By **Closing Balance**				75,700.00
				75,700.00	**75,700.00**

Fig 21-11: Cash / Bank Book

21.4.4 Multi-Column Cash/Bank Book

Multi Column Cash / Bank book shows a separate column for each selected cash / bank account showing the details of opening balances, transactions & closing balances.

At Multi *Account Books Printing* menu (Fig 21-7), select Multi-Column Cash/Bank to get Multi column Cash Bank Book printing options (21-12) to print a multi columnar Cash / Bank Book for several Cash Bank Accounts (Fig 21-13).

At Multi Column Cash Bank Book print dialogue (Fig 21-12), select the Cash / Bank ledger accounts for each Cash / Bank column (Maximum 3).

Report Titles

Multi Column Cash/Bank Book

(with Print Preview)

From (blank for beginning)	:	**1-4-2005**
To (blank for end)	:	**31-3-2007**
Cash/Bank A/c for 1st Column	:	**Indian Bank**
for 2nd Column	:	**Bank of India**
for 3rd Column	:	**Cash**
Format	:	**Detailed**
Show Billwise Details also	?	**No**
Show Cost Centre Details also	?	**No**
Show Inventory Details also	?	**No**
Show Narrations also	?	**No**

Fig 21-12: Multi Column Cash Book configuration Options

Agni Computers
21, Lenin Sarani
Kolkata-700013

Multi Column Cash/Bank Book
1-Apr-2005 to 31-Mar-2007

Page 1

Date	Particulars	Voucher Type	Number	Indian Bank Dr	Bank of India Dr	Cash Dr	Date	Particulars	Voucher Type	Number	Indian Bank Cr	Bank of India Cr	Cash Cr
1-Apr-2005	To Opening Balance			50,000.00	2,10,000.00	17,850.00							
1-Apr-2005	To M/s Raj Enterprise	Rcpt	1			50,000.00	1-Apr-2005	By (as per details)	Pymt	1	5,300.00		
1-Apr-2005	To Gayatri Software	Rcpt	2	1,35,000.00				Salary to Krishnan [illegible] Dr					
1-Apr-2005	To Bit Software Education	Rcpt	3			25,000.00		PF 800.00 Cr					
1-Apr-2005	To Abc Computers Ltd.	Rcpt	4	50,000.00				P.Tax 50.00 Cr					
1-Apr-2005	To Servo Ltd.	Rcpt	5	60,000.00				Esi 50.00 Cr					
1-Apr-2005	To Bit Software Education	Rcpt	6	30,000.00			1-Apr-2005	By (as per details)	Pymt	2	7,100.00		
1-Apr-2005	To Devan Contractors	Rcpt	7	50,000.00				Salary to Sunil [illegible] Dr					
1-Apr-2005	To Motor Car	Rcpt	8	45,000.00				PF 800.00 Cr					
1-Apr-2005	To Abc Computers Ltd.	Rcpt	9	2,000.00				Esi 50.00 Cr					
1-Apr-2005	To Abc Computers Ltd.	Rcpt	10	2,000.00				P.Tax 50.00 Cr					
							1-Apr-2005	By Conveyance	Pymt	4			850.00
							1-Apr-2005	By Electricity	Pymt	5	2,500.00		
							1-Apr-2005	By Office Rent	Pymt	6	5,000.00		
							1-Apr-2005	By Salary to Sweeper	Pymt	7			300.00
							1-Apr-2005	By Telephone	Pymt	8	2,000.00		
							1-Apr-2005	By A.K Shina	Pymt	9			10,000.00
							1-Apr-2005	By Abc Computers Ltd.	Pymt	10			5,000.00
							1-Apr-2005	By Bit Software Education	Pymt	11			5,000.00
							1-Apr-2005	By A.K Shina	Pymt	12			6,000.00
1-Apr-2005	To Indian Bank	Ctra	1			10,000.00	1-Apr-2005	By Cash	Ctra	1	10,000.00		
					2,10,000.00								
	To							By Closing Balance			3,92,100.00	2,10,000.00	
					2,10,000.00							2,10,000.00	

Fig 21-13: Multi Column Cash / Bank Book

21.4.5 Multi Ledger printing

At Account Books Printing menu (Fig 21-7), select Ledger to get Multi Ledger printing menu (Fig 21-14).

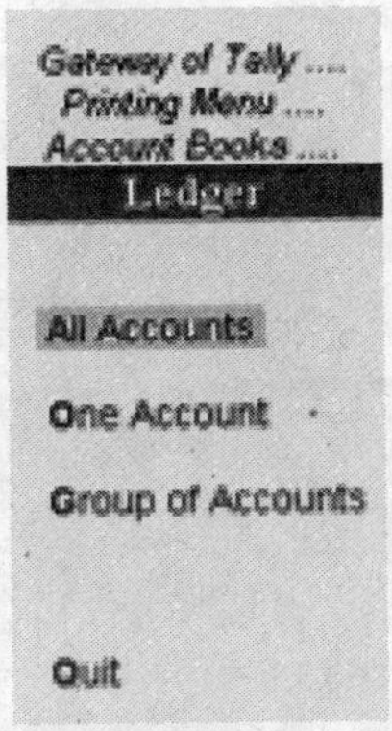

Fig 21-14: Multi Ledger printing Menu

At Multi Ledger printing menu (Fig 21-14), select the desired option as follows to get Multi Ledger Printing configuration option screen (Fig 21-16).

- **All Ledgers**: Select *All Accounts* to print all Ledger Accounts.
- **One Ledger Account**: Select *One Account* and then select the Ledger Account to be printed from the list of Ledger Accounts.
- **All Ledgers of an Account Group**: Select *Group of Accounts* to print all Ledgers placed under one Account Group.

At Style of Report, select Normal ledger to print Ledger Book (Fig 21-15):

Agni Computers
21, Lenin Sarani
Kolkata-700013

Aditya Enterprise

Ledger Account
1-Apr-2005 to 1-Feb-2006

Page 1

Date		Particulars	Vch Type	Vch No.	Debit	Credit
1-4-2005	By	**Purchase**	Purchase	1		28,000.00
	By	**Purchase**	Purchase	3		7,900.00
						35,900.00
	To	**Closing Balance**			35,900.00	
					35,900.00	**35,900.00**

Fig 21-15: Ledger Book

21.4.6 Confirmation of Accounts

To print Confirmation of Accounts (Fig 21-17), select *Confirmation of Accounts* at Style of Report field (Fig 21-16) at Multi Ledger Printing Configuration screen.

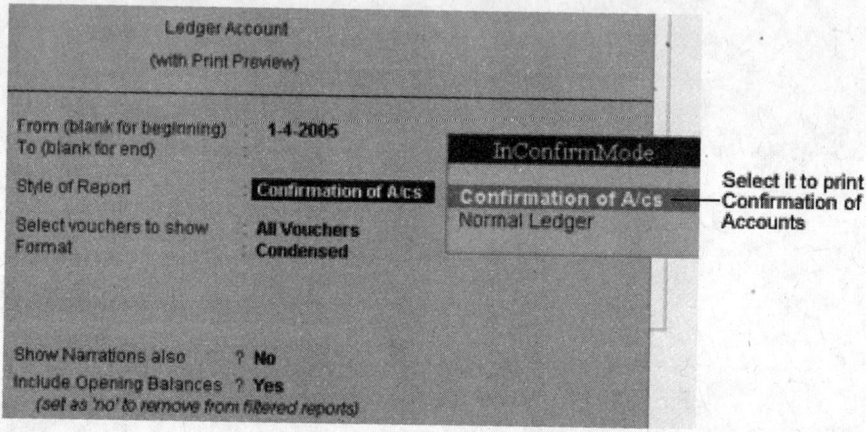

Fig 21-16: Option for Multi ledger printing

To : **Arun Kumar Sinha**
12 A. J. C. Bose Road
Kolkata 700135

From : **Agni Computers**
21, Lenin Sarani
Kolkata-700013

Dear Sir/Madam,

Dated : **1-Apr-2007**

Sub : Confirmation of Accounts
1-Apr-2005 to 31-Mar-2007

Given below is the details of your Accounts as standing in my/our Books of Accounts for the above mentioned period.

Kindly return 3 copies stating your I.T. Permanent A/c No., duly signed and sealed, in confirmation of the same. Please note that if no reply is received from you within a fortnight, it will be assumed that you have accepted the balance shown below.

Date	Particulars	Debit Amount	Date	Particulars	Credit Amount
1-May-2006	Cash *Loan given*	30,000.00			
31-Oct-2005	Interest Received on Loan	229.00	31-Oct-2006	Cash *received from Arun kumar sinha*	25,000.00
		30,229.00			25,000.00
				Closing Balance	5,229.00
		30,229.00			30,229.00

I/We hereby confirm the above

Yours faithfully,

I.T. PAN No. : S4F5J78K5Q

Our I.T. PAN No. : a323456L

Fig 21-17: Confirmation of Accounts

Self Test Questions

STQ 21.1: Explain the options to print Multi Column Cash Bank Book (One Cash Account, One Bank Account & One Bank OCC Account), for a specified period (in Detailed format)

STQ 21.2: Explain the options to print all Customer Ledger Accounts

STQ 21.3: Explain the options to print Confirmation of Accounts for all ledgers under the Group Unsecured Loans.

Data Maintenance

22

In this Chapter we discuss about Housekeeping chores like Backup, Restore, New Year Books etc.

22.1 Backup

Backup means keeping a copy of working data at another place for safety.

Select *Backup* from Company Info menu (Ref Fig 7.2) to get Backup screen (Fig 22-1).

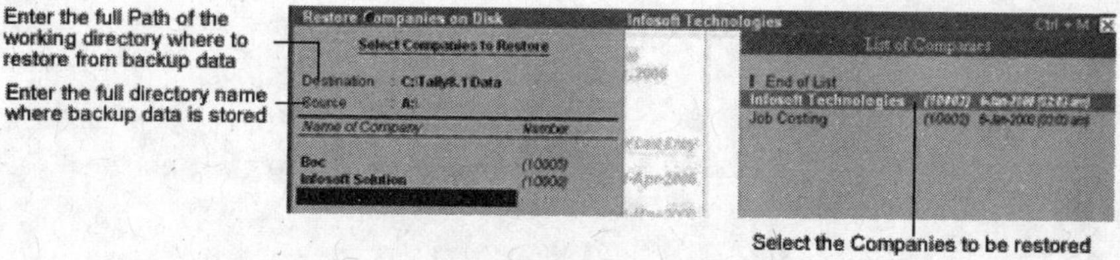

Fig 22-1: Backup screen

22.1.1 Back Up Data Source

At *Source* field in Back Up screen (Fig 22-1), enter the full directory name where the Company data is stored (Tally proposes the folder name of currently selected Company - press Backspace to get back to this field and change if necessary), as demonstrated in Fig 22-2 to 22-4.

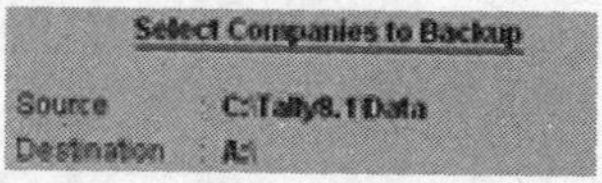

Fig 22-2: Default Source pathname

Fig 22-3: Change of Source pathname

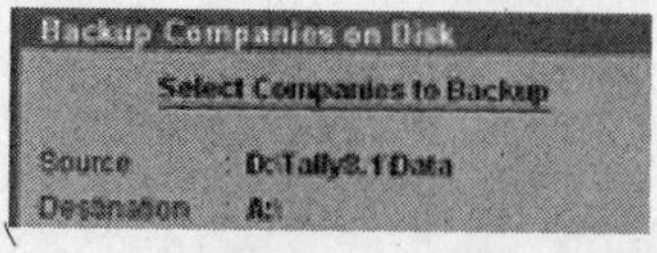

Fig 22-4: Changed Source pathname

22.1.2 Back Up Data Destination

At *Destination* field in Back Up screen (Fig 22-5), enter the full directory name where you like to keep the Back Up data (normally A: to back up in floppy disk – Fig 22-1). You may also specify a network drive name.

Fig 22-5: Changed Destination Drive

22.1.3 Back Up Company Names

At *Name of Company* field in Back Up screen (Fig 22-1), select the Company (Fig 22-6) to be backed up. You may select several companies one by one. Press *End of List* to terminate selection of Company (it is recommended to take back up of one company at a time).

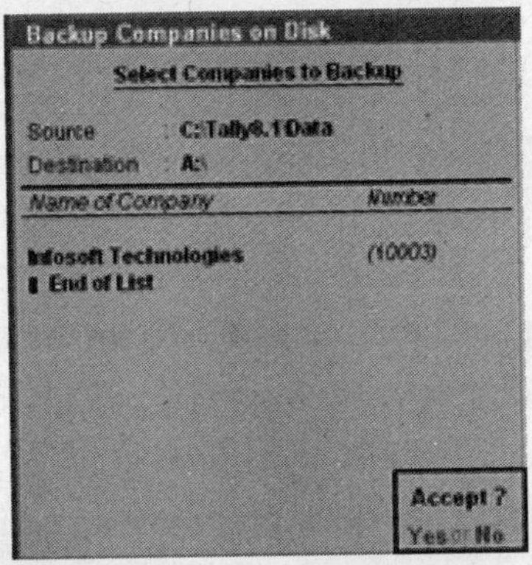

Fig 22-6: Selection of Company for Back Up

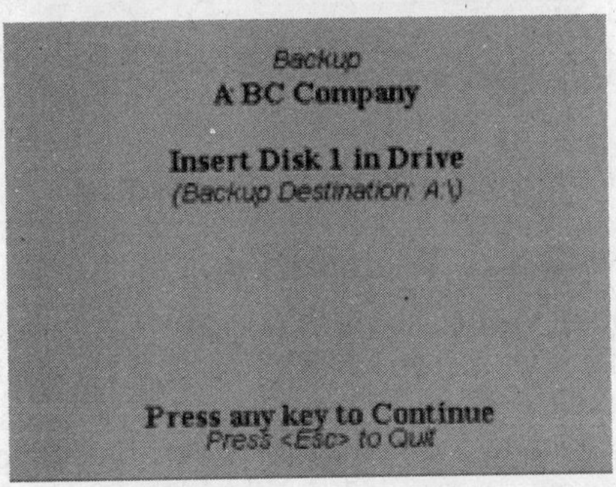

Fig 22-7: Back Up Process message

Click *Yes* to start Back up (Fig 22-6). Follow the messages shown by Tally for the back Up process (Fig 22-7).

22.1.4 Back Up Files

After the Back Up process, you always get the Backed up file named tbk900.001 file in the destination drive, irrespective of which or how many companies you back up (Fig 22-8 / Fig 22-9). So, from the Back Up filename, you will not be able to distinguish the Company Names backed up.

If you take Back Up of one company and then another company at the same destination, the earlier back up will be overwritten as Tally always creates Back Up with same file name.

Fig 22-8: Single Company Back Up file

Fig 22-9: Multi Company Back up file

22.2 Restore

Restore means getting back the backed up data for working.

Select **Restore** from Company Info Menu (Fig 7-13) to get Restore screen (Fig 22-10).

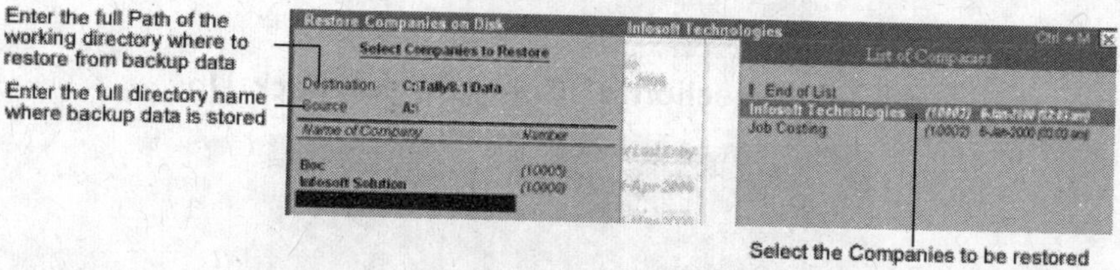

Fig 22-10: Data Restoration

22.2.1 Restore Data Destination

At *Destination* field of Restore screen (Fig 22-10), enter the full name of the working directory where you like to restore Backed Up data (Tally proposes the data folder name of the currently selected company- press Shift+Tab or Backspace to get back to this field and change if necessary).

22.2.2 Restore Data Source

At *Source* field of Restore screen, enter the full directory name (Fig 22-10) from where the Company data is to be restored (normally A: to restore from floppy disk).

22.2.3 Restore Company Names

The companies available at Directory specified at source field (22-10) are listed. Select the Companies to be restored (Fig 22-11).

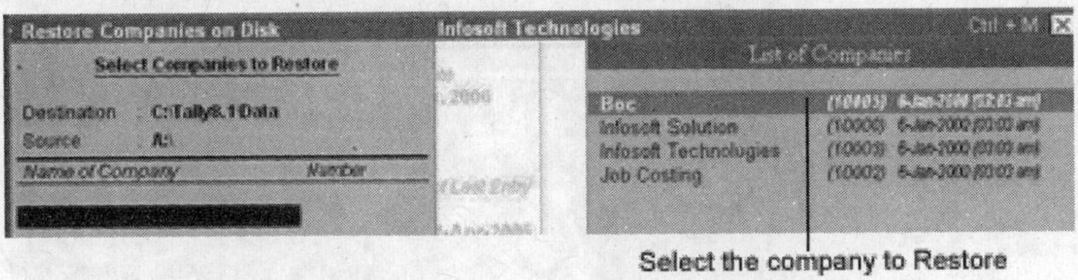

Fig 22-11: Selection of Company to Restore

Click *Yes* to start Restoration (Fig 22-12).

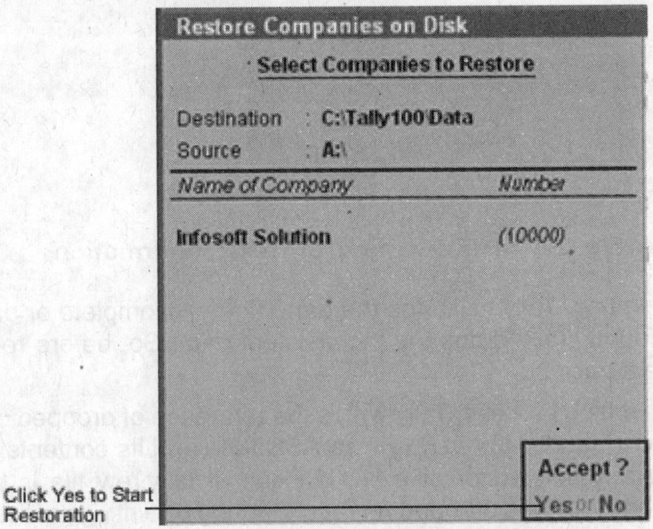

Fig 22-12: Confirmation for Restoration

22.3 Rewriting

Sometimes, the data may get damaged and Tally cannot open a Company. In such case, you have to repair the data (called re-writing). You may also need to re-write when you open a company created with earlier version of Tally.

To re-write data of a company, press Ctrl+Alt+R at Gateway and select the Company you wish to re-write (Fig 22-13). A confirmation will be sought for re-writing (Fig 22-14). Press *Y* to re-write the data (Fig 22-14).

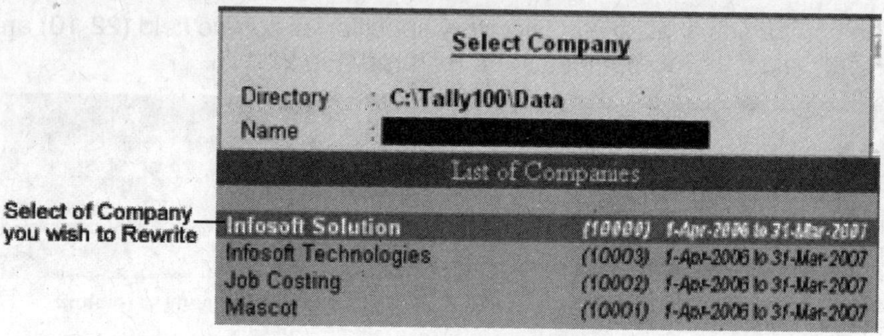

Fig 22-13: Selection of Company to re-write

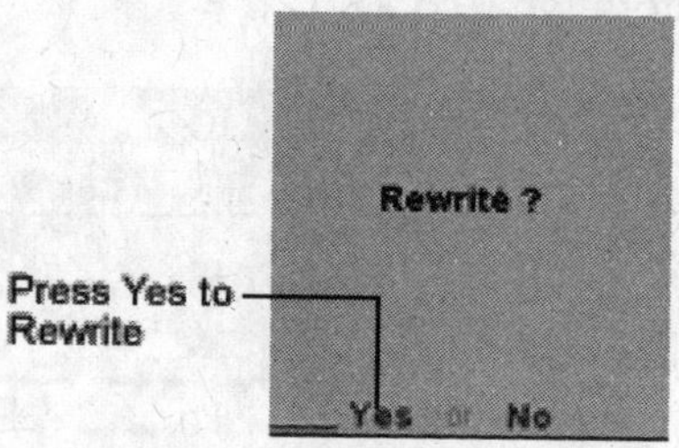

Fig 22-14: Re-writing process confirmation

During re-writing, Tally validates the data. If any incomplete or damaged record is found, Tally drops the inconsistent data. So, before re-writing, better take a back up.

During Re-writing process, Tally writes the reference of dropped data in a file *tally.rew* (Fig 22-15). *Tally.rew* an ASCII file and its contents may be viewed by any text editor (like NOTEPAD). If tally.rew file is blank, it indicates that Tally has dropped no record during re-writing process.

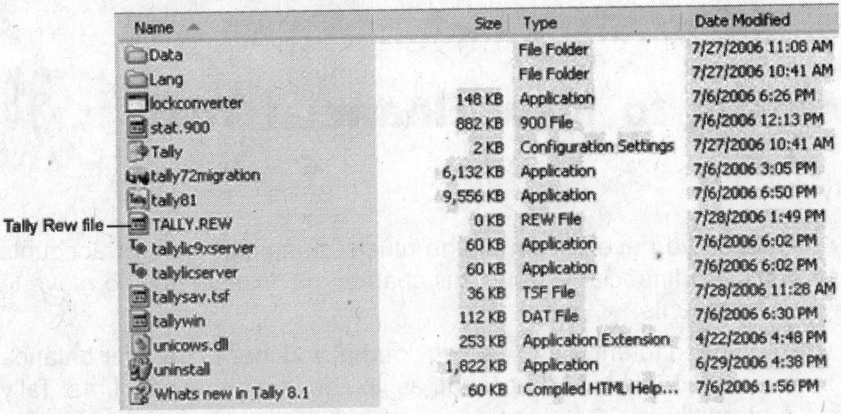

Fig 22-15: Tally.rew file created on re-writing of data

Fig 22-15 shows tally.rew file created in the Tally folder (Ref 1.3).

Self Test Questions

STQ 22.1: Explain how to keep Back Up of a company data at C:\tallybackup\ directory.

STQ 22.2: What is the Back Up filename created by Tally

STQ 22.3: Explain how you can Restore data from C:\tallybackup\ directory to Tally\data directory.

STQ 22.4: Currently there are 3 Company data (Company # 1,2 & 3) at c:\tally\data. You restore data of a Company from C:\tallybackup\data directory (which contains back of Company # 5) to the working directory c:\tally\data. Now what would be Company Number of the restored company?

STQ 22.5: What is Re-writing of Data? Why do you need to re-write. Explain the step of Re-writing.

Moving to New Financial Year 23

By this time, we have shown all the rituals of maintenance of accounts for a complete financial year. In this chapter, we explain how to move to new year accounts.

You do not need to enter any closing Journal voucher to transfer balance of revenue accounts to P L Account, as you do in manual accounts. Tally does it internally.

23.1 Appropriation of Profit

At year-end, you may enter a Journal voucher to appropriate the Profit (Fig 23-1) to Ledgers under Capital Accounts group (or sub-groups like Reserves & Surplus). You may even leave entire Profit or a part as balance which would be carried forward to next year and appear in next year's Balance Sheet as Opening Balance for Profit & Loss A/c (normally applicable for Companies).

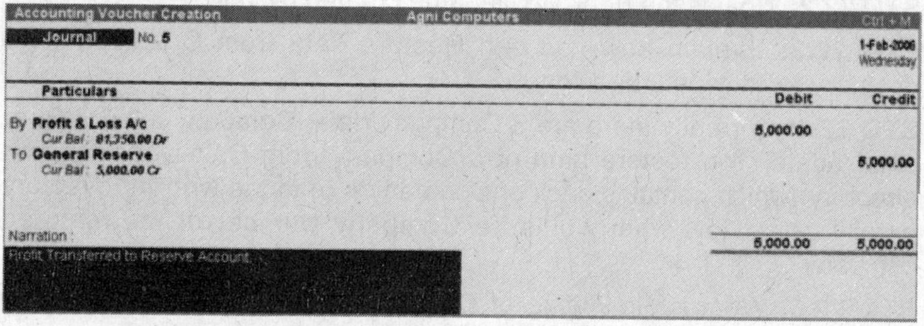

Fig 23-1: Journal Voucher appropriation of Profit

Similarly, following Journal voucher explains transfer of the entire amount of current year profit of Rs 120750.00 to Proprietor's Capital account

Particulars	*Dr*	*Cr*
Profit & Loss A/c	120750.00	
Proprietor's Capital A/c		120750.00
Narration Transfer of current year Profit to Proprietor's Capital A/c		

Further, following Journal voucher explains transfer of the entire amount of current year profit of Rs 120000.00 to Partner's Capital account in ration of 60:40

Particulars	*Dr*	*Cr*
By Profit & Loss A/c	120000.00	
Capital A/c – Partner Mahesh Goyal		72000.00
Capital A/c – Partner Anita Goyal		48000.00

NarrationTransfer of current year Profit to Partner's Capital A/c in ratio of 60:40

23.2 Extension of Financial Year

Tally initially creates a Financial Period of 12 months from the *Financial Year From* date (Fig 2.5) entered in *Company Creation* screen (e.g when *Financial Year From* Date is 1-4-2006, the FY is 1-4-2006 to 31-3-2007).

To enter data for next year (FY07-08), press *F2: Period* button to get Change Period screen (Fig 23-2) and enter the next year closing date (e.g 31-3-2008) at To field (DO NOT change the *Financial Year From* date through Alter option from Company Info menu – Fig 3.17). The accounts are extended till 31-3-2008.

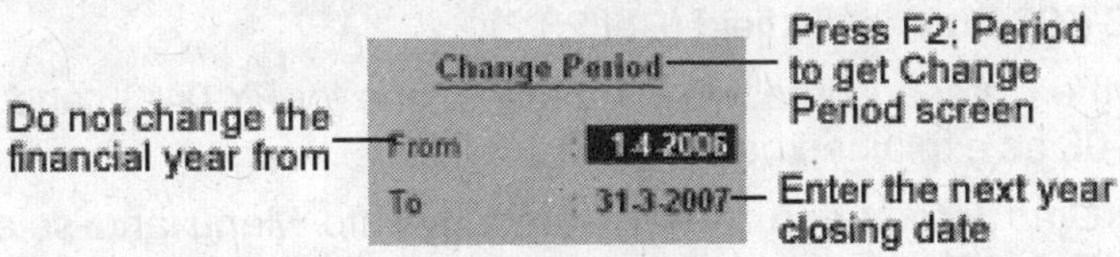

Fig 23-2: Extension of Accounting period for next Financial Year

This way, you may continue working without closing the FY06-07 or transferring closing balances of FY 06-07 to Opening balance of FY 07-08. Thus, accounts in Tally are always open and contiguous (so you may get report for any period – one year or several years together).

Having extended the F Year, you may enter voucher for any date by setting the *F2: Period* and *F2: Date*. To enter voucher for FY 06-07, click *F2: Period* (or press *Alt+F2*), set 1-4-2006 (at From) and 31-3-2007 (at To). Press *F2: Date* and set the Voucher Date (within 1-4-2006 to 31-3-2007). To enter voucher for FY 07-08, click *F2: Period* (or press Alt+F2), set 1-4-2007 to 31-3-2008. Press *F2: Date* and set the current date (within 1-4-2007 to 31-3-2008).

23.3 Creating a New Company for New Year A/c

Instead of extending the Financial Year and keeping several years data in one company, you may create a new company with new financial period. At Company creation screen (Ref 7.2), specify the next F Year Start Date (i.e.1.4.2006) at Financial Start From (Fig 23-3).

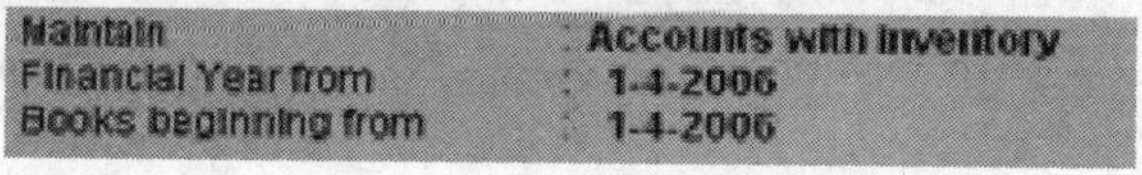

Fig 23-3 : Creation of New Company for New Financial Year

23.4 New Year Company creation through Splitting

After extending the Financial Year (Ref 23-2), split the Company into 2 years to get the New Year Company with Opening Balances carried from the Closing Balances of previous year. First extend the Financial Year of the existing Company (Ref 23.2). For example, to extend the period of the Company for FY 04-05 to 05-06, press *F2: Period* button and enter the Date 31-03-2006 at *To* field (Ref 23.2).

Now split the Company into two companies, one for FY 04-05 and another for FY 05-06 as explained below.

Click F3: *Cmp Info* button to get Company Info Menu and select *Split Company Data* (Fig 23-4).

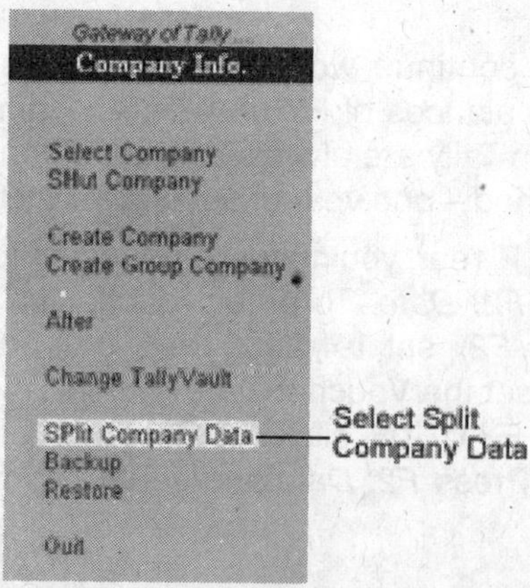

Fig23-4:Company Splitting option at Company Info menu

At Split Company data screen (Fig 23-5), enter the Date from which you like to split the Data (e.g 1-4-2006). Tally will show the period of two companies (Fig 23-5). Press *Yes* to continue.

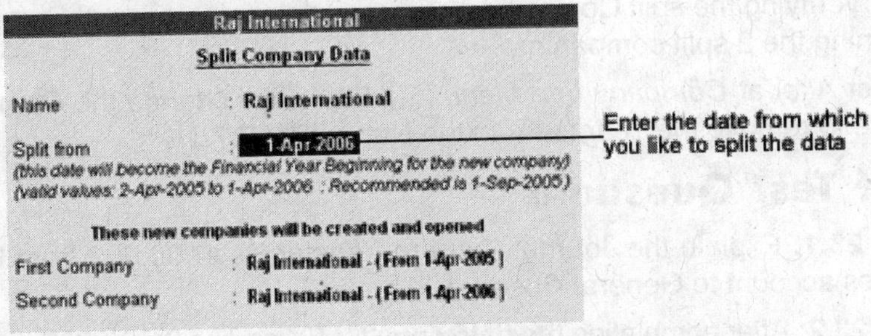

Fig 23-5: Splitting of a Company into 2 years

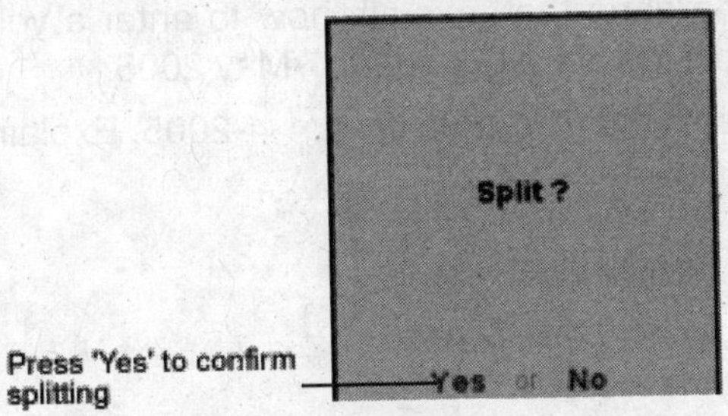

Fig 23-6: Splitting Confirmation

Press *Yes* to confirm splitting (Fig 23-6).

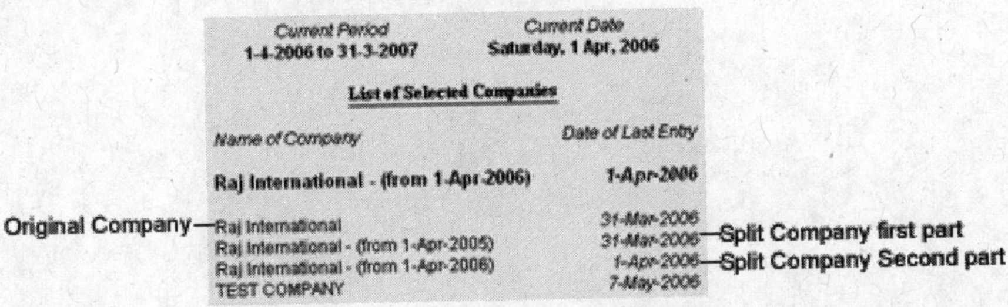

Fig 23-7: Split & Original company at list of selected companies, after splitting

Tally creates 2 new companies data files, showing the progress status (do not interrupt till the process is over). The original company data is also retained. *Financial Year From* date is added (suffixed) to the Name of the Split Company for identification (Fig 23-7).

Tally, adds the beginning date in *Name* only but *Mailing Name* remains intact. Thus in external reports, *Mailing Name* would be printed while in internal report, Company Name along with beginning date would be printed.

After verifying the split Companies, you may delete the original Company, retaining the 2 split companies.

Select *Alter* at *Company Info Menu* (Fig 23-4) and change the Company Name to remove the Year suffix in the Name (Ref 7.7.1).

Self Test Questions

STQ 23.1: Explain the Journal Entry to transfer Rs 1, 00,000 from Profit & Loss account to General Reserve.

STQ 23.2: After completing the data entry for FY ending 31-3-2005, extend the Accounting period till 31-Mar 2006.

STQ 23.3: Having done that, explain how to enter a voucher dt 31-Mar 2005 and then how to enter voucher dt 1-May 2005.

STQ 23.4: Now split the Company from 1-4-2005. Explain the steps.

Inventory Set Up

24

We have so far discussed about Accounts, involving transaction and accounting of money only. But in any trade, Items are also traded and stock accounts maintained.

Now we discuss about maintaining Inventory :

- Creation of Company to maintain Inventory
- Creation of Ledger Accounts like Customers & Suppliers, Sales & Purchase
- Creation of Inventory Masters like Stock Item Group, Unit of Measure & Stock Items
- Create Inventory Vouchers and Invoices like Sale, Purchase, Debit & Credit Notes
- Print Inventory Documents like Sales & Purchase vouchers & Invoices, Debit & Credit Notes
- Print Inventory Reports like Invoice Registers, Item Group & Item Ledgers, Analysis Reports and Stock Statements

24.1 Company Creation to maintain Inventory

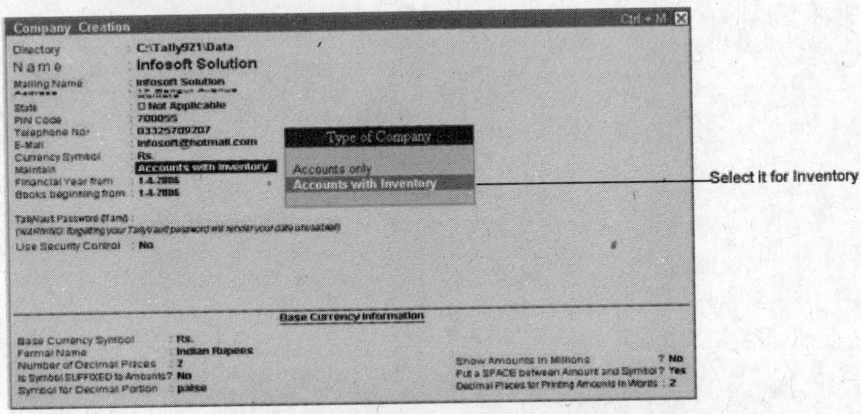

Fig 24-1: Creation of Company for Accounts with Inventory

We have discussed Creation of Company (Ref 7.2). To maintain Inventory, at *Maintain* field, select *Accounts with Inventory* (Fig 24-1)

Self Test Questions

STQ 24.1: What option you need to set up for Inventory maintenance during Company Creation

Inventory Masters

25

Having created the Company for *Accounts with Inventory,* you may now create following Masters:

Accounts Masters

- Customer Ledger Accounts
- Supplier Ledger Accounts
- Sales Ledger Accounts
- Purchase Ledger Accounts

Inventory Masters

- Stock Group
- Unit of Measurement
- Stock Item

25.1 Configuration for Customer & Supplier Ledger Accounts

At Ledger Accounts entry screen (Ref 10.3), click F12:Configuration button to get Masters Configuration screen (Fig 25-1). Now set the following options for Accounts Masters as required :

- **Allow Advanced entries in Masters :** Set No (Advanced topics are not discussed in this book)
- **Add Notes for Ledger Accounts :** Set No (not discussed in this book)
- **Use Address for Ledger Accounts :** Set Yes to get prompt for Mailing Details & Tax Details in ledger creation screen (Fig 25-3)

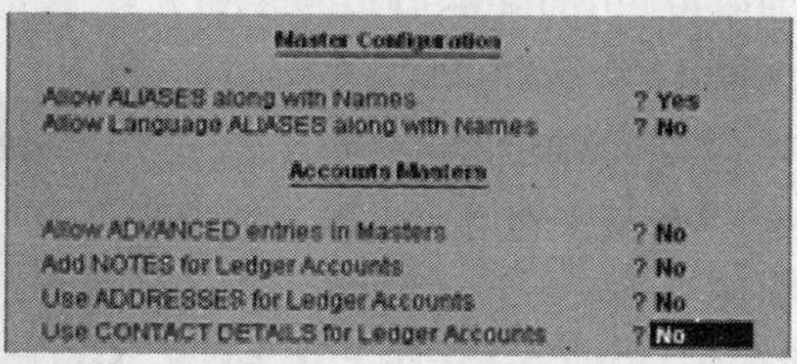

Fig 25-1: Configuration set up for Masters

- **Use Contact details for Ledger Accounts :** Set Yes to get prompt for entering Contact Person, Telephone No, Fax , e-mail also (Fig 25-4)

25.2 Customer & Supplier Ledger Accounts

We have discussed creation of Ledger Accounts (Ref 10.3). We now explain the details specific for Customer & Supplier Ledger Accounts.

Parent Group : At *Under* field, select Sundry Debtors or its subgroup for Customer Ledgers or select Sundry Creditors or its subgroup for Supplier Ledgers (Fig 25-2).

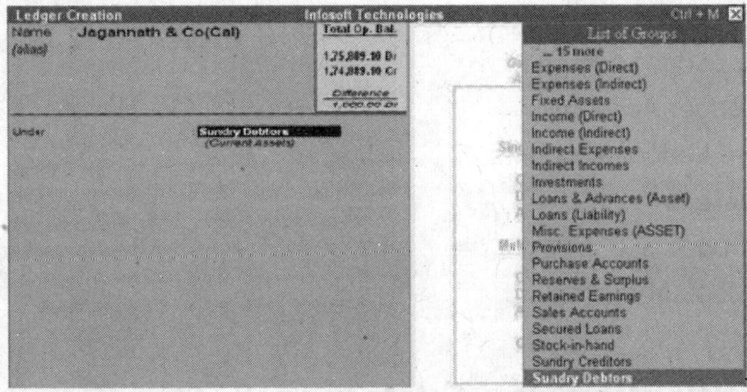

Fig 25-2 : Customer Ledger Account

Mailing Details

You may enter the following details (Fig 25-3) if you have set Yes at *Use Address for Ledger Accounts* at Masters Configuration (Fig 25-1)

- **Name :** Enter the legal Name of the Party which will be printed in all invoice and all external documents. Normally this is same as Ledger Name, but may be different when you have more than one party having similar name.
- **Address :** Enter the full Address as you like to print in Invoice & other documents. You may enter in multiple lines. Press <enter> at blank line to terminate address entry.
- **State :** Select the State from the list
- **PIN Code :** Enter the PIN code

You may also enter the following Tax details, where necessary :

- **PAN/IT No :** Income Tax PAN #, if any
- **Sales Tax No :** Sales Tax or VAT TIN #, if any

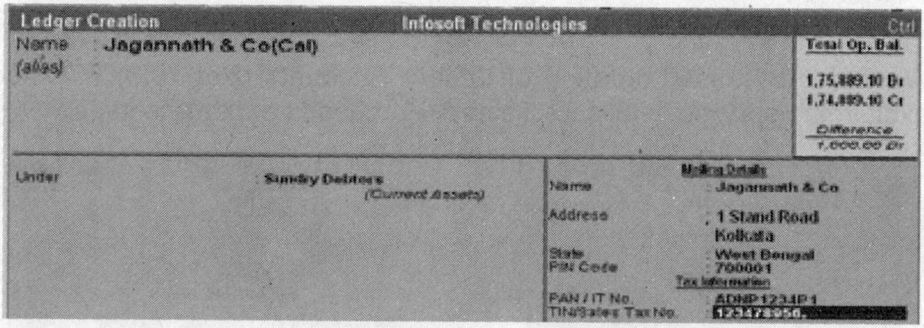

Fig 25-3: Customer Ledger with Address fields

Contact Details

You may enter the following details (Fig 25-4) if you have set Yes at *Use Contact Details for Ledger Accounts* at Masters Configuration (Fig 25-1)

- **Contact Person :** Enter the Name of Contact person(s) for your ready reference.
- **Telephone Number :** Enter the Telephone Number (s), with area code for outstation parties, for your ready reference
- **Fax No :** Enter the Fax Number (s), with area code, for your ready reference
- **E-Mail :** Enter the e-mail address, if any, for your ready reference

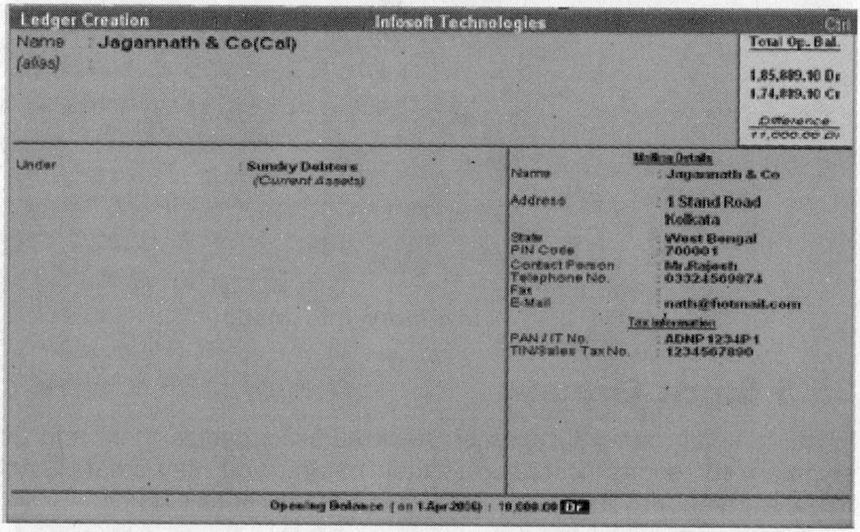

Fig 25-4: Customer Ledger with Address & Contract details fields

25.3 Sales & Purchase Ledger Accounts

We have discussed creation of Ledger Accounts (Ref 10.3). We now explain the specific details for Sales & Purchase Ledger Accounts.

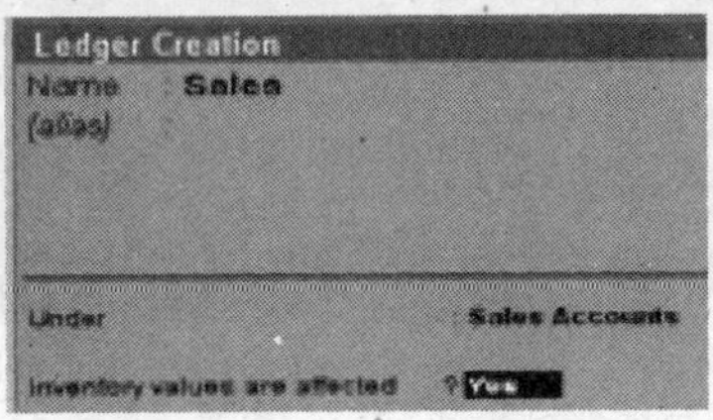

Fig 25-5 Sales Ledger Account

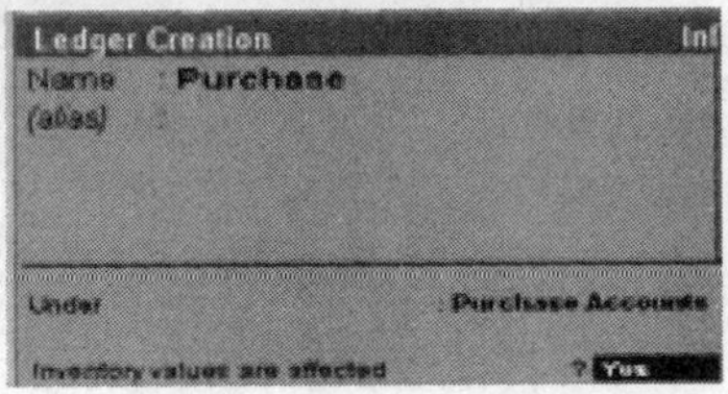

Fig 25-6 Purchase Ledger Account

Parent Group : At *Under* field, select Sales or its subgroup for Sales Ledgers (Fig 25-5) or select Purchase or its subgroup for Purchase Ledgers (Fig 25-6).

Set Yes at the field *Inventory values are affected* (Fig 25-5 & 25-6).

25.4 Inventory Masters

To create Inventory Masters, select Inventory Info at Gateway to get Inventory Info Menu (Fig 25-7)

Fig 25-7 : Inventory Info Menu

25.5 Stock Group

If you maintain several types of Stock Items, organize them and get summarized reports according to their nature, you may create Stock Groups. Later on, you link the Stock Items to the Stock Groups.

At *Inventory Info* menu (Fig 25-7), select Stock Group to get Stock Group Menu (Fig 25-8).

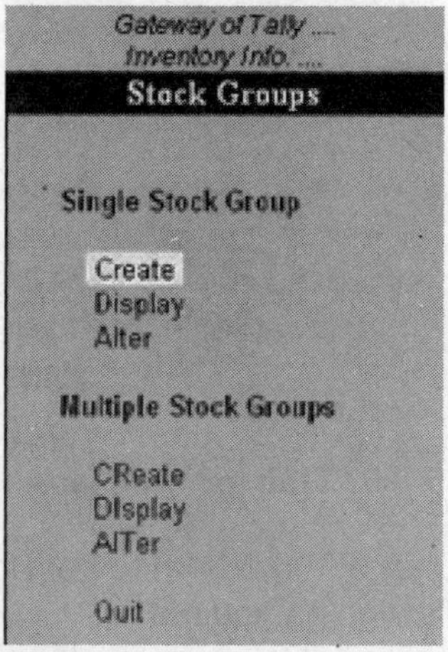

Fig 25-8 : Stock Group Menu

At Stock Group Menu (Fig 25-8) select Create under Single Stock Group to get Stock Group Creation screen and enter the following Particulars (Fig 25-9) .

- **Stock Group Name**: Enter Name of Stock Group.
- **Parent Stock Group**: At *Under* field, select the parent Stock Group for the Stock Group being created (select *Primary* to create top level Group). The first Stock Group created must be Primary. To create a new parent Group (if the Parent Stock Group is not existing, press Alt+C to create the parent Stock Group).
- **Stock Group Quantity**: At the *Can Quantities of Items be Added*, set *Yes* to get Total Stock Quantity of the child Stock Items under the Stock Group (if all child Stock Items are measured in same UoM), else set *No* (Stock Group Quantity is not summed up).

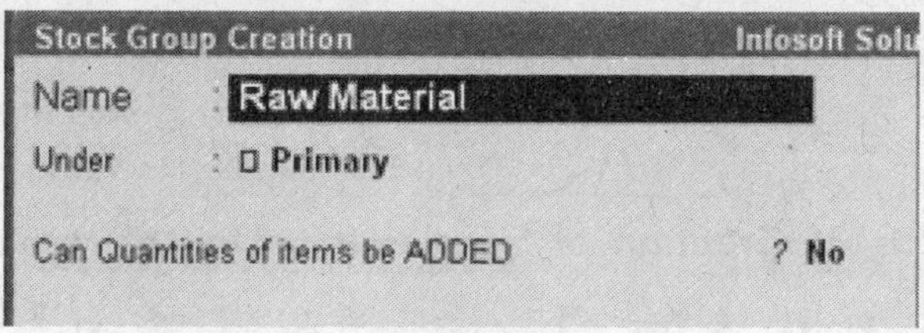

Fig 25-9: Stock Group Entry

25.6 Simple Unit of Measure

At *Inventory Info* menu (Fig 25-7), select Units to get Units Menu (Fig 25-10)

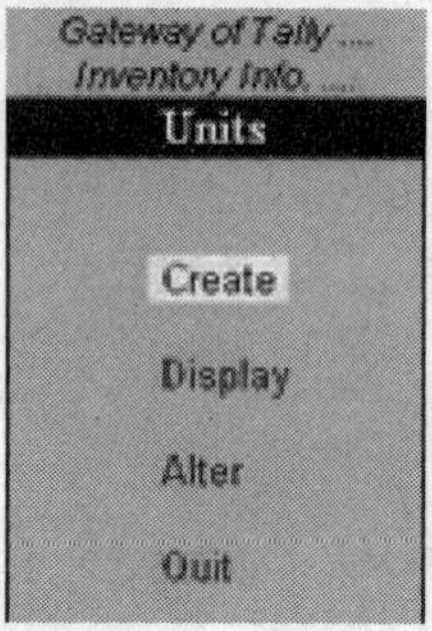

Fig 25-10: Unit of Measure Menu

At Units Menu, select Create (Fig 25-10) to get Unit Creation screen (Fig 25-11) and enter the following particulars :

- **UoM Type**: At Type *field*, cursor normally skips showing Simple as selected to create a Simple Unit.
- **UoM Symbol**: At *Symbol* field, enter the symbol to denote the Unit (e.g., Kg. Ltr.). This is normally printed in all reports to indicate the UoM.
- **UoM Name**: At *Formal Name* field, enter full Name of the Unit (e.g., Kilogram, Litre etc) different from UoM Symbol.
- **UoM Decimals**: At *Number of Decimal Places*, specify maximum number of decimal places (between 0 to 4) in which the quantity for the Unit may be specified (like 3 to show 1.234 MT, 0 to show 29 Pcs).

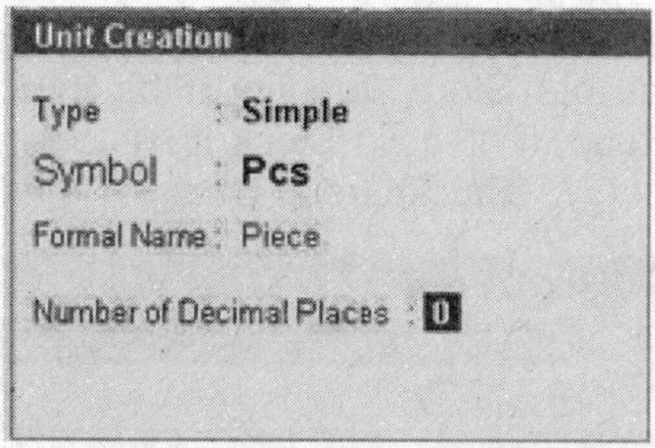

Fig 25-11: Creation of Simple Unit (Unit of Measure)

25.7 Stock Items

To maintain transaction details and stock figures, you must create unique Stock Items. For example, you may create *Flour* as a stock Item to maintain total stock quantity and stock ledger for all sizes of Flour Bags. You will not get details for each bag size. To get stock and transaction details for each type of Flour Bags (e.g for each brand, for each bag size), then you must create separate Stock Items like Annapurna Flour 5kg, Pahalwan Flour 2kg etc.

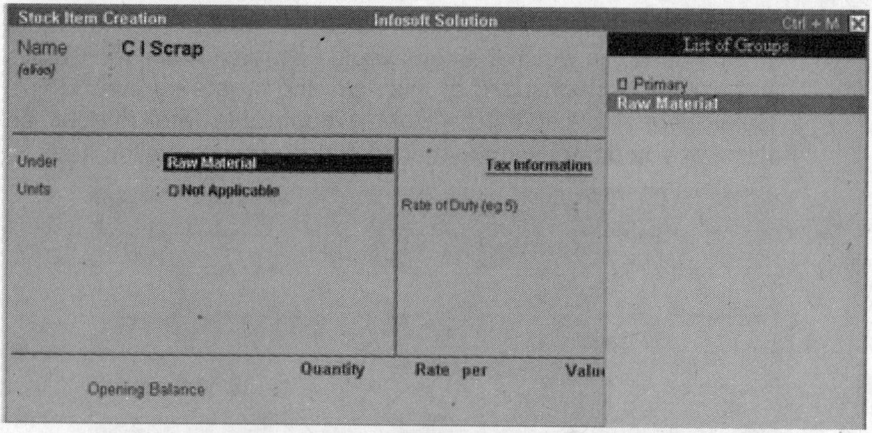

Fig 25-12: Stock Item Creation – selection of Parent Stock Group

At *Inventory Info* menu (Fig 25-7), select Stock Items to get Stock Item Menu (Fig 25-13).

Fig 25-13: Stock Item menu

At Stock Item Menu (Fig 25-13), select Create at Single Stock Item to get Stock Item creation screen (Fig 25-12) to enter the following particulars (Fig 25-14)

- **Stock Item Name**: At *Name* field, enter a unique Name of the Stock Item.

- **Parent Stock Group**: At *Under* field, select the Parent Stock Group (if the Parent Stock Group is not existing, press Alt+C at this field and create the Parent Stock Group).
- **Stock Item UoM**: At *Units* field, select the Unit of Measurement (from pop-up) in which the Item would be measured (if the UoM is not existing, press ***Alt+C*** at this field and create the new UoM). Select *Not Applicable* if no UoM is applicable (e.g, for Service Item) or you do not want to maintain stock figures for the Item.

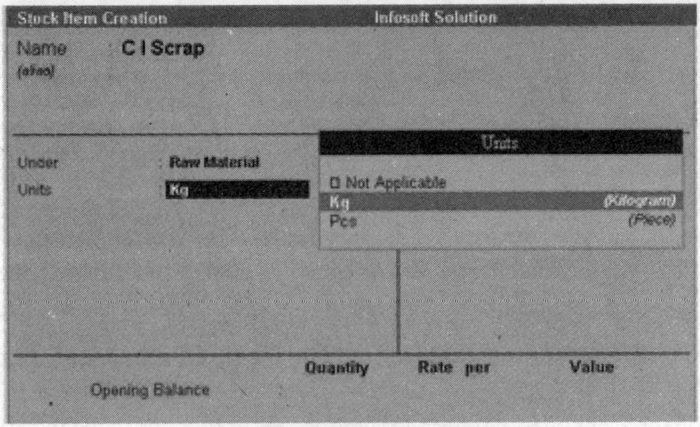

Fig 25-14: Stock Item Creation

Opening Stock Details : At *Opening Balance* field (Fig 25-15), enter Opening Stock details as on the *Books Beginning From Date*, as explained below:

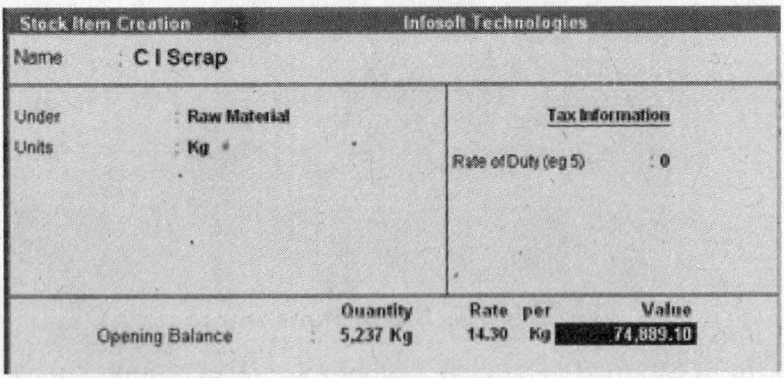

Fig 25-15: Opening Stock Details entry in Stock Items§

- **Opening Stock Quantity**: At *Quantity* field, enter the Opening Stock Quantity as on *Books beginning from date.*

- **Opening Stock Rate**: At *Rate* field, enter the Opening Stock Rate (if you do not know the Rate, leave it blank, and enter the Opening Stock value, Tally will compute & fill up the Rate).
- **Opening Stock Value**: The Opening Stock value is computed from the Opening Stock Quantity & Opening Stock Rate as entered and displayed at Value field. However, you may change the Amount. The Rate will get changed accordingly.

25.8 Display of Inventory Masters

To Display Inventory Masters as discussed above, select *Display* from the respective Menu in the same way. All the records will be displayed. Now select the record to get complete details displayed. In Display mode, you cannot modify the record.

- **Display of Stock Group**: Select Inventory Info > Stock Group > Display to view a Stock Group (but you cannot Alter), choose the Group you wish to view from *List of Stock Group*.
- **Display of Stock Item**: Select Inventory Info > Stock Item > Display and select the Stock Item to Display (you cannot Alter).
- **Display of Unit of Measure**: Select Inventory Info > Units > Display and select the Unit to Display (you cannot Alter).

25.9 Alteration / Deletion of Inventory Masters

To Alter / Delete Inventory Masters as discussed above, select *Alter* from the respective Menu in the same way. All the records will be displayed. Now select the record to *Alter* or *Delete*.

- **Alteration / Deletion of Stock Group**: Select Inventory Info > Stock Group > Alter to Alter a Stock Group, choose the Group you wish to Alter from *List of Stock Group*. Make the necessary modification and press Ctrl+A to save. To Delete the Group, press Alt+D and click *Yes* to confirm.
- **Alteration / Deletion of Units of Measure**: Select Inventory Info > Units > Alter and select the Unit to Alter. Carry out the Alteration (if the unit has been referred in any voucher, number of decimal places cannot be changed) and press Ctrl+A to save. To Delete any Unit, press Alt+D and click *Yes* at *Delete Yes or No?* to confirm Deletion.
- **Alteration / Deletion of Stock Item**: Select Inventory Info > Stock Items > Alter and select the Unit to Alter. Carry out the Alteration (if the unit has been referred in any voucher, UoM cannot be

changed) and press Ctrl+A to save. To Delete any Stock Item, press Alt+D and click *Yes* at *Delete Yes or No?* to confirm Deletion.

25.9.1 Restriction in Deletion of Stock Item Masters

However, in following cases, the Record cannot be Deleted and hence Deletion Confirmation screen does not appear.

- **Stock Group**: The Group would not be deleted if it is parent of any Stock Group or Stock Item.
- **Stock UoM**: The Stock UoM cannot be deleted if is has been referred in any Stock Item.
- **Stock Item**: The Stock Item cannot be deleted if it has been referred in any Voucher.

Self Test Question

STQ 25.1 : How to create an Unit of Measure for '*M Tons'* to enter data like 25.321 MT, 32.000 MT, 27.005 MT etc in inventory vouchers.

STQ 25.2 : Write the respective Parent Group (at *Under* field) to create Stock Group / Stock Items as per following hierarchy

Raw Materials

- Iron Scraps
  - ❋ Pig Scraps
    - ❑ Low Silica Pigs
  - ❋ M S Scraps
    - ❑ M S Flat scraps

Group / Stock Item	*Parent Stock Group at Under Field*
Iron Scraps	
Pig Scraps	
Low Silica Pigs	
M S Scraps	
M S Flat scraps	

STQ 25.3: How to enter Opening Stock Quantity & value in Stock Items

STQ 25.4: Explain how create a Service Item and Unit of Measure for which only values are to be entered in vouchers (no Quantity).

STQ 25.5: Explain how to create a Service Item for which the Rate is to be charged in Hours.

Inventory Voucher

26

Having created Inventory Masters, you may start Inventory transaction (Vouchers) entry. Like Accounting transactions, Inventory transaction details are entered in voucher.

26.1 Inventory Vouchers

Inventory Transactions may be entered in Voucher mode and in Invoice Mode. In Voucher mode, the Ledger Amount is entered first (in the respective Debit / Credit columns) and then the corresponding Itemwise allocations are entered. In Invoice mode, the Item details are entered first. Like Single entry voucher mode, you do not have to specify the Debit / Credit. These are properly recognized by Tally,when entered 'As Invoice'. However when entered as 'As Voucher' you need to specify Dr/Cr.

So, in voucher mode entry, you enter the Net Amount first in the Party Account and then the amount for each Ledger Account (Like Sales Account etc). This means that you must have all the Amounts computed first. So, voucher mode is suitable when you have got all the amounts already computed (e.g you enter sales voucher from manual sales bills).

In Invoice mode entry, you enter the Stock Item Data first (Rate, Quantity etc). Tally computes the Item Value etc and posts into Sales Ledger. You then enter Tax Rates etc. Tally computes Taxes etc and posts into the respective ledger. Finally, Tally computes the Net Bill Amount and posts to the Party Ledger Account.

In this chapter, we discuss about Voucher Entry Mode, which is similar to Accounts Voucher Entry as discussed in Chapter 11.

26.2 Debit/Credit Notes Set Up

To enter Debit/Credit Note, click *F11: to get Company Features* Menu (Fig 26-1).

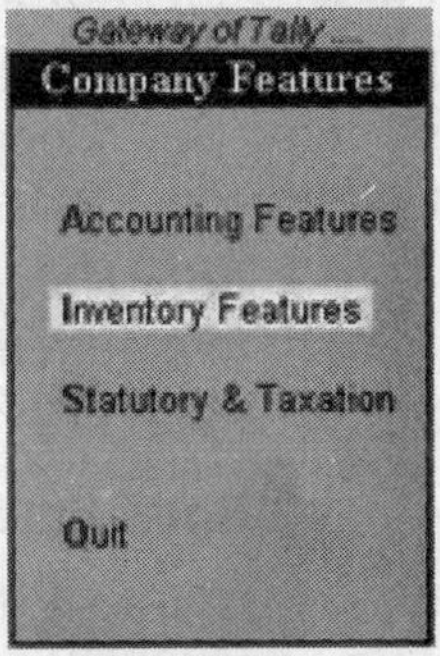

Fig 26-1: Company Features Menu

At Company Features Menu (Fig 26-1), select Inventory Features to get Inventory Features set up screen (Fig 26-2).

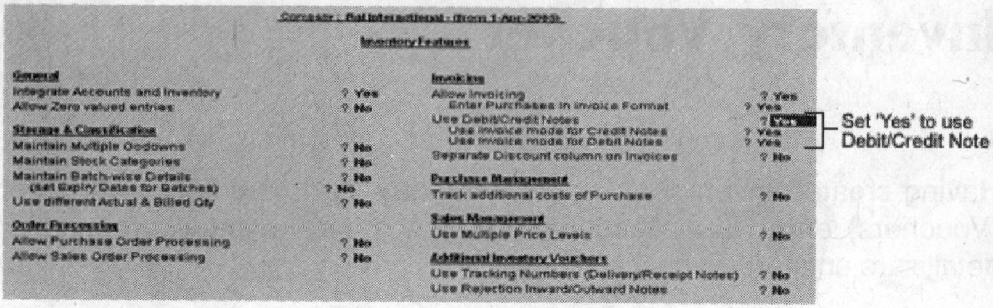

Fig 26-2: Activation of Debit / Credit Note option at Configuration

At Inventory Features set up screen (Fig 26-3), set *Yes* at *Use Debit/ Credit Notes* (Fig 26-3) (else such entries are to be entered in Journal Voucher only).

26.3 Inventory Voucher Entry

Now we discuss the steps for Inventory Voucher Entry (Sales, Purchase, Debit Note & Credit Note) in Voucher mode.

At Gateway, select Accounting Voucher (Ref 11.3) to get Voucher Entry screen. The entry process is similar to Accounts Voucher (Ref 11.3). We discuss the additional steps for Inventory.

26.3.1 Sales Voucher Entry

At Voucher screen, click *F8:Sales* button at Vertical button bar to get Sales Voucher Entry screen

In first line, select the Customer Ledger for Credit Sale or Cash/ Bank Account for Cash Sale and enter the net voucher amount in Debit column.

At the second line of Voucher, select Sales Ledger Account and enter the amount in Credit column.

If you have set *Yes* at *Inventory Values are affected* (Fig 25-5) for the selected Sales ledger, you get the Item allocation screen to enter the Item Details (Fig 26-4) as follows:

- **Item Name:** At *Name of Item* field, select the Item (Press Alt+C to create new Item).
- **Quantity:** Enter the Quantity. The UoM is displayed.
- **Rate:** Enter the Rate per Unit.
- **Item Value:** At *Amount* field, the computed Amount (as per Quantity & Rate) is displayed, which you may change if required.

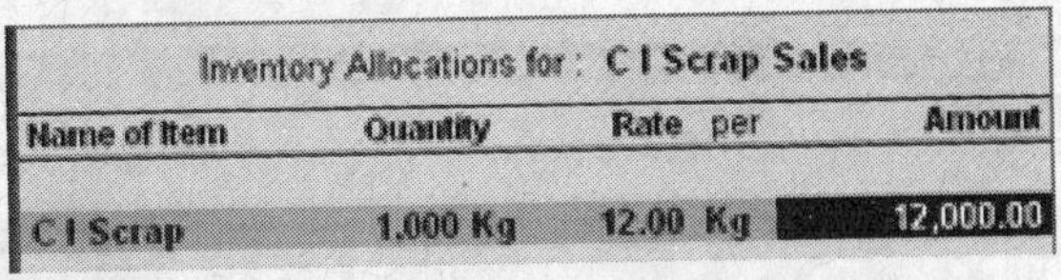

Fig 26-3: Item Allocation for Sale Ledger

This way enter the Items to complete the Ledger allocation. The total Item Value must match the entered Ledger Amount.

You may enter several such ledger accounts (and the Item allocations for each Sales Ledger Account).

The ledger entries are terminated, when the total of Debits equals to total of Credits.

Now you may enter the Voucher Narration (Ref 11.3.3).

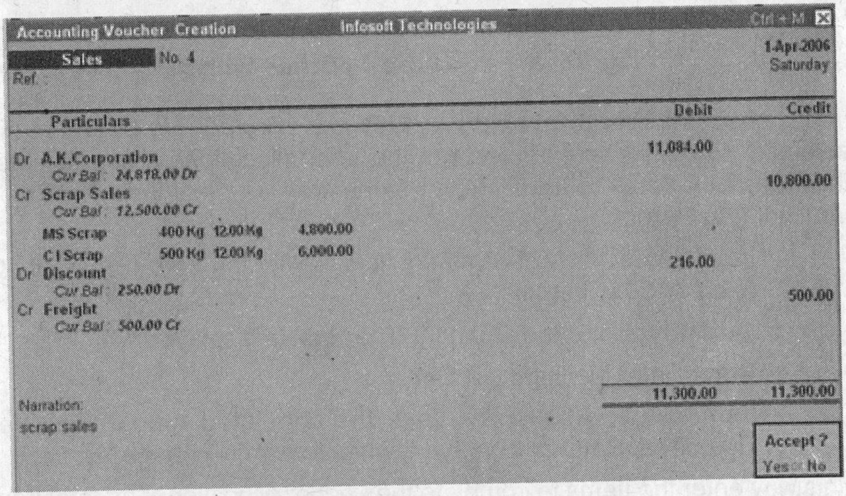

Fig 26-4: Sales Voucher entry

26.3.2 Purchase Voucher Entry

At Voucher screen, click *F9:Purchase* button at Vertical button bar to get Purchase Voucher Entry screen (Fig 26-5)

In first line, select the Supplier ledger for Credit Purchase or Cash/ Bank Account for Cash Purchase and enter the net voucher amount in Credit Column.

At the second line of Voucher, select Purchase Ledger Account and enter the amount in Debit Column.

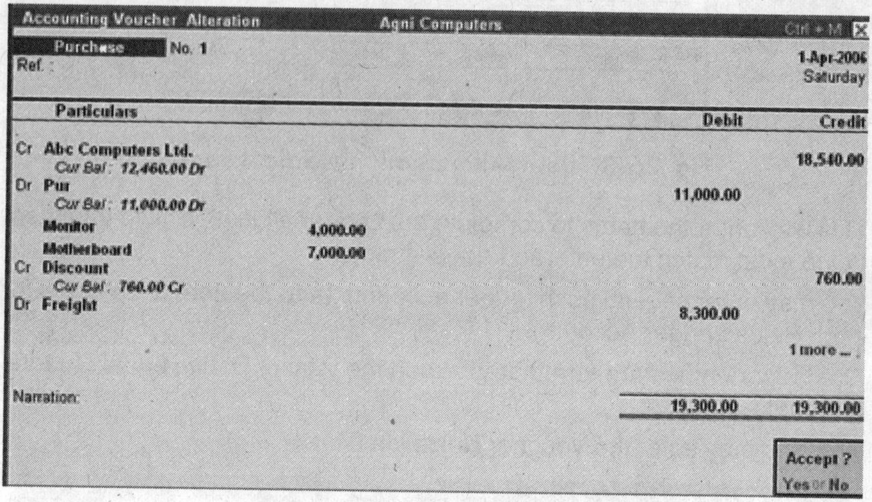

Fig 26-5 : Purchase Voucher Entry

If you have set *Yes* at *Inventory Values are affected* (Fig 25-6) for the selected Purchase Ledger, you get the Item allocation screen to enter the Item Details as follows, in the same way as described for Sales Voucher (Fig 26-3)

- **Item Name:** At *Name of Item* field, select the Item (Press Alt+C to create new Item).
- **Quantity:** Enter the Quantity. The UoM is displayed.
- **Rate:** Enter the Rate per Unit.
- **Item Value:** At *Amount* field, the computed Amount (as per Quantity & Rate) is displayed, which you may change.

This way enter the Items to complete the Ledger allocation. The total Item Value must match the entered Ledger Amount.

You may enter several such ledger accounts (and the Item allocations for each Purchase Ledger Account).

The ledger entries are terminated, when the total of Debits equals to total of Credits.

Now you may enter the Voucher Narration (Ref 11.3.3).

In the same way, you may enter Debit / Credit Note. In second entry onwards, you may enter Sales / Purchase, Duties & Taxes or any other ledger account.

26.3.3 Debit Note voucher Entry

At Voucher screen, click *F9:Debit Note* button at Vertical button bar to get Debit Note Voucher Entry screen (Fig 26-6)

In first line, select the Party ledger or Cash/ Bank Account and enter the net voucher amount in Debit Column.

From second line onwards, you may enter any other ledger account.

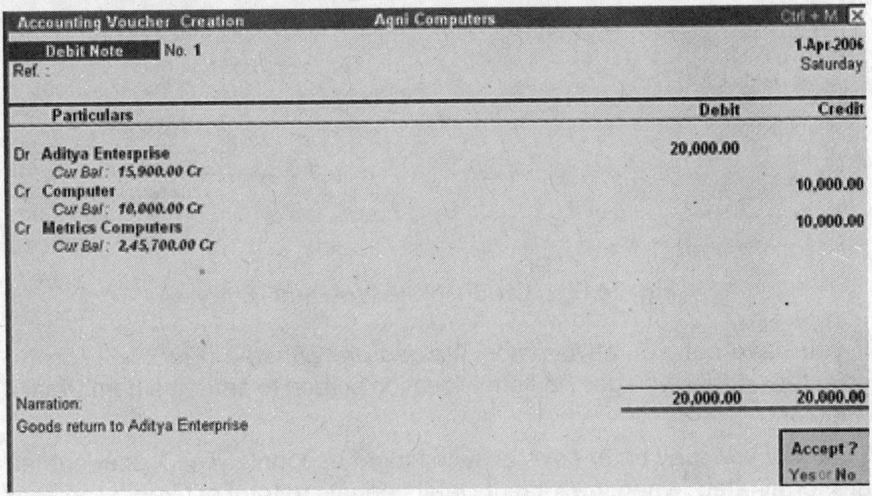

Fig 26-6 : Debit Note Voucher Entry

If you have set *Yes* at *Inventory Values are affected* (Fig 25-6) for the selected Ledger, you get the Item allocation screen to enter the Item Details (Fig 26-3).

This way you may enter several such ledger accounts. The ledger entries are terminated, when the total of Debits equals to total of Credits.

Now you may enter the Voucher Narration (Ref 11.3.3).

26.3.4 Credit Note voucher Entry

At Voucher screen, click *F8:Credit Note* button at Vertical button bar to get Credit Note Voucher Entry screen

In first line, select the Party ledger or Cash/ Bank Account and enter the net voucher amount in Credit Column.

From second line onwards, you may enter any other ledger account.

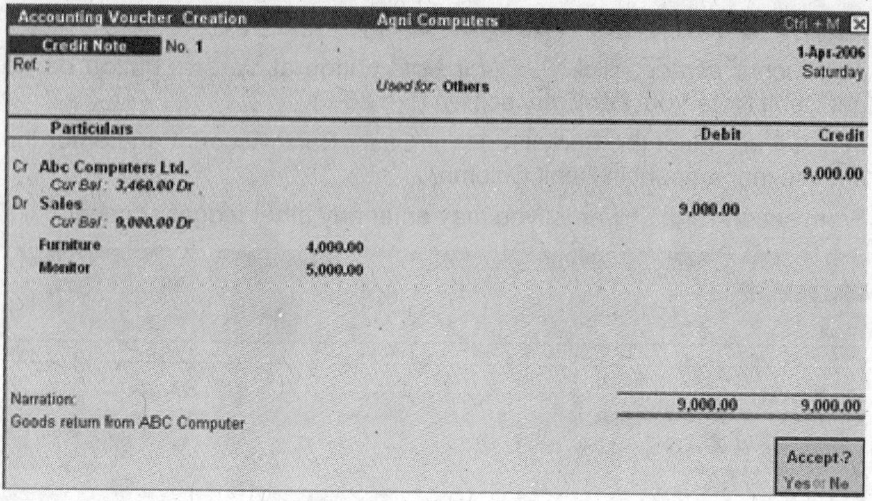

Fig 26-7 : Credit Note Voucher Entry

If you have set *Yes* at *Inventory Values are affected* (Fig 25-6) for the selected Ledger, you get the Item allocation screen to enter the Item Details (Fig 26-3).

This way you may enter several such ledger accounts. The ledger entries are terminated, when the total of Debits equals to total of Credits.

Now you may enter the Voucher Narration (Ref 11.3.3).

Self Test Questions

STQ 26.1 : Explain the options to be set up to enter Debit & Credit Note vouchers

STQ 26.2 : Explain how to enter the following Cash Sales voucher

- MS Scrap – 12.310 MT @ 1220 / M Ton
- Pig Scrap – 11MT @ 1300 / M Ton
- Less Cash Discount – Rs. 3000
- Add Freight – Rs. 4000

STQ 26.3: Explain how to enter the following Credit Note on S K Enterprises for return of materials sold, due to defect in quality

- MS Scrap – 4.310 MT @ 1220 / M Ton
- Less Freight 500.00

Invoicing

27

We have explained Inventory Voucher Entry in Voucher mode. In this chapter we discuss Invoice Entry (Inventory Voucher in Invoice Mode).

27.1 Company Features set up for Invoicing

At Company features screen (Fig 27-1), set *Yes* at *Allow Invoicing* to enter Sales Invoice in Invoice Format (Fig 27-1).

To enter Purchase Invoice also in Invoice format, set *Yes* at *Enter Purchases in Invoice Format* in the next line (Fig 27-1).

To enter Debit Note & Credit Note also in Invoice format, set *Yes* at *Use Debit / Credit Notes* and then set Yes at *Use Invoice Mode for Debit Notes* and set *Yes* at *Use Invoice Mode for Credit Notes* (Fig 27-1).

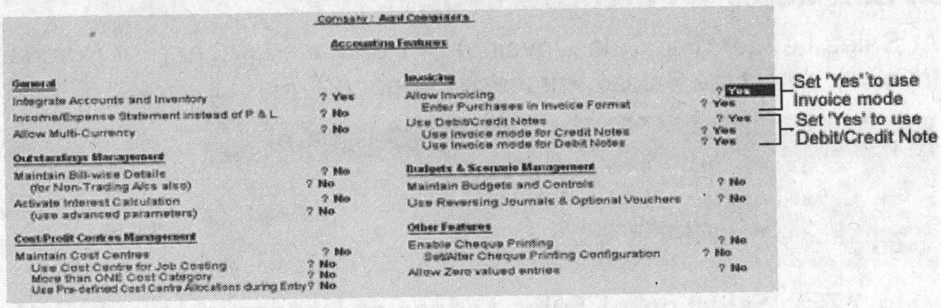

Fig 27-1: Invoicing option set up at Company Operations

To enter Invoice, select the toggle buttons *As Invoice* and & *Item Invoice* at Sales, Purchase, Debit Notes and Credit Notes entry.

Fig 27-2: As Voucher / As Invoice toggle button

Fig 27-3: Item / Account Invoice toggle button

27.2 Invoice Entry

At Gateway, select Accounts Voucher entry and then click the respective voucher type button (Fig 26-3) to get the respective Invoice entry screen.

In this chapter, we discuss about simple Invoice entry where all particulars are entered in main screen.

The entry process is similar to Inventory Voucher entry (Ref 26.3). We explain the additional steps.

27.2.1 Party Ledger Account

At *Party's A/c Name* field, select the Party from *List of Ledger Accounts* field (press Alt+C to create a new Ledger). All the Ledger accounts placed under Sundry Debtors, Sundry Creditors, Cash, Bank, Bank OCC, Branch & Divisions are available here.

In case of Cash Sales, you may select *Cash* ledger. If payment is received by Cheque, you may select the respective Bank Ledger (to eliminate entry of another Receipt voucher).

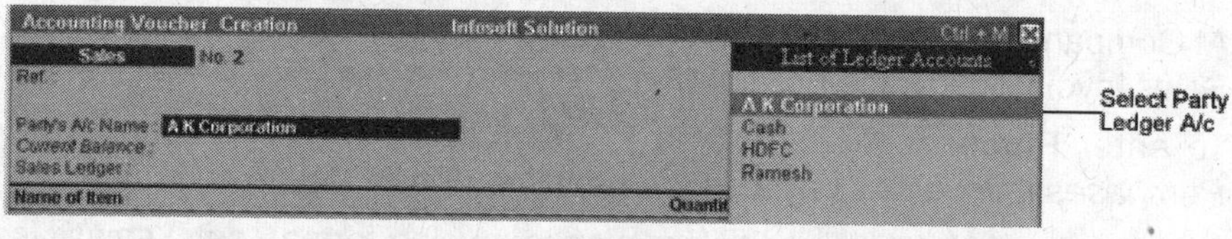

Fig 27-4: Selection of Party Ledger in Invoice

27.2.2 Sales / Purchase Ledger

At Sales Ledger (For Sales Invoice) or Purchase Ledger (For Purchase Invoice), select the Sales / Purchase Ledger (27-5)

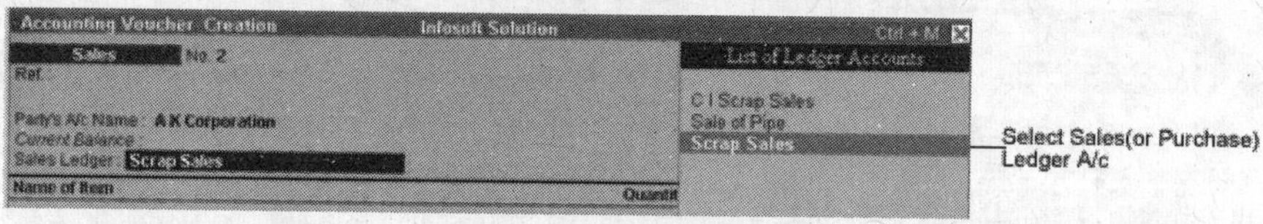

Fig 27-5: Selection of Sales Ledger at Header in Invoice Entry

27.2.3 Item Details Entry in Invoice

Now enter the Item details as explained for Inventory Voucher (Fig 26-3), as shown in Fig 27-6

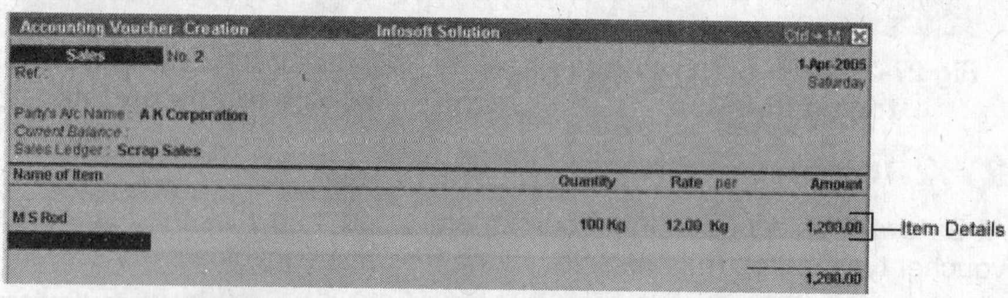

Fig 27-6: Item details entry in Sales Invoice

This way, enter Item details for all the Items. To terminate Items entry, press ↵ at *Name of Item* field to enter Accounting Allocations, as explained below:

27.2.4 Accounting Allocations in Invoice entry

Now you may enter details of other ledger accounts (like Sales Tax, Discount, Freight etc - Fig 27-7):

- **Ledger Account**: Select the Ledger Account from the list.
- **Ledger Amount**: Enter the Amount (to reduce the amount, enter in negative figure).

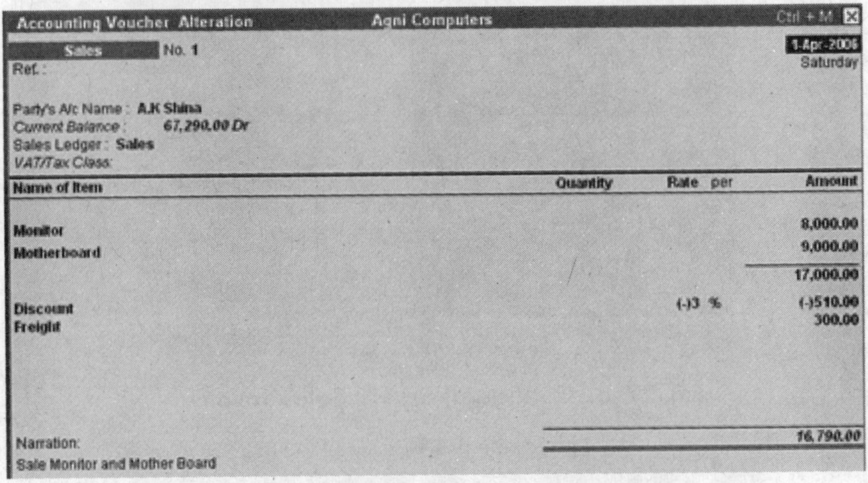

Fig 27-7: Sales Invoice entry

27.2.5 Inventory Voucher Alteration, Deletion & Cancellation

You may perform Voucher Alteration, Deletion & Cancellation at Voucher in Alteration Mode in the same way, as discussed for Accounts Vouchers (Ref 11.8.1)

27.3 Invoice Printing

The steps of Invoice printing is similar to Accounts Voucher Printing described in Chapter 13

27.3.1 Inventory Voucher Printing Configuration

As explained in Chapter 13, you may change the default configuration of Sales, Purchase, Debit & Credit Notes printing (Ref 13.2).

At Voucher printing screen (Fig 27-8, 27-9, 27-10), click *F12: Configure* to get the Voucher printing Configuration Screen for the respective voucher types. Set the configuration options as desired.

The standard values in the configuration screen are pre set to fit voucher in A4 size stationery. However, you may change them to adjust according to the size of stationery you use.

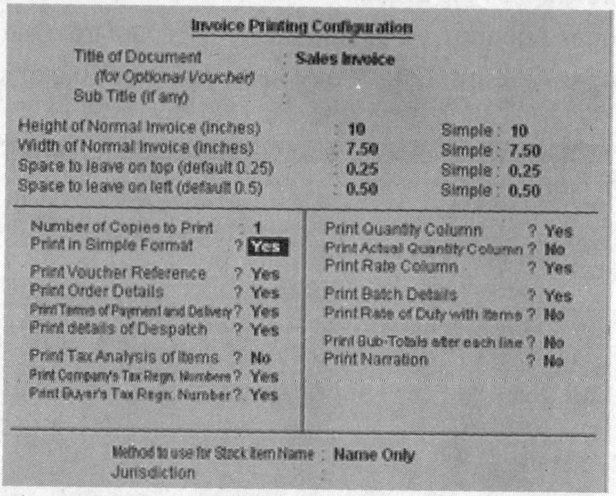

Fig 27-8: Configuration for Sales Invoice

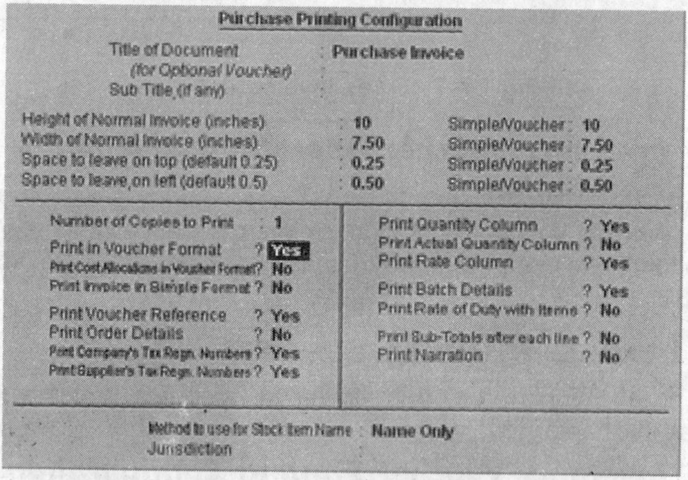

Fig 27-9: Configuration for Purchase Invoice

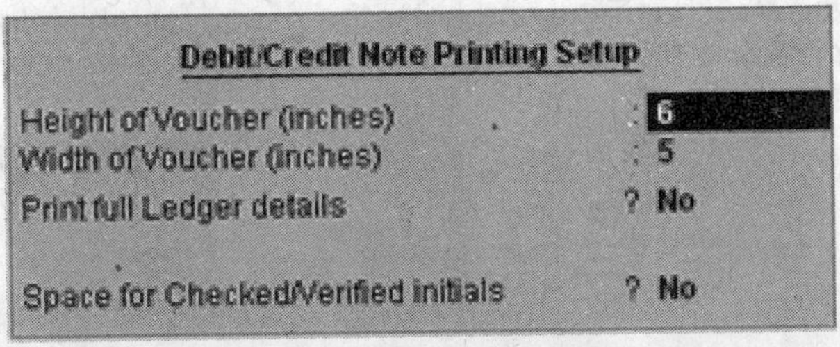

Fig 27-10: Configuration for Debit /Credit Note

27.3.2 On Line Invoice Printing

To print the Invoice before saving, press Alt+P (or click *Print* button) at Invoice entry screen (Fig 27-7). You will get the Invoice Printing dialogue (Fig 27-11).

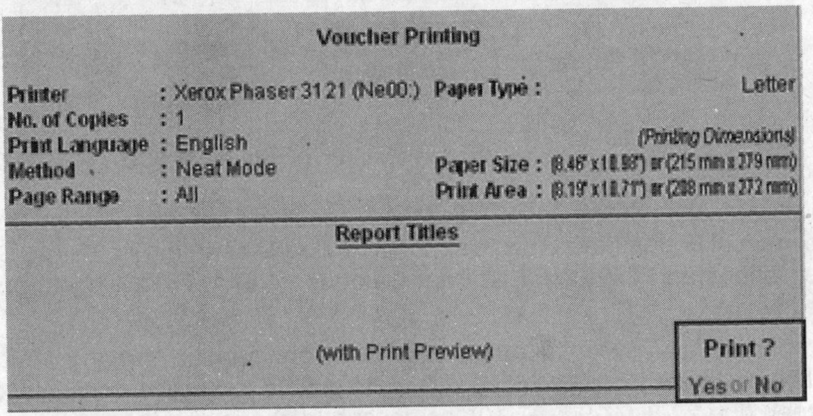

Fig 27-11: Online Invoice Printing dialogue

Click *Yes* at *Print? Yes or No*. (Fig 27-11) to print the Invoice as per existing Printing Configuration (Fig 27-8, 27-9, 27-10). To change any configuration options or any printing options, set *No*. Now you may change any printing option or Print Configuration through the buttons available at the vertical button bar (Fig 20-3). Having changed the configuration option, now click *Yes* at the voucher printing dialogue (Fig 27-11) and print the voucher.

27.3.3 Off Line Invoice Printing

In on-line Invoice printing during entry, you print the current Invoice only, before saving it. To print several Invoices at a time (which have been saved), at Tally Main Menu select Multi Account Printing to get Multi Account *Printing Menu* (Fig 21-1). At Multi Account Printing menu, select Multi Account Voucher Printing to get *Multi Voucher Printing Dialogue* (Fig 27-

12) Select the Voucher Type and enter the period for which Invoice to be printed and press Y (for Yes) to print Invoice as per current configuration and options set up.

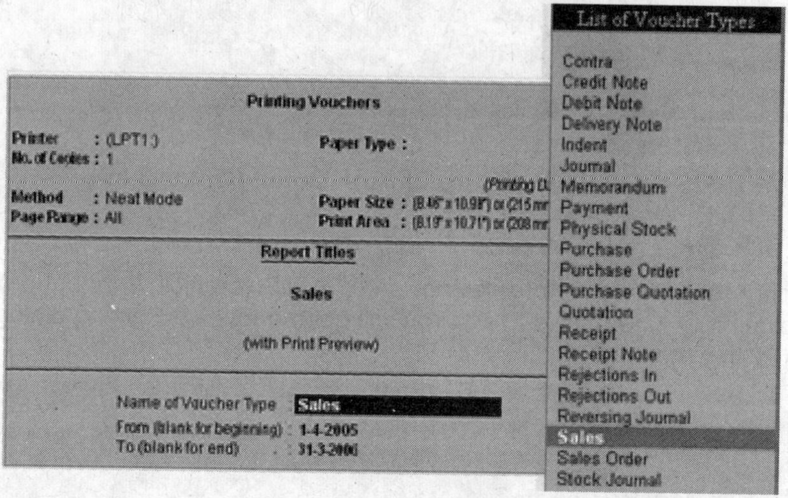

Fig 27-12 : Multi Invoice Printing dialogue

To change any printing option, click the respective print option button from the vertical button bar at Invoice printing dialogue screen (Fig 27-12). Set the options and then set Y at Print dialogue screen (Fig 27-12) to print the Invoice.

To change Invoice Configuration, click F12:Configuration from the vertical button bar at the Invoice printing screen, to get the respective Configuration screen (Fig 27-8, 27-9 & 27-10), as described above. Set the options and then set Y at Print dialogue screen (Fig 27-12).

27.3.4 Invoice output Format

Tally provides two output formats for Invoices, namely (a) Simple and (b) Comprehensive. Comprehensive format is primarily meant for Exporters incorporating additional information for shipping etc while simple format is for general purpose with bare minimum additional information.

If you select Dot Matrix Format, the printing will always be in simple format, sample shown in Fig 27.13.

Invoice No. 2 Dated 1-Apr-2006
Ref. No. :

Disha Infotech
17 Bangur Avenue
Kolkata

Sales

Party : **A.K.Corporation**
B/206

Description of Goods	Quantity	Rate	per	Amount
M S Scrap	**100 Kg**	12.00	Kg	**1,200.00**
C I Scrap	**50 Kg**	10.00	Kg	**500.00**
				1,700.00
Less: ***Discount***		(-)2	%	**(-)34.00**
Output Vat 4%		4	%	**68.00**
Total	**150 Kg**			**1,734.00**

E. & O. E.

Amount Chargeable (in words)
Rs. One Thousand Seven Hundred Thirty Four Only

Inter State Sales Tax No. : **85665666**

Declaration
We declare that this invoice shows the actual price of the goods described and that all particulars are true and correct.

for **Disha Infotech**

Authorised Signatory

This is a Computer Generated Invoice

Fig 27-13 : A Sales Invoice in Simple Format

Should you select 'Neat Format' printing, you may print Invoice in either format. To print in comprehensive format (Fig. 27-14), respond 'No' at Print in Simple Format in the Invoice Printing configuration (Fig. 27-8).

Sales

Disha Infotech 17 Bangur Avenue Kolkata	Invoice No. 2	Dated 1-Apr-2006
	Delivery Note	Mode/Terms of Payment
	Supplier's Ref.	Other Reference(s)
Buyer **A.K.Corporation** B/206	Buyer's Order No.	Dated
	Despatch Document No.	Dated
	Despatched through	Destination
	Terms of Delivery	

Description of Goods	Quantity	Rate	per	Amount
M S Scrap	**100 Kg**	12.00	Kg	**1,200.00**
C I Scrap	**50 Kg**	10.00	Kg	**500.00**
				1,700.00
Less: *Discount*		(-)2	%	(-)34.00
Output Vat 4%		4	%	68.00
Total	**150 Kg**			**1,734.00**

Amount Chargeable (in words) E. & O. E.

Rs. One Thousand Seven Hundred Thirty Four Only

Remarks :
Scrap sales

Inter State Sales Tax No. : **85665666**

Declaration
We declare that this invoice shows the actual price of the goods described and that all particulars are true and correct.

for **Disha Infotech**

Authorised Signatory

This is a Computer Generated Invoice

Fig 27-14: A sales Invoice in Comprehensive Format in English language

बिक्री

Disha Infotech 17 Bangur Avenue Kolkata	इनवॉइस नं. 2	दिनांकित 1-अप्रै.-2006
	सुपुर्दगी नोट	भुगतान के तरीके/शर्तें
	आपूर्तिकर्ता का संदर्भ	अन्य संदर्भ
क्रेता **बिक्रमजित सरकार** 123 ए. जे. सि. बोस रोड कोलकाता 700135	खरीददार का ऑर्डर नं.	दिनांकित
	प्रेषण दस्तावेज नं. :	दिनांकित
	द्वारा प्रेषित किया गया	गन्तव्य
	सुपुर्दगी की शर्तें	

माल का विवरण	मात्रा	दर	प्रति	राशि
एम. एस. स्क्राप	**100 Kg**	12.00	Kg	**1,200.00**
सि. आइ स्क्राप	**50 Kg**	10.00	Kg	**500.00**
				1,700.00
शर्तें : *डिसकाउन्ट*		(-)2 %		(-)34.00
आउटपुट वैट		4 %		68.00
कुल(योग)	**150 Kg**			**1,734.00**

E. & O. E.

टिप्पणियाँ :
माल बिक्री कर हुआ
अंतर्राज्यीय बिक्री कर नं. : 85665666
घोषणा
हम घोषणा करते हैं कि यह इनवॉइस वर्णित माल के वास्तविक मूल्य को दर्शाता है और सभी विवरण सत्य एवं सही हैं

के लिए **Disha Infotech**

अधिकृत हस्ताक्षरकर्ता

This is a Computer Generated Invoice

Fig. 27-15 shows comprehensive Invoice in Hindi

Fig 27-15: A Sales Invoice in Comprehensive Format in Hindi language

To print in Simple format, respond 'Yes' at 'Print in Simple Format' in the Invoice Printing configuration (Fig. 27-8).

For printing of Invoice in comprehensive format, it is always recommended to use non-impact printers (e.g., Laser or Inkjet) since Dot Matrix Printers will take long to time to print in graphics mode and clarity will also be compromised.

Self Test Questions

STQ 27.1: Explain the set up options to create Sales and Credit Note voucher in Invoice Mode, Purchase & Debit Note in Voucher mode.

STQ 27.2: Explain how to enter the following Sales Invoice on 'Angel Distributors'

- MS Scrap – 12.310 MT @ 1220 / M Ton
- Pig Scrap – 11MT @ 1300 / M Ton
- Less Cash Discount – Rs. 3000
- Add Freight – Rs. 4400

STQ 27.3: Explain how to enter the following Credit Note (in Invoice format) on 'Angel Distributors' for return of materials sold, due to defect in Quality

- MS Scrap – 4.310 MT @ 1220 / M Ton
- Less Freight 500.00

Inventory Reports

28

Having entered Inventory Voucher / Invoice, you may get various Inventory Reports

28.1 List of Stock Items

Select *Display > List of Accounts*. Click the button *Stock Items* to get the List of Stock Groups & Stock Items in hierarchical order (Fig 28-1).

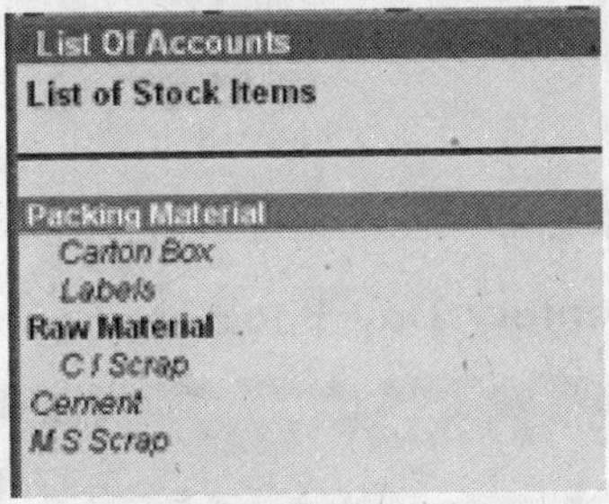

Fig 28-1: List of Stock Items

28.2 Stock Summary

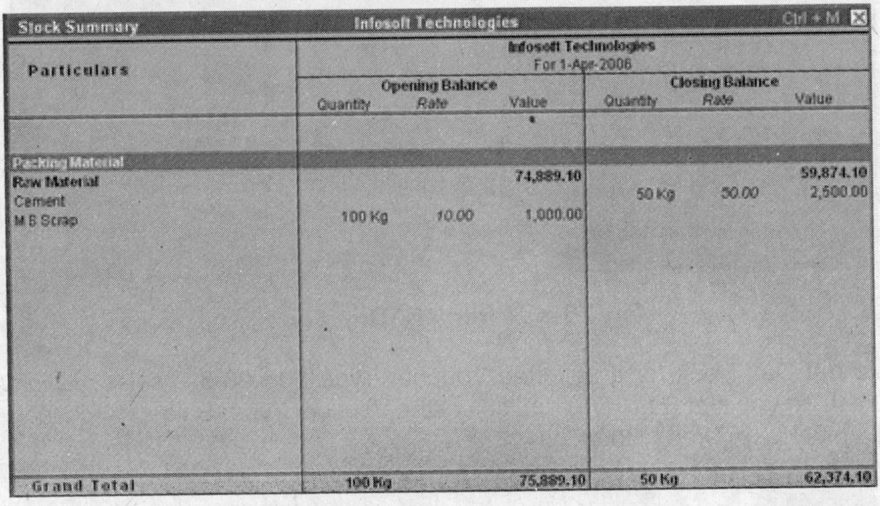

Stock Summary — Infosoft Technologies — Ctrl + M

Infosoft Technologies
For 1-Apr-2006

Particulars	Opening Balance			Closing Balance		
	Quantity	Rate	Value	Quantity	Rate	Value
Packing Material						
Raw Material			74,889.10			59,874.10
Cement				50 Kg	50.00	2,500.00
M S Scrap	100 Kg	10.00	1,000.00			
Grand Total	100 Kg		75,889.10	50 Kg		62,374.10

Fig 28-2: Stock Group Summary

This Report (Fig 28-2) displays Item Summary for Items of a selected Stock Group. Select *Gateway of Tally >Stock Summary.* Select a Stock Group to get Item Summary of all child Stock Items for the selected Item Group. You also get similar report from Gateway of Tally>Display>Inventory Books>Group Summary.

28.3 Day Book

We have discussed Day Book in chapter 15 (Ref 15.1.2). At Day Book Configuration (Fig 28-3), set *Yes* at *Show Inventory Details also* (Fig 28-3) to get Inventory Day Book (Fig 28-4).

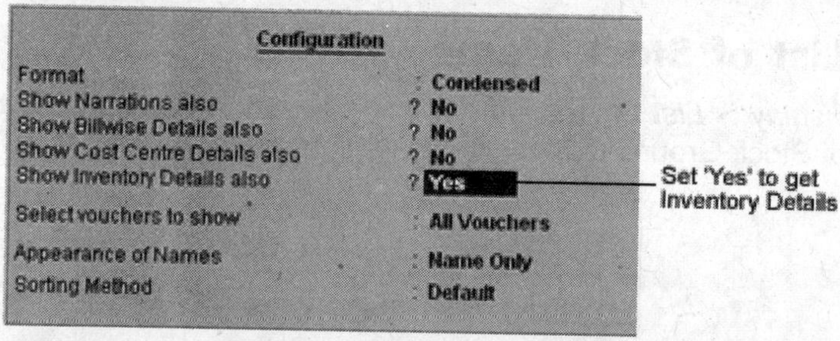

Fig 28-3: Inventory Day Book configuration option

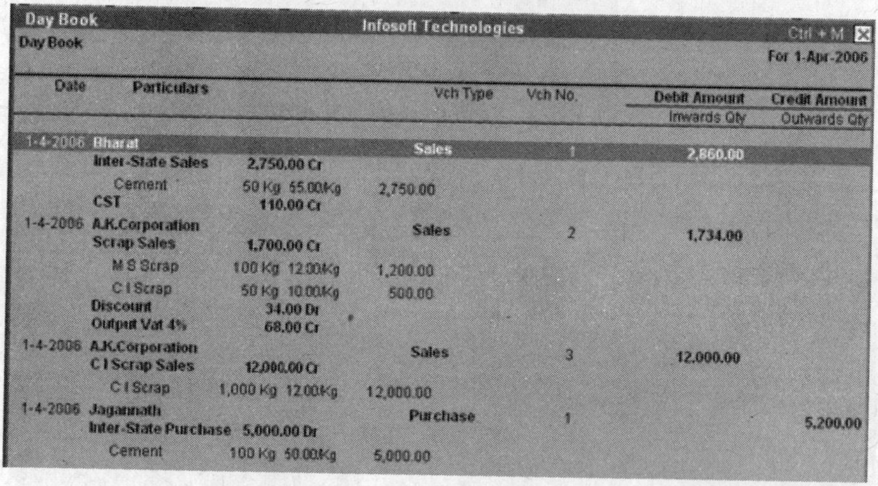

Fig 28-4: Inventory Day Book

To get Day Book for a selected Voucher Type (Fig 28-5 – sales), Click *F4: Chg* Voucher (Fig 15-8) and select the Voucher Type (Sales, Purchase, Debit Note & Credit Note).

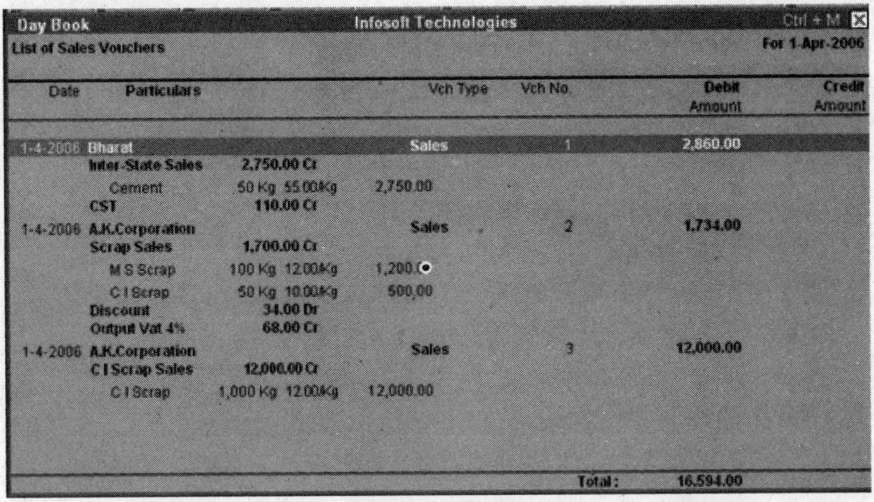

Day Book — Infosoft Technologies — Ctrl + M

List of Sales Vouchers — For 1-Apr-2006

Date	Particulars				Vch Type	Vch No.	Debit Amount	Credit Amount
1-4-2006	Bharat				Sales	1	2,860.00	
	Inter-State Sales	2,750.00 Cr						
	Cement	50 Kg	55.00/Kg	2,750.00				
	CST	110.00 Cr						
1-4-2006	A.K.Corporation				Sales	2	1,734.00	
	Scrap Sales	1,700.00 Cr						
	M S Scrap	100 Kg	12.00/Kg	1,200.00				
	C I Scrap	50 Kg	10.00/Kg	500.00				
	Discount	34.00 Dr						
	Output Vat 4%	68.00 Cr						
1-4-2006	A.K.Corporation				Sales	3	12,000.00	
	C I Scrap Sales	12,000.00 Cr						
	C I Scrap	1,000 Kg	12.00/Kg	12,000.00				
					Total :		16,594.00	

Fig 28-5: Sales Day Book with Inventory details

28.4 Stock Movement Analysis

To get Stock group Movement Analysis (Fig 28-7) at Gateway of Tally select Display>Inventory Books>Movement Analysis>Stock Group Analysis, select an Account Group.

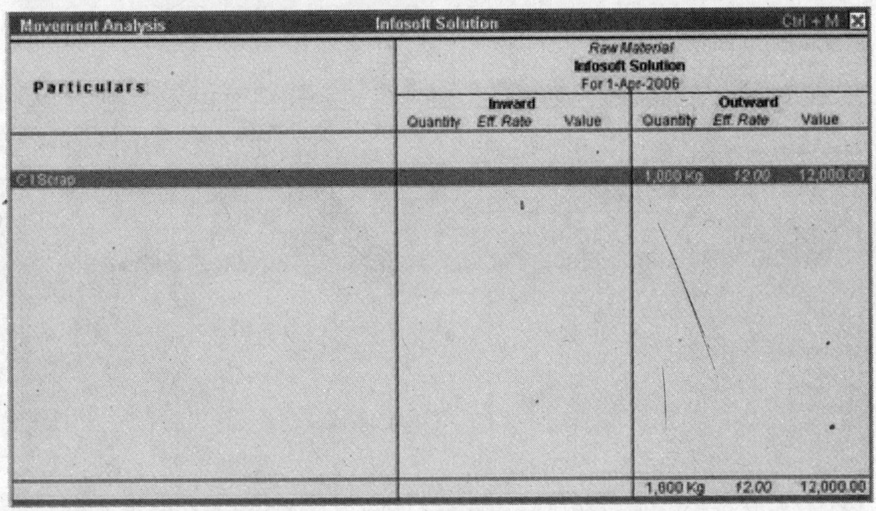

Movement Analysis — Infosoft Solution — Ctrl + M

Raw Material — Infosoft Solution — For 1-Apr-2006

Particulars	Inward Quantity	Inward Eff. Rate	Inward Value	Outward Quantity	Outward Eff. Rate	Outward Value
C I Scrap				1,000 Kg	12.00	12,000.00
				1,000 Kg	12.00	12,000.00

Fig 28-6: Stock Group Movement Analysis

To get Stock Item Movement Analysis, at Gateway of Tally select Display>Inventory Books>Movement Analysis>Stock Item Analysis, select a Stock Item to get the report (Fig 28-7)

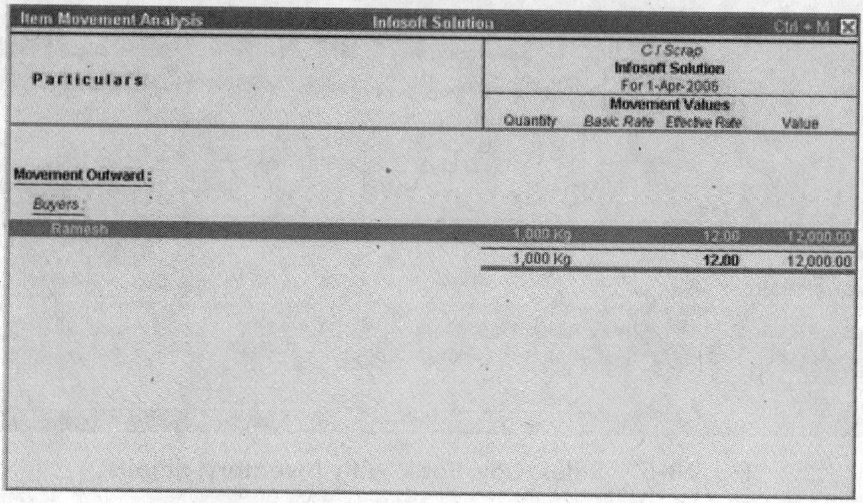

Item Movement Analysis — Infosoft Solution — Ctrl + M

Particulars	C I Scrap Infosoft Solution For 1-Apr-2006 Movement Values			
	Quantity	Basic Rate	Effective Rate	Value
Movement Outward :				
Buyers :				
Ramesh	1,000 Kg		12.00	12,000.00
	1,000 Kg		12.00	12,000.00

Fig 28-7: Stock item Movement Analysis

28.5 Stock Item Monthly Summary

At Stock Summary (Fig 28-2), select a Stock Group and then select a Stock Item to get Item Monthly Summary (Fig 28-8). You may also get this report through Display>Inventory Book>Stock item and then select a Stock Item from the list.

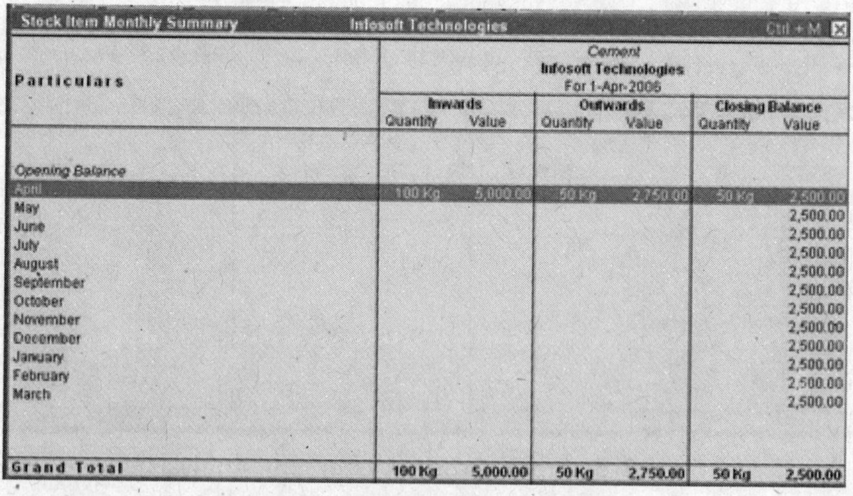

Stock Item Monthly Summary — Infosoft Technologies — Ctrl + M

Particulars	Cement Infosoft Technologies For 1-Apr-2006					
	Inwards		Outwards		Closing Balance	
	Quantity	Value	Quantity	Value	Quantity	Value
Opening Balance						
April	100 Kg	5,000.00	50 Kg	2,750.00	50 Kg	2,500.00
May						2,500.00
June						2,500.00
July						2,500.00
August						2,500.00
September						2,500.00
October						2,500.00
November						2,500.00
December						2,500.00
January						2,500.00
February						2,500.00
March						2,500.00
Grand Total	**100 Kg**	**5,000.00**	**50 Kg**	**2,750.00**	**50 Kg**	**2,500.00**

Fig 28-8: Item Monthly summary

28.6 Stock Item Ledger

At Stock Item monthly summary (Fig 28-8), press <enter>

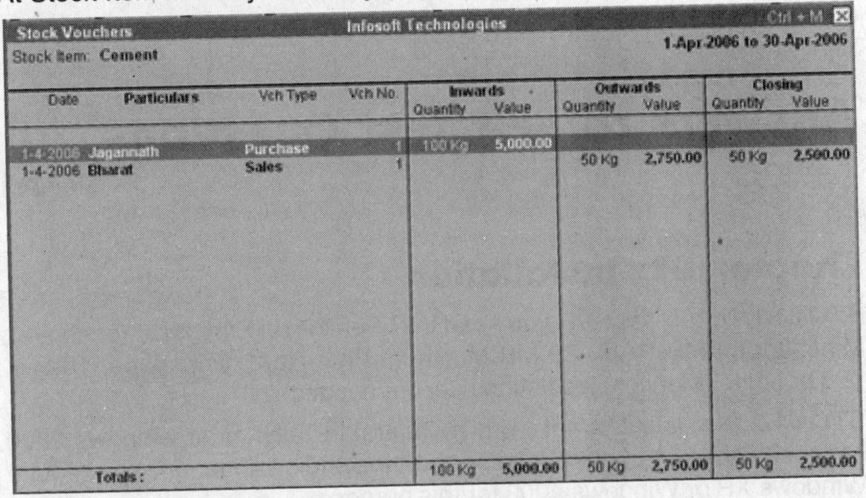

Fig 28-9: Stock Voucher

Self Test Questions

STQ 28.1: Explain how to print list of Stock Groups & Stock Items in hierarchical order.

STQ 28.2: Explain how to print Stock Summary of all Raw Materials only

STQ 28.3: Explain how to get list of Sales Vouchers for the period from 1.5.2006 to 31.5.2006

STQ 28.4: Explain how to print Movement Analysis of all Finished Products only

STQ 28.5: Explain how to print monthly summary of the Stock Item 'M S Scrap'

Answers to Self Test Questions

A

Chapter 01: Installation

STQ 01.1: To run Tally 8.1, you need Intel Pentium III Processor (or above), Minimum 64 MB RAM, 30 MB Minimum Free Hard disk space, 1024 X 768 or higher Monitor Resolution (Recommended).

STQ 01.2: No, you can not work in Gujarat in Tally under windows 2000 because windows 2000 will not support this Indic Language. You require Windows XP or Windows 2003 for this purpose.

STQ 01.3:

Field Name	*Directory Name*
Application Directory	c:\tally81
Data Directory	d:\Tally\81data
Configuration Directory	c:\tally81
Language Directory	c:\tally81\language

STQ 01.4: The following Information are needed to be entered at Activation screen, to Activate Tally 8.1.

- Serial Number
- Key Number
- E-mail Id

If these are not correctly entered at Activation, Tally will run in *Educational* Mode.

Chapter 02: Upgrading

STQ 02.1:Tally Currency coupons are to be bought from Tally Authorized Dealers to make payment for Tally Products

Each coupon envelop contains a scratch card with a serial number and covered key number. You have to scratch to uncover the Key Number (like the kind of scratch card you get for pre paid Phone coupons),.You will have to type the Key Number at the time of on-line up gradation.

STQ 02.2:

Load Tally 7.2.

- At Gateway of Tally screen, click F12: Configuration to get Configuration Menu.
- At Configuration menu select Shop to get Shop Menu.
- At Shop Menu select Online to get Online Menu.
- At Online Menu select Buy to get Shop screen.

At Shop screen:

- At *Select* Currency field, select the Currency INR,
- At *Category* field, select Upgrades from the list.
- Select the respective upgrade option from the List of Add Ons (depending upon the existing User level (Silver/ Gold etc).
- Enter the Tally Currency Key Numbers scratching the Tally Currency Coupons, one by one, in each line.
- Press any key to get connected to Tally Website and get the Location selection screen.

At Location selection screen

- At Location field, select the Country India from the list to get Tally 8.1 screen.
- At Tally 8.1 screen, click the Download button to get Download Tally 8.1 screen.
- At Download Tally 8.1 screen, click the Download Now button at Tally 8.1 box to get the Tally 8.1 Registration screen.

At Download submission screen enter the following to download the Tally 8.1 Upgrade

- At Serial Number field, enter the Tally Serial Number (your old version serial number) very carefully.
- At Activate Code e-mail id filed, enter your e-mail id carefully. This e-mail id will have to be entered at the time of Activation of Tally.

Now click at Submit button List.

- Upon down load, install Tally 8.1

Chapter 03: Data Migration

STQ 03.1: You can use Tally 7.2 data into Tally 8.1 only after migrating Tally 7.2 data into Tally 8.1 data format through Data Migration utility.

STQ 03.2: The name of migration utility file is tally72migration.

At Tally System file folder click the tally72migration file to get the Data Migration screen.

Alternately, you may load the migration tool from Start>Programs>Tally 8.1>Tally Migrate Data.

STQ 03.3:

First the Tally 7.2 data is to be converted into 8.1 formats through Data as follows:

At Tally System file folder, click the tally72migration file to get the Data Migration screen. The Data Migration screen contains 2 parts. In the left part, you get Migrate Company Menu. In the right part, Migration information gets displayed as the Migration process goes on. At Migrate Company Menu, click Migrate Data to get Select Company for Migration screen. At *Select Company for* Migration screen, select the Company for which data to be migrated from 7.2 to 8.1 ver. After the data is loaded, you get a confirmation screen. Click Yes to confirm.

At the right side, statistical figures about the migration data are shown. At the end of Migration process, the two panes show the comparative statistics of Data of 7.2 ver & 8.1 ver. You see an information in the box to compare and ensure that all data have been migrated properly. Having compared the statistics at both pane, press <enter>. You get a Congratulation message. Press <Enter> to get back to the Migrate Company Menu. Press <Esc> to get Quit box to get a confirmation screen (Quit box) to exit from Migration application. Type Y to quit from the Migration utility.

After you exit from Migration tool, explore the old 7.2 ver data folder. You will find 2 data folders there.

1. Old data folder with 4 digit number (7.2 ver data)
2. New migrated data folder in 8.1 ver format under a five digit numbered folder (like 00001).

Now copy the 5 digit data folder from 7.2 data folder to Tally 8.1 data directory. Run Tally 8.1 version. You will now be able to open the Company in 8.1 ver as usual.

Chapter 04: Language Setup

STQ 04.1: In the Gateway of Tally at horizontal button bar select L: Language and then select Bengali from the drop down list.

Chapter 05: Multilingual Operation

STQ 05.1: At ledger creation field press F12 to get the Master configuration screen. At master configuration screen set 'Yes' at ' Allow language

Aliases along with names' and save the configuration. Now. During Ledger creation, select the language (English / Hindi) and enter the name in that language.

STQ 05.2: At ledger creation field press F12 to get the Master configuration screen.

Select L:Language button at Horizontal button bar and select English from the list

At master configuration field set 'No' at Allow language Aliases along with names and save the configuration. Now you can enter the enter all other master and voucher data in English.

STQ 05.3: At Printing Dialogue screen, select L: Print Language button from vertical button bar and select Hindi from the list to Invoice in Hindi Language.

Everything will be shown in Hindi expect Numeric data and master created in English.

Chapter 06: Basic Concepts of Accounting

STQ 06.1

(a) Asset, (b) Asset, (c) Asset, (d) Expense, (e) Income, (f) Expense, (g) Income, (h) Liability, (I) Expenses, (j)Expenses (k) Liability, (l) Asset, (m) Liability, (n) Asset, (o) Liability, (p) Liability, (q) Liability, (r) Asset, (s) Liability, (t) Liability, (u) Asset.

STQ 06.2

(i)

Depreciation A/c	Increase in Expenses	2000	
Motor Car A/c	Decrease in Assets		2000

(ii)

Cash A/c	Increase in Asset	1000	
Sales A/c	Increase in Income		1000

(iii)

Purchased A/c	Increase in Expenses	4000	
A.K. Enterprise A/c	Increase in Liability		4000

(iv)

Cash A/c	Increase in Assets	200	
Professional Fees A/c	Increase in Income		200

(v)

Professional Fees A/c	Increase in Expenses	1000	
A.K.Tewari A/c	Increase in Liabilty		1000

(vi)

Salary A/c	Increase in Expenses	4000	
Cash A/c	Decrease in Assets		3960
Professional Tax A/c	Increase in Liability		40

(vii)

Cash A/c	Increase in Assets	2200	
Sales A/c	Increase in Income		2000
Sales Tax A/c	Increase in Liability		200

(viii)

Bank of India Current A/c	Increase in Assets	20000	
A.K. Sinha A/c	Decrease in Assets		20000

Chapter 07: Company Creation

STQ 07.1: (a), **STQ 07.2** – (c), **STQ 07.3** – (b) **STQ 07.4** – (b) & (c), **STQ 07.5**: (a).

STQ 07.6: The Company Name & Company Mailing Name may be different when you create several Tally Companies for the same Legal Company. For example, you maintain separate Tally Companies for HO, Branch of same legal company, in one computer, e.g Mascot (Calcutta) & Mascot for the legal company Mascot. So, in such case, enter the Company Legal Name (e.g.Mascot) at mailing name for both the Tally Companies. Company Name cannot be duplicate but Mailing Name may be duplicate.

STQ 07.7: At Books Beginning From field, the Financial Year from Date is carried. If you start Accounts in Tally for the first time, from middle of the Financial Year (say you start Accounts entry in Tally from 1.8.2006 for FY 1.4.2006 to 31.3.2006) then change and enter the books starting date (i.e 1.8.2006 at *Books Beginning From* field). This field cannot be left blank.

When you start Accounts in Tally for the first time, from middle of the Financial Year (say you start Accounts entry in Tally from 1.8.2006 for FY 1.4.2006 to 31.3.2006) then change and enter the books starting date (i.e 1.8.2006 at *Books Beginning From* field).

STQ 07.8: Tally shows the current directory name (where the Tally software is located) to store the data under the current directory and skips this field. To keep Company data in any other place, press <backspace > (or <Shift> + <Tab> buttons) to move cursor to *Directory* field and enter the Path. where you wish to keep data files for the Company (Tally would create the Directory, if not existing).

STQ 07.9: To delete the currently active Company, press ***Alt+D***, at Company Alteration screen. A confirmation 'Delete? *Yes or No*' appears. Type Y (Yes) to confirm Deletion. Next, you again confirm yes at Are you sure? The Data files of the Company are deleted.

Chapter 08: Gateway of Tally

STQ 08.1: (d), **STQ 08.2-** (c)

STQ 08.3: (a) Company number #1 to #5

(b) #2

(c) #1, #2, #4, #5

STQ 08.4: When the software has not been registered.

The Main difference is Educational version is not registered version and Regular version is registered version.

STQ 08.5: The period within which the current date can fall.

Press Alt+F2 and enter From And To dates.

Press Alt+F2 and set the current period to prevent accidental change in any voucher prior to 1 Aug-2006.

STQ 08.6: The last selected company is Active Company.

Active company is running company in which you are working. Selected company is all the selected company in the Gateway of Tally. Company on Disk is all the company you have created.

STQ 08.7: At Gateway press Esc key. You will get a confirmation screen for "Quit". Press 'y' to exit from Tally.

Chapter 9: Charts of Accounts

STQ 9.1: (I) B, (II) C, (III) A, (IV) B, (V) A, (VI) C, (VII) B, (VIII) C, (IX) D, (X) D, (XI) A, (XII) B, (XIII) B, (XIV) A, (XV) A, (XVI), (XVII) B.

STQ 9.2:

Capital Account

(Redeemable Preference Shares)

Reserves & Surplus (Retained Earnings)

(Shares Premium)

Loans (Liability)

Bank OD A/c (Bank OCC A/c)

Secured Loans

(HDFC Bank Cash Credit Account)

Unsecured Loans

Current Liabilities

(Legal Expenses Payable to Lawyer (for previous year)

Duties & Taxes

(TDS deducted on interest paid on Loans Taken)

(Sales VAT)

Provisions

(Provision for Bad Debt)

Sundry Creditors

A Mohan & Co. (Supplier of Goods)

Fixed Assets

Motor Car (used by a Company)

Investments

Current Assets

(TDS on interest received on Fixed Deposit deducted by Bank)

Bank Accounts

Cash-in-hand

Deposits (Asset)

Loans & Advances (Asset)

Stock-in-hand

Motor Car (for sale by a Motor Car dealer)

Sundry Debtors

Premier Trading (Customer)

Branch / Divisions

Misc. Expenses (ASSET)

Suspense A/c

Direct Expenses (Expenses (Direct))

Direct Incomes (Income (Direct))

Indirect Expenses (Expenses (Indirect))

(Expenses on Fixed Assets)

(Employers Contribution to Provident Fund)

(Conveyance Expenses)

Indirect Incomes (Income (Indirect))

Purchase Accounts

Sales Accounts

Chapter 10: Account Masters

STQ 10.1: (c), **STQ 10.2:** (b), **STQ 10.3:** (a),

STQ 10.4: The opening balance as on 1-Aug-2005 will be enter because the books is beginning from 1-Aug-2005.

STQ 10.5: At under field press Alt+C to get a group master entry screen. Create the new parent group and save it.

STQ 10.6: At Gateway of Tally select Accounts Info>Ledger>Alter, select the ledger, press Alt+D and press 'y'.

A ledger account can be deleted if the account has opening balance.

A ledger account can not be deleted if it is referred in any voucher.

STQ 10.7: At Gateway of Tally select Accounts Info>Ledger>Alter, select the ledger(Raw Materia Stock), at closing balance field enter date(30 Jun,2006) and amount. Again in the next line enter date(30 sep,2006) and amount.

At Gateway of Tally select Accounts Info>Ledger>Alter, select the ledger (Finished Products Stock), at closing balance field enter date (30 Jun, 2006) and amount. Again in the next line enter date (30 Sep, 2006) and amount.

STQ 10.8: At Gateway of Tally select Accounts Info>Ledger>Alter, select the ledger cash, at opening balance field enter the opening balance.

The process is different from other ledger because cash ledger tally create automatically.

STQ 10.9: At Gateway of Tally select Display>Statement of Accounts>Statistics.

Chapter 11: Voucher Entry

STQ 11.1: (c), **STQ 11.2:** (c), **STQ 11.3:** (c), **STQ 11.4:** (a), **STQ 11.5:** (a), **STQ 11.6:** (d),

STQ 11.7:

(a)

Voucher Type	*A/c Name*	*DEBIT*	*CREDIT*
Contra	Cash	1000	
	HDFC Cash credit A/c		1000

(b)

Voucher Type	*A/c Name*	*DEBIT*	*CREDIT*
Contra	Syndicate Bank Current A/c	1000	
	HDFC Cash credit A/c		1000

(c)

Voucher Type	*A/c Name*	*DEBIT*	*CREDIT*
Receipt	Cash A/c	120	
	Sales A/c		120

(d)

Voucher Type	*A/c Name*	*DEBIT*	*CREDIT*
Sales	Bank A/c	120	
	Sales A/c		120

(e)

Voucher Type	*A/c Name*	*DEBIT*	*CREDIT*
Payment	Salary A/c	3500	
	Cash A/c		3150
	P.F A/c		350

(f)

Voucher Type	*A/c Name*	*DEBIT*	*CREDIT*
Journal	Depreciation A/c	2500	
	Furniture A/c		2500

STQ 11.9:- At particulars field press Ctrl+R.

STQ11.10: At Voucher narration field press Alt+R.

STQ 11.11: At Voucher narration field press Ctrl+R.

STQ 11.12: At Gateway of Tally select Display>Day Book, select the voucher and press Alt+D

STQ 11.13: Gateway of Tally selects Display>Day Book, select the voucher and press Alt+X.

STQ 11.14: At Gateway of Tally select Display>Statements of Account>Statistics.

The cancelled vouchers are also included in the number of voucher shown and also separately shown in the bracket.

Chapter 12: Single Mode Voucher Entry

STQ 12.1: (d), **STQ 12.2:** (a), **STQ 12.3:** (a), **STQ 12.4:** (c), **STQ 12.5:** (b), **STQ 12.6**: (b),

STQ 12.7: In single mode voucher cash/Bank A/c always entered in header without amount. Insigne mode voucher no Debit/Credit is to be specified in any ledger Account.

Receipt, Payment and Contra voucher can be entered in the single mode voucher

STQ 12.8:

(a)

Header Account	Cash A/c	1000	
Line Account	HDFC Cash credit A/c		1000

(b)

Header Account	Syndicate Bank current A/c	3000	
Line Account	Cash A/c		3000

(c)

Header Account	Syndicate Bank current A/c	1000	
Line Account	HDFC Cash credit A/c		1000

(d)

Header Account	Cash A/c	120	
Line Account	Sales A/c		120

(e)

Header Account	Bank A/c	120	
Line Account	Sales A/c		120

(f)

Header Account	Cash A/c	3500	
Line Account	Salary A/c		3150
	P.F A/c		350

Chapter 13: Accounts Voucher Printing

STQ 13.1: (b), **STQ 13.2:** (c), **STQ 13.3:** (a),

STQ 13.4: At voucher types set 'yes' Print Formal Receipt after saving. After setting this pass the voucher and must enter the mane of the receipt at the voucher field then press Alt+P.

Chapter 14: Accounts Master Lists

STQ 14.1: At Gateway of Tally select Display>List of Accounts, by default the screen will show the List of Ledgers. At the right side of the screen clicks on the Groups.

STQ 14.2: At Gateway of Tally select Display>List of Accounts.

STQ 14.3: At the List of Ledger select the group and modify.

STQ 14.4: At the list of Ledger select the ledger and then press Alt+D.

Chapter 15: Accounts Voucher Lists

STQ 15.1: To use Shift+Enter.

STQ 15.2: At voucher List select the voucher And press Alt+R to hide the voucher and use Alt+S to restore it.

STQ 15.3: At Gateway of tally select Display>Accounts Books>Group Summary, select the group. For ledwise summary use F5 key. For Specified period use F2 keys..

STQ 15.4: At Gateway of Tally select Display>Day Book, at the right sight of the button bar click on the F4: Chg Vch to get a list a list of voucher. From the list of voucher select the Receipt voucher type.

STQ 15.5: At Gateway of Tally Select Display>Account Books>Group Voucher, select Sundry Debtors.

STQ 15.6- Creation of a new voucher by copying another voucher. Select a Voucher from the list and press Alt+2 to duplicate the voucher.

Chapter 16: Day Book Summaries

STQ 16.1: At Gateway of Tally select Display>Account Books>Group summary, select the group and then press F6 for Monthly Summary.

STQ 16.2: At gateway of Tally select Display>Account Books>Ledger, select the ledger and press F7 for Monthly Summary.

Chapter 17: Columnar Account Voucher Register

STQ 17.1: At Gateway of Tally Display>Account Books>Ledger, select the ledger and then Press F8 and set the option

STQ 17.2: At Gateway of Tally Display>Account Books>Ledger, select the ledger and then Press F8 and in the type of column set All Items(automatic columns)

Chapter 18: Trial Balance

STQ 18.1: At Gateway of Tally Select Display> Trial Balance, pressAlt+F1 for detailed trial balance and then press F12 configuration for set 'yes' opening balance, Transaction and closing balance option and Expand all levels in Detailed Format.

STQ 18.2: At Gateway of Tally Select Display> Trial Balance, press F5 with all ledger with alphabetical order and use F2 keys for period.

Chapter 19: Final Accounts

STQ 19.1: At Gateway of Tally select Balance Sheet, press Alt+F1 for detailed Balance Sheet, and then press F12 configuration and set 'yes' show percentages to show Balance Sheet with percentage figure.

STQ 19.2: At Balance Sheet drill down through Current Asset to get the Group Summary. At Group Summary again drill down through closing stock. You will get the stock Group Summary of Raw Materials. Again Drill Down through Raw Materials. You will get the Raw Material Ledger Alteration Screen. At the Ledger Alteration screen in the closing stock field enter the closing balance of 31-12-2005.

Chapter 20: Reports Printing

STQ 20.1: To print only specified pages of the report, click Page No button and set the page filter to print specified pages of the report. At Page Number Starts from field enter the starting page number you like to allot to the first page. Here to start Cash Book of May from page 22 (instead of 1), enter 22.

STQ 20.3: To save the report on any Media (if you have selected Quick/ Draft at Print Format), click Select Printer button and then specify as follows:

Print to a file: Set *Y* (for Yes) to save the Report on media.

File Name: Tally proposes a filename depending on the selected report (like BSHEET.PRN). Change the filename if you like to. The report will be saved in the designated file at the specified directory.

Chapter 21: Multi Accounts Reports Printing

STQ 21.1: At Gateway of Tally select Multi Account Printing>Account Books>Multi column cash/Bank, you will get print dialogue box, at print dialogue box set the specified period at the period field, at Cash/Bank A/c column set the specified column.

STQ 21.2: At Gateway of Tally select Multi Account Printing>Account Books>Ledger>Group of Accounts, then select sundry debtors to print the all customer Ledger Accounts.

STQ 21.3: At Gateway of Tally select Multi Account Printing>Account Books>Ledger>Group of Accounts, select Unsecured Loans, after selecting of Unsecured Loans you will get print dialogue box. At print dialogue box Style of Report field select confirmation of Accounts to print confirmation of Accounts for all ledgers under the group unsecured loans.

Chapter 22: Data Maintenance

STQ 22.1: At Gateway of Tally press Alt+F3 to get the company Info Menu, select Back up, at source field enter the company data c:\tallybackup\directory.

STQ 22.2: tbk900.001

STQ 22.3: At Gateway of Tally press Alt+F3 to get the company Info Menu, select Restore, at destination field enter Tally\data directory and source field enter C:\tallybackup\ directory.

STQ 22.4: The company number will be 5.

STQ 22.5: Rewriting means repairing of data (when Tally encounters some problem in reading the data smoothly).

When data file of older version is opened by newer version of tally.

Press Ctrl+Alt+R at Gateway and select the Company for re-write and press 'y'.

Chapter 23: Moving to new financial year

STQ 23.1:			
	Profit & Loss A/c	100000	
	To General Reserve		100000

STQ 23.2: At Gateway of Tally press Alt+F2 to get the change period field. At change period in the To field extend the period till 31 March 2005.

STQ 23.3: Again press Alt+F2 to get the change period field. At change period in the To field enter the date 31-5-2005. Now you can enter 1st May, 2005 Voucher.

STQ 23.4: At Gateway press Alt+F3 and press split company data in the company Info Menu. You will get a Split Company Data field. At Split Company Data field split from field enter the date 1-4-2005 to split the company from 1-4-2005.

Chapter 24: Inventory Set up

STQ 24.1: To maintain Inventory, at *Maintain* field, select *Accounts with Inventory* in the company creation screen.

Chapter 25: Inventory Master

STQ 25.1:

At Units Menu, select *Create* to get Unit Creation screen and enter the following particulars:

- At Type *field*, cursor normally skips showing Simple as selected to create a Simple Unit.
- At *Symbol* field, enter the symbol MT.
- At *Formal Name* field, enter full Name M Tons.
- At *Number of Decimal Places* enter the decimal number 3 to get the data like 25.321 MT, 32.000 MT, 27.005 MT etc in the Inventory Voucher.

STQ 25.2:

Group / Stock Item	*Parent Stock Group at Under Field*
Iron Scraps	Raw Material
Pig Scraps	Iron Scraps
Low Silica Pigs	Pig Scraps
M S Scraps	Iron Scraps
M S Flat scraps	M S Scraps

STQ 25.3: At stock Item Entry Screen

- At *Quantity* field, enter the Opening Stock Quantity.
- At *Rate* field, enter the Opening Stock Rate (if you do not know the Rate, leave it blank, and enter the Opening Stock value, Tally will compute & fill up the Rate).
- The Opening Stock value is computed from the Opening Stock Quantity & Opening Stock Rate as entered and displayed at Value

field. However, you may change the Amount. The Rate will get changed accordingly.

STQ 25.4: At Stock Item Creation, at Unit field select *Not Applicable* to enter only values without Quantity.

STQ 25.5: First create a simple Unit called Hr (Hour), At Stock Item Creation at Unit field select Hr to create a service Item for which the Rate is to be charged in Hours.

Chapter 26: Inventory Voucher

STQ 26.1:

- To enter Debit/Credit Note, click *F11: to get Company Features* Menu.
- At Company Features Menu, select Inventory Features to get Inventory Features set up screen.
- At Inventory Features set up screen, set *Yes* at *Use Debit/Credit Notes.*

STQ 26.2: First compute the Net Bill Amount before you can enter the voucher.

The Net Bill Amount is 30,318.50, received in Cash.

Now enter the Sales Voucher as follows

At Gateway, select Account Voucher. Click F8: Sales button (Click As Voucher button) at Vertical button bar to get Sales Voucher entry screen.

At first ledger, select the Cash account and enter the amount 30318.20 in Debit column. At the second ledger account, select the Sales ledger. You will get an Item allocation screen to enter the Item details as follows:

In first line, select the Item MS Scrap, at Quantity field, enter 12.310, At Rate field, enter 1220. the Item value is displayed.

In the same way, in second line, select the Item Pig Scrap, at Quantity field, enter 11.000, At Rate field, enter 1300. the Item value is displayed.

Press <enter> or select <End of List> to terminate Item entry.

You will get back to the main screen showing the amount Rs 29318.30 displayed at Credit column against the Sales Ledger Account.

Now select Cash Discount ledger and enter 3000 at Debit ColumnIn the next line, select Freight ledger and enter 4000 at Credit Column

At Narration field, you may enter an appropriate narration, say, the name of the customer for your reference.

Press Ctrl+A to save the voucher.

STQ 26.3: At Gateway, select Account Voucher. Click F8:Credit Note button(Click As Voucher button) at Vertical button bar to get Credit Note entry screen.

At first ledger, select the party S K Enterprises and enter the amount 4758.20 at Credit column. At second ledger, select Sales (or Sales Return, as the case may be). You will get a sub screen to enter the Item details, as follows :

Select the Item MS Scrap, at Quantity field, enter 4.310, At Rate field, enter 1220. the Item value is displayed.

Press <enter> or select <End of List> to terminate Item entry.You will get back to the main screen showing the amount Rs 5258.20 displayed at Debit column against the Sales (or Sales Return) Ledger Account.

Now select Freight ledger and enter 500 at Debit Column

Press Ctrl+A to save the voucher.

Chapter 27: Invoicing

STQ 27.1: At Company features Inventory option screen, set *Yes* at *Allow Invoicing* to enter Sales Invoice in Invoice Format.

To enter Credit Note in Invoice format, set *Yes* at *Use Debit / Credit Notes* and then set *Yes* at *Use Invoice Mode for Credit*

STQ 27.2: At Gateway, select Account Voucher. Click F8:Sales button at Vertical button bar to get Sales Invoice entry screen. Then Click the following button

- As Invoice
- Item Invoice

At Party's A/c Name field select the Party name *Angel Distributors.*

At Sales ledger field, select Sales

At Item Table (Line Area), enter as follows:

At first line in Line Area, at Name of the Item field, select the Item M S Scrap, At Quantity field enter 12.310, at Rate field enter 1220. At Amount field, the computed Item value will be shown automatically.

At second line in Line Area, at Name of the Item field, select the Item Pig Scrap, At Quantity field enter 11.000, at Rate field enter 1300. At Amount field, the computed Item value will be shown automatically.

Press <enter> or select <End of List> to terminate Item entry.

Now select Cash Discount ledger and enter -3000 at Amount columnIn the next line, select Freight ledger and enter 4000 at Amount Column

At Narration field, you may enter an appropriate narration, if necessary

Press Ctrl+A or <enter> to save the Invoice

STQ 27.3: At Company Features Inventory option Screen set 'Yes' *Use Invoice Mode for Credit Notes* to get Invoice format in credit note.

At Gateway, select Account Voucher. Click F8:Credit Note button at Vertical button bar to get Credit Note entry screen. Then Click the following button

- As Invoice
- Item Invoice

At Party's A/c Name field select the Party name *Angel Distributors.*

At Sales ledger field, select SalesAt Item Table (Line Area), enter as follows:

Select the Item MS Scrap, at Quantity field, enter 4.310, At Rate field, enter 1220. The Item value is displayed.

Press <enter> or select <End of List> to terminate Item entry.

Now select Freight ledger and enter -500 at Amount column

At Narration field, you may enter an appropriate narration (e.g reason of goods return), if necessary

Press Ctrl+A to save the Invoice

Chapter 28: Inventory Reports

STQ 28.1: To print list of Stock Groups & Stock Items in hierarchical order, Select *Display > List of Accounts*. Click the button *Stock Items* to get the List of Stock Groups & Stock Items in hierarchical order.

STQ 28.2: To print Stock Summary of all Raw Materials only, Select *Gateway of Tally >Stock Summary*, Press F4: Group Button and select the Stock Group ' Raw Materials'

STQ 28.3: To get list of Sales Vouchers for the period from 1.5.2006 to 31.5.2006, Select Display>Account Books>Sales Register for May'06.For period selection press *F2: Period* button and enter the period 1.5.2006 to 31.5.2006.

STQ 28.4: To print Movement Analysis of all Finished Products only, at Gateway of Tally select Display>Inventory Books>Movement Analysis>Stock Group Analysis, select 'Finished Products' stock group.

STQ 28.5: To print monthly summary of the Stock Item 'M S Scrap' Select Display>Inventory Book>Stock item and then select stock Item M S Scrap from the list.Answers to Self Test Questions